In an era that is focused on the here and now, it is good to hear a balanced teaching that is awakening the human conscience to the reality of hell and eternity. Bill's vision has penetrated millions of hearts and is bringing the message of eternity back to the forefront.

—Jentezen Franklin
Senior Pastor, Free Chapel
Author of *New York Times* Best Seller *Fasting*

For the last thirty years I have interviewed many people who have had out-of-body experiences and visited heaven or hell. Bill Wiese's story is the most credible I have ever investigated.

—Sid Roth
Host, *It's Supernatural!* TV

This could be one of the most valuable books you have ever read. It could save your life out of the grips of hell and get you on the right road to heaven. Bill Wiese is a man living for God and doing his best to take a lot of people to heaven. I am glad to call Bill Wiese my good Christian friend whom I trust very much. I believe this book will be a great blessing to those who read it.

—Dr. Norvel Hayes
Founder and President, Norvel Hayes Ministries
Founder, New Life Bible College and New Life Bible Church

Riveting. Powerful. God is pleading through this man for America to wake to biblical reality.

—Doug Chambers
Senior Pastor, Full Gospel Church
Bellflower, California

D0037304

Spas

Bill Wiese is an anointed author and speaker who unashamedly answers the most difficult questions that have been asked about hell. Because of his impeccable character and integrity, one finds it easy to accept his remarkable testimony. God has given Bill a unique gift to teach the Word of God with simplicity and clarity, confirming his experience and putting even the most skeptical hearts at rest. Bill and Annette have served the Lord faithfully for many years and are dear and fine people. I highly recommend Bill's new book to all who want real answers that very few can explain, from a reliable and credible source.

—Pastor Theo Wolmarans, ThD, DD
Christian Family Church International

BILL WIESE

Charisma
HOUSE
A STRANG COMPANY

Most Strang Communications/Charisma House/Christian Life/Excel Books/FrontLine/Realms/Siloam products are available at special quantity discounts for bulk purchase for sales promotions, premiums, fund-raising, and educational needs. For details, write Strang Communications/Charisma House/Christian Life/Excel Books/FrontLine/Realms/Siloam, 600 Rinehart Road, Lake Mary, Florida 32746, or telephone (407) 333-0600.

Hell by Bill Wiese
Published by Charisma House
A Strang Company
600 Rinehart Road
Lake Mary, Florida 32746
www.strangdirect.com

Unless otherwise noted, all Scripture quotations are from the New King James Version of the Bible. Copyright © 1979, 1980, 1982 by Thomas Nelson, Inc., publishers. Used by permission.

Scripture quotations marked AMP are from the Amplified Bible. Old Testament copyright © 1965, 1987 by the Zondervan Corporation. The Amplified New Testament copyright © 1954, 1958, 1987 by the Lockman Foundation. Used by permission.

Scripture quotations marked KJV are from the King James Version of the Bible.

Scripture quotations marked NIV are from the Holy Bible, New International Version. Copyright © 1973, 1978, 1984, International Bible Society. Used by permission.

Scripture quotations marked NLT are from the Holy Bible, New Living Translation, copyright © 1996, 2004. Used by permission of Tyndale House Publishers, Inc., Wheaton, IL 60189. All rights reserved.

AUTHOR'S NOTE: In quotes from Scripture, and in many cases of quotes from others, I have added italics to denote emphasis on a specific phrase or meaning.

Design Director: Bill Johnson
Cover Designer: Justin Evans

Library of Congress Cataloging-in-Publication Data:

Wiese, Bill.
  Hell / Bill Wiese.
      p. cm.
  Includes bibliographical references.
  ISBN 978-1-59979-339-9
  1. Hell--Christianity. 2. Private revelations. I. Title.
  BT838.W46 2008
  236'.25--dc22

                                              2008025329

First Edition

08 09 10 11 12 — 987654321
Printed in the United States of America

ACKNOWLEDGMENTS

I WOULD LIKE TO FIRST THANK THE LORD, WHO HAS SO BLESSED MY life. I am extremely grateful for His help in writing this book. His wisdom is infinite, and I hope I was able to convey a small piece of it here.

I most certainly want to thank my exceptional and most beautiful wife, whom I love with all my heart. I could not have written this book without her. Her commitment to the Lord and to me is priceless.

I also want to thank my wonderful parents, who have prayed so much for my wife and me, this ministry, and this book. I deeply appreciate their example of integrity throughout my life and their wholehearted support for us.

CONTENTS

INTRODUCTION

I F ANY OF US TRAVEL TO ANOTHER COUNTRY, WE USUALLY RESEARCH THE hotels, restaurants, climate, places of interest, and so forth—and this is just for a short stay! Yet, when it comes to where we will go after we die, most do little or no research. We invest more time into a short vacation than we do for our own eternity. Why so little effort or interest? I believe it is because, whatever beliefs we were brought up with, we tend to stay with and not question them. Now, that might be a good thing, but what if you were raised with something that is not true?

The wisest man who ever lived, except for Jesus, was King Solomon. He said in Proverbs 14:12, "There is a way that seems right to a man, but its end is the way of death." Due to no investigation, we would remain uninformed on the subject. The adage "never discuss religion or politics" comes into play. If we do not discuss something, and if we do not research it, we will be left in an uneducated state of mind. Mark Twain said, "We are all ignorant; just about different things."[1] Jesus said in Luke 11:35, "Make sure that the light you think you have is not actually darkness" (NLT).

When learning any new subject, most people realize that in order to learn, they must be willing to submit themselves to someone who does have the knowledge. And most are not only willing, but they are also anxious to learn. I know that sometimes we don't always enjoy corrective learning, but if we can humble ourselves, we can surely benefit from it. So why do we have such difficulty even discussing the topic of our eternal destination? Is it because we remember a preacher shouting at us when we were young that we will "burn in hell"? Or is it because we were told by our parents that God would "get us" if we didn't straighten up? Are those the emotional triggers that cause us to shut down the matter?

If you think about it, it doesn't even make sense as to why we get so defensive in our unwillingness to be open for an intelligent discussion! We defend our right *not* to discuss it, just like a military man defending his entrenched position. Yet we pride ourselves on being "open-minded" and "logical." Most of us think we are mature enough to engage in discussion on any topic—except when it comes to religion! We say, "Let's not go there, because I'll get upset or angry. My convictions are not open for discussion." That stance will leave us uninformed, leaving our strong personal convictions based on nothing concrete. Why? We haven't even investigated the subject. We simply believe whatever we were told or whatever we have formulated in our minds. Winston Churchill said, "Personally, I'm always ready to learn, although I do not always like being taught."[2]

The reason most people are defensive is because discussing our eternal destination does not simply involve mental comprehension and logic. It is spiritual as well. You see, we as people have an enemy to our souls. That enemy wants us to remain ignorant about the subject, because if we investigate, we will discover his deceit. What if heaven and hell really do exist?

We are going to take a look at the most tolerant, loving, and good individual in all of history—God. That's right, the God of the Bible. But before we do, if you are already offended by the fact that this "loving" God allows millions to suffer in absolute torment for eternity, then you won't read the rest of this book with a heart open to learn. We are appalled when someone unjustly "judges" or "condemns" us without even knowing us. Yet we do the very same thing to God. So before you shut down and reject this God of the Bible, be the very person you pride yourself on being—one who is rational, logical, and nonjudgmental. One thing is certain: all of us are going to die!

In this book I will address the questions that many have in regard to what happens to us after we die. I will attempt to shed some light on the misconceptions and erroneous ideas that some have conceptualized. If you can set aside your presuppositions, by the end of this book you will hopefully have the information necessary to make an informed decision. If you decide to throw it all out, that is your choice. But at least hear the facts first.

During the fall of 1998, I experienced overwhelming terror, dreadful fear, penetrating horror, untold misery, and total exhaustion and despair. There was never-ending trauma, burning fire, unquenchable thirst, and endless hunger. I was in a place of complete isolation and unending torment, a place where I was hopelessly lost and without human intervention. Yes, this is a place—an actual reality that exists now, this very moment, for untold millions of people. This place is hell, where I found myself for twenty-three minutes on November 23, 1998. I tell of this entire experience in explicit detail in my first book, *23 Minutes in Hell*.

This was an out-of-body experience that is referred to as a vision in the Bible. I will give an explanation of this ahead. No, I didn't have a bad dream, I don't take drugs or medications, nor do I have any psychological or mental issues. My wife and I do not ever see dark or evil movies, nor do we allow any evil music, artifacts, cultish symbols, or cursed objects into our home. (See Deuteronomy 7:26.) I didn't ask for this, nor did I ever seek after spiritual experiences. In fact, to be associated with something as radical as this is uncomfortable for me. I'm a conservative man by nature, a real estate broker for over thirty-five years, and a Christian since 1970. I had never researched the topic of hell, nor had I ever had a desire to learn about it. I knew there was an afterlife and that I was going to heaven. I believed hell existed, but since I wasn't going there, I didn't see the need to study it. After seeing firsthand the absolute misery and horror that exists for so many, I wanted to warn everyone I could how to avoid this place. It was then that I began to research the subject of hell. And, as I pointed out in *23 Minutes in Hell*, my desire is not to convince anyone to believe my experience was real but to believe what the Bible says is real. That is all that matters.

As eternal beings, our souls will live forever in either heaven or hell. There is no other place that exists for the soul to go. We cannot quite grasp eternity here. Time is linear in our minds with a beginning and an end, but in hell, I could not get my mind around it.

The impact of knowing I would never, ever, get out of that place was the worst part. Obviously, I'm still here on Earth. I didn't die. This was not a near-death experience. This was a vision, and while I was in this vision, the knowledge of my being a Christian was kept hidden from my mind. I will explain further on this in a later chapter. This was the only way I could experience the total hopelessness of those who are there. The souls of people who walked the earth, just as you and I do, are still alive suffering extreme torment. They are in the realm of the dead. They are the living dead.

The purpose for writing this book is threefold. First, I would like to answer some of the most frequently asked questions in regard to hell and the afterlife. Many think that Christians are narrow-minded and that only a very mean God would send people to hell. I will address these thoughts. Secondly, I would like to expound on some of the events I experienced and how this could take place scripturally. I will give additional verses to help clarify, and include many of the commentaries, opinions, and views from current and past reputable leaders. Thirdly, I would like to share some of the responses we have received from others, what the Lord has done, and about the many souls saved as a result of people reading *23 Minutes in Hell*. Christians have become more committed, ceased living a compromised life-style, and have a renewed passion for the lost. There have been thousands of positive e-mails and letters, many from prisoners, with heart-wrenching stories that we are honored to share. The questions you have asked based on your reading of *23 Minutes in Hell* will be answered thoroughly in the pages ahead.

My wife and I wish to thank all those who have read our first book and have written to us, as we are so very appreciative and grateful to you for opening your heart to us and sharing your situations. If it were possible, we would like to meet every one of you and personally thank you. Your letters and e-mails are highly valued.

PART ONE

CHAPTER 1

AGE-OLD QUESTIONS—
ARE THERE ANSWERS?

SINCE I HAVE BEGUN TO TELL MY TESTIMONY ON THE RADIO, TELE-vision, and at other events, I have been asked many questions and have heard a wide variety of comments—some sound very reasonable and logical. They range in emotion from fear to downright anger:

- "How can a loving God send anyone to hell? If He is all loving, as we have been told, how could He be so merciless as to torment people for all eternity?"

- "Why would He make such a horrible place?"

- "How could a temporary time of sin cause a justification of an eternal punishment? The punishment doesn't seem to fit the crime."

- "What about all those other religions out there? There are many different religions with people who are as dedicated to their beliefs as you Christians. What about those religions? Are you telling me that they are all wrong and only you are right? That is really being narrow-minded, judgmental, and condemning. You really can't believe that way!"

- "What about the one who never heard of the Bible or Jesus, the one who lives up in the remote mountains, who doesn't hurt anyone? Are you going to tell me that just because they didn't 'believe' the way you 'believe' that they will suffer forever? That's crazy."

- "What about my neighbor? He works hard every day taking care of his family, loves them dearly, and is a really good man. He helps everyone. He is involved in a city program to help the poor and handicapped children. Are you telling me that even he will go to hell because he doesn't know Jesus? I don't think so!"

- "If your God would send all those good people to hell, then He is an unreasonable God, and I wouldn't want anything to do with Him."

This is how many people feel, and I can understand their line of thinking. These are just a few of the thoughts someone might have, especially if they don't know what the only true God is really like! Many think God is inconsiderate of others who don't have the same beliefs. To send someone to hell just because they don't believe in Jesus and don't repent of sin seems very unreasonable, especially if they are good people, right?

Before I address those issues, I would like you to view these questions from a different perspective. I would like you to contemplate what would be your thoughts if you were lying on a hospital bed right now. Your doctor has informed you that you only have several hours to live. Your disease is in the very final stages. You will probably not last the night. What would be important to you during those last remaining hours you have on this earth? I'm sure that the usual things we all are concerned with, such as seeing family members, spending each cherished moment with your spouse, and making sure financial affairs are in order, would be prominent. However, would you think about things such as, "Is there life after death? Is there such a place as heaven or hell? If there is, where will I go—heaven or hell?

Would I be accepted into heaven, and if so, why? Will the deciding factor be based on my being 'good' or 'bad'?"

Perhaps you might believe in hell but think that hell is simply a state of mind. If that is true, then why did Jesus warn us so much about its horrors? You might think, "Well, I don't believe in an afterlife. I believe that we simply cease to exist." If that is the case, then you have to ask yourself this question: What about the Hitlers and the child molesters of the world? If there is no life after death, then there would be no justice ever served. Is that fair?

On the other side of the coin, what about those who have done so much good for humanity? To not acknowledge and reward those would also be an injustice. Nothing would matter since everyone "ceases to exist." If there is no justice, and the killers get off scot-free, is that a fair and proper ending to this life? If there is no one to answer to, then what is life's purpose?

In chapter 16, "Are You In, or Are You Out?" my wife and I will share a recent true story from a man who recently faced that exact situation. He was a wealthy man who didn't believe in God and found himself at death's door. How did he respond, and what happened to him?

What if you didn't have that opportunity to think on these things while in a hospital because your life ended suddenly? If your thoughts are, "Well, who really knows? I will find out when the time comes," would that be considered prudent? If we took that attitude where our retirement years are concerned, we know that would be foolish. If we said, "I will just wait until I'm sixty-five; I will think about saving and planning then," it could be too late at that point. Wouldn't that be ill considered? Even more so, to ignore something of such importance as your own eternity, one would be considered unwise. Proverbs 19:2 says, "That the soul be without knowledge, it is not good" (KJV). Proverbs also says, "A prudent man foresees evil and hides himself; the simple pass on and are punished" (Prov. 27:12). If you are one who hasn't investigated, then are you willing to risk so much on just your opinion?

CHAPTER 2

HOW CAN A LOVING GOD SEND PEOPLE TO HELL?

I F THERE IS ONE QUESTION THAT I HAVE BEEN ASKED COUNTLESS TIMES, it is this one. Many assume it is God sending even good people to an eternal, fiery torment. "How could a loving God do such a thing?" they ask.

There are many misconceptions regarding the subject of divine judgment, hell, and God's justice. Some have commented that God is mean and inconsiderate of others who disagree with biblical views. In addition, they have stated that Christians are unreasonable and narrow-minded to believe that they are the only ones who will be admitted through the pearly gates. I can understand why many would come to these conclusions, as it doesn't seem to make sense. However, once the nature of God is understood, and the fact that He is *not* sending anyone to hell, we will see that our own concepts and presuppositions are simply in error.

Because many refuse to even discuss the topic, there exists a lack of knowledge regarding these issues. Without the correct information, many have formed a god in their minds that doesn't exist. Their view of God is one who is either merciless in sending people to hell, or He is one who excuses their sin altogether. Either way, both concepts are misguided. I will answer these questions throughout the rest of these chapters, and I truly believe that, if you will read all the information herein, you will gain clarity. Only after obtaining the information can you make an informed decision. King Solomon said in

Proverbs 18:13, "He who answers a matter before he hears it, it is folly and shame to him."

This subject is so vitally important that we absolutely must know the truth in order to avoid making the wrong decision. There is no turning back. One second after we die, it's too late. Please don't take this lightly. With all sincerity, I wouldn't want my worst enemy to end up in hell. My intent in this book is not to denigrate anyone's beliefs, but I will attempt to dissuade you from your believing anything other than the Bible.

ARE WE "ENTITLED" TO LIVE AT GOD'S HOUSE?

Suppose you knocked on the door of the most expensive home in the country and told the owners, "I'm moving in with you." What do you think they would say? Of course they would say no! And you wouldn't expect them to welcome you. You have no relationship with them. So you, who question God's fairness, live your entire life having nothing to do with Him, even denying that Jesus is the Son of God; you then come knocking on God's door at your death and say, "Excuse me, I'm moving in with You!"

Why would you think that you have a right to move into His house? Why should He let you in? You never asked Him to be your Father, as He has offered Himself to you during your life on Earth. As a matter of fact, you denied His Son as your Lord and Savior, who He told you was the only way into heaven (John 3:36; 11:25–26; 14:6; Acts 4:12; Rom. 3:30; 10:9–10; 1 Tim. 2:5; 1 John 5:12). Therefore, there is no relationship that exists between you and Him (John 1:12). He is not your Father, only your Creator (Col. 1:16).

You say, "But He knows me, and He is supposed to be a loving God!" He knows you exist, but He doesn't know you personally. In Matthew 7:23, Jesus said, "And then will I profess unto them, I never knew you: depart from me, ye that work iniquity" (KJV). How terrible would that be to hear from His lips? The fact that He gives us a choice to be in relationship with Him proves He is a loving God. It is up to us to choose whether we do so or not.

If a stranger came to you and said that he was moving into your home, would I be justified in calling you "mean" for not allowing him access? Would I be justified in saying that you were "unloving"? No, because their moving in with you is not based on the question of whether you are "loving" or not, but it is based on your "relationship" with them.

So it is with us. If we do not have a relationship that exists with Jesus, then we are not in His family, and we have no right to enter His home. Now tell me, who here is the inconsiderate and unreasonable one? I don't know if you are ready for this or not, but Jesus actually said in John 8:44, "For you are the children of your father the Devil..." (NLT). He says this because His message did not find a place in the people's hearts (John 8:37). In other words, either God is your Father, or the devil is your father. I know that is strong language, but most don't realize that we all have a spiritual father, and there are only two choices. If we haven't made Jesus our Lord, then we have a father whether we know it or not. If you think that is foolish, then you have a right to disagree with Jesus, but it won't change the facts. I know many assume we are all "the children of God." That is a misnomer.

In addition to John 8:44 above, John 1:12 says, "But to all who believed him and accepted him, he gave *the right to become* children of God" (NLT). Again, when speaking to the Father, Jesus said in John 17:9, "I pray for them. I do not pray for the world but for those whom You have given Me, *for they are Yours*" (NKJV). According to Galatians 3:26, our faith or belief in who Jesus is makes us children of God. It says, "For ye are all the children of God *by faith in Christ Jesus.*"

Ephesians 1:5 states, "His unchanging plan has always been to *adopt us into his own family* by bringing us to Himself *through Jesus Christ*" (NLT). (See also Matthew 5:45; Luke 6:35–36; Romans 9:7–8; Galatians 4:19; Ephesians 5:1; 1 Thessalonians 5:5.)

For us to show up at heaven's gates and expect to just move in without a relationship would be as foolish as expecting to live in that expensive home. Our lack of knowledge is no excuse. It is just as if we were speeding and told the policeman, "I didn't see the sign!"

GOD IS NOT TO BLAME—THE CHOICE IS YOURS

In blaming God for the many tragedies that take place on this earth, many assume He is the one responsible for sending people to hell also. To accuse God of evil is completely misguided. The possibility of Him causing bad things to happen to us is the antithesis of His nature. The truth is, because God has given man a free will, man can choose whatever he wants to do and to believe.

Yet many are quick to respond, "Where was God when this flood occurred, or the fire, or the earthquake? How is it that He let this happen?" We ask these questions as if we were in a higher moral position than God Himself. We infer that we would not have allowed such a horrible thing to happen. We would have prevented the disaster. We accuse God and question, "You didn't stop this and why not?" We question God in our arrogance and lack of knowledge. God said to Job in Job 40:8, "Will you condemn Me, that you may be righteous?"

Dr. Erwin Lutzer said, "Often the same people who ask where God was following a disaster thanklessly refuse to worship and honor Him for years of peace and calmness. They disregard God in good times, yet think He is obligated to provide help when bad times come."[1] Dr. Walter Martin also said, "Don't call into question God's attributes of mercy and compassion. Call into question the mess that we made of the earth in which we live. When God created it, it wasn't intended to be this way. The beauty that's in the world was God's idea. The mess was ours. And now, when we look around and see a world cursed by sin, and we see judgment in that world...we blame God."[2]

To sum it up, many blame God for the disasters that take place, yet in the good times, they deny His very existence. Man has free will, and therefore he has the freedom to sin. God has established a universal law: we reap what we sow (Gal. 6:7). Perhaps, there is a connection with all the terrible things that take place upon the earth and our blatant rejection of God and His Word. Rather than take responsibility, man chooses to believe that God is the author of evil. That way, we can question God's love and fairness. If we travel this path, we will eventually reject God, and along with that, we most certainly will reject the reality of hell. In addition, we will conclude that it is foolishness to suggest that demons are real and that they can influence our thoughts.

In the garden, God told Adam, "But of the tree of the knowledge of good and evil, thou shalt not eat of it: for in the day that thou eatest thereof thou shalt surely die" (Gen. 2:17, KJV). Man had a choice to obey or not to obey God's command. The devil came along and said, "Ye shall not surely die" (Gen. 3:4, KJV). Satan lied, of course, since he is the father of lies (John 8:44), and Adam and Eve fell for his deception. Billy Graham says that Lucifer lied, saying that "God does not know what He is talking about. Satan often works by interjecting a question to raise doubts. It is deadly to doubt God's Word! Satan's strategy is to persuade us to rationalize....Eve foolishly parleyed with the tempter."[3]

It is the same way today. Many "parley" with the tempter, and in so doing, make the wrong decision. However, this decision happens to be permanent. That is why our contemplation in regard to this matter deserves a most careful consideration. Perhaps this next analogy will help us further see that we do have that choice.

Suppose I invited you over for dinner but told you not to open the large steel door that is next to the garage because there is a lion behind that door. Would you still open it? I even posted warning signs all over the door that a deadly lion is behind the door. The warning reads, "Do not open the door under any circumstance, or you will die." You, then, have a choice. You can deliberately not listen, think you know all there is to know about lions, and lose your life by opening the door. Or you could heed the warning and choose not to open the door. My desire is that you never open the door. However, you decide to open the door and you die. It wasn't my will or my desire that you die. I didn't "send" you to your death. It's the same way with God. The Bible says that it isn't God's will for any to perish (2 Pet. 3:9). Just because it is God's will for you to receive eternal life and not perish doesn't mean you'll listen to Him and make that choice.

THE ENEMY

In researching the Scriptures, we find that God is not the one sending us to hell; neither is He causing the tragedies that take place in everyday life. If we can understand this, then perhaps it will be possible for many to see that man has a very real enemy who seeks to destroy us by any means necessary—and it is *not* God. Jesus said in John 10:10, "The thief [Satan] cometh not, but for to steal, and to kill, and to destroy: I am come that they might have life, and that they might have it more abundantly." First John 3:8 also states why Jesus came. It says, "For this purpose the Son of God was manifested, that He might destroy the works of the devil. During Jesus's earthly ministry, we see Him healing the sick, casting out devils, raising the dead, preaching and teaching the kingdom of God and repentance. (See also Matthew 8:3, 16–17; Mark 7:32–35; 10:52; Luke 4:18–21, 40–44; 5:12–13; 8:48; 13:3, 16; Acts 10:38.) Jesus just stated in those verses that evil comes from the devil. Demonic powers exist and cause evil. In addition, man has a free will to cooperate with evil and to disobey God's instructions if he so chooses.

Many do not realize that evil powers are very real. Now, I am not talking about seeing a demon behind every tree. As a matter of fact, most of the times the evil and troublesome things that occur are a result of man's own disobedience, not the devil. However, we have seen many of the despicable acts some have committed, with the kidnapping and torture of little children or all the shootings that have taken place in our schools, universities, and shopping centers. We have seen the heinous and wicked acts perpetrated by the terrorists, some even sawing people's heads off right on the TV. How merciless and evil is that? There are some wicked people out there, but to do something like that is beyond "mean." That kind of evil can only come from the demonic realm. You are dealing with not just a messed-up person but also a demonic spirit.

Billy Graham says, "In his warfare against God, Satan uses the human race, which God created and loved. So God's forces of good and Satan's forces of evil have been engaged in a deadly conflict from the dawn of our history....Satan and his demons are known by the discord they promote, the wars they start, the hatred they engender, the murders they initiate, the opposition to God and His commandments. They are dedicated to the spirit of destruction."[4]

In 2 Corinthians 2:11, the apostle Paul speaks to believers and tells us that we are not to be ignorant of Satan's devices. Therefore, it is possible for us to be ignorant. You might say, "I don't believe in the demonic realm or Satan." Well, let me ask you a question. Where do you think all the evil in the world originated from? These things are very real, whether you believe them or not. First Peter 5:8 says, "Be sober, be vigilant; because your adversary the devil, as a roaring lion, walketh about, seeking whom he may devour" (KJV). This verse indicates that there are those the devil *may not* devour. We have a part to play in this. James 4:7 says, "Submit yourselves therefore to God. Resist the devil, and he will flee from you" (KJV). In other words, if you are not submitted to God, the devil won't flee from you. Jesus, on the other hand, said that He came to give us abundant life, not death. So why do many blame God for the death and tragedies?

There is a comment spoken by many when a tragic loss of a loved one occurs. They sometimes will say, "Well, the good Lord took them home." Now, I am aware that people are well intentioned and are trying to offer comfort with this statement. But would that be scripturally true? Is it the Lord's doing? We just pointed out in John 10:10 that the thief Satan comes to steal, kill, and destroy—not God. You say, "But why did God allow it? Since He is God, He could have stopped it!" First of all, the Bible calls Satan the *god of this world* and he is the one causing the destruction (2 Cor. 4:4, KJV). Secondly, there are areas of entrance the enemy can find to gain access into our lives. Many times it is due to a lack of knowledge on our part.

The Bible gives us instructions on how to avoid many problems; however, we either don't read it and are therefore unaware of the warnings, or we don't obey them. Now I know the loss of a loved one is devastating and great compassion should be given to those in such a hurting circumstance. We are not to judge others, nor judge God. However, we can't continue to blame God just to comfort ourselves. I want to be very careful here not to cause anyone to feel condemnation, as that is not the purpose or the issue.

But I also would like people to see that we sometimes falsely accuse God. I'd rather offend someone and perhaps cause them to examine themselves, rather than hear God get the blame again for taking a life. It is usually the devil who stole the loved one's life. We must also realize that many people are not even in God's family and, therefore, according to Scripture, have no protection from the evil one, because "the angel of the LORD encamps all around *those who fear Him*, and delivers them" (Ps. 34:7). Those who don't know Him and don't fear Him have no angels of protection. Proverbs 15:29 says, "The LORD is far from the wicked." However, if they happen to be blessed with a family member who prays for them, then for a time they will have God's mercy extended to them.

LIFE, DEATH, AND THE SOVEREIGNTY OF GOD

Another thought you may now have is, "What about the sovereignty of God? He chooses when someone will die." Yes, God is sovereign, but there are two things to consider. First, if you are not in His family, you have no assurance of a long life whatsoever. Deuteronomy 28:66 says, "Your life shall hang in doubt before you; you shall fear day and night, and have no assurance of life." Second, if you are a child of God, the Bible is full of promises of long life, but they are based on us taking hold of those promises and obeying His Word. (See Deuteronomy 25:15; 1 Kings 3:14; Proverbs 3:2, 16; 4:10; 7:1–2; 9:11; 10:27; 14:27; 19:23; 28:16; Ephesians 6:3.)

As you can see from the verses above, we have a responsibility to keep His Word, thereby receiving the promise of a long life. This is not overstepping the sovereignty of God, by any means. It is simply taking Him at His Word. He is the one who stated the promises. He wants us to discover them in His Word and believe and trust Him for them. Psalm 91:16 says, "With long life will I satisfy him and show him my salvation."

My earthly dad is a man of his word. Over the years, I have watched my dad exercise great integrity and keep his word throughout his life even during some of the toughest real estate transactions. If he said it, he will do it—even if it is to his own hurt. Suppose I asked my dad for ten thousand dollars and he told me, "Son, you'll have it by Friday this week." Later that day, my dad overhears me talking with my wife. I say, "Honey, I don't know how we're going to pay these bills. I don't know if my dad will come through. What are we going to do?" How do you think my dad would feel?

Well, this is exactly what we do with God. My wife and I have found out that God honors childlike faith and that He means what He says. You may not take His Word literally, but we have found out that is exactly what He wants us to do. It certainly has resulted in answered prayer for us.

It will take some faith to appropriate those promises, and it takes faith to please God (Heb. 11:6). Also, we are held accountable to God to know the Scriptures. Jesus held Israel accountable to know who He was and His time of visitation because it was foretold in Scripture (Luke 19:44). Deuteronomy 6:6–9 speaks of committing ourselves wholeheartedly to learning the Word of God. It tells us to repeat God's commands over and over to our children, talk about them when we're at home or on a journey, and to keep them before our eyes as a reminder. (See Joshua 1:8.) If we truly love the Lord, as we may say, then we will obey Him (John 14:23). Many say they love God, but they don't obey Him. To obey Him would mean to worship Him, feed the poor, tithe, witness, and read His Word daily (Deut. 6:1–9; Matt. 19:21; Mark 16:15; Luke 18:22; 2 Cor. 9:9).

I'm not saying we can prevent all trials, tragedies, or difficulties in our lives, but I am saying we will be in a place to at least examine ourselves to see if we are off in some area, and thereby correct ourselves and eliminate many mishaps.

My point is, we can't automatically assume when loss or tragedy occurs that it was God's fault or even His will. Psalm 119:67 records David saying, "*Before* I was afflicted I went astray: *but now* have I *kept thy Word*." Notice his affliction occurred after he went astray. It doesn't mean it was God's will for him to be afflicted. In fact, David tells us that he was responsible for his troubles. Throughout the Scriptures, David examined himself against God's Word. We should all do the same. And Hosea 4:6 says, "*My people* are destroyed for a lack of knowledge."

Here are some areas we can look at to see where we may be putting ourselves in the path of destruction. Please keep in mind these are just a few examples. God's Word is full of instruction for every area of our life.

SIN

Psalm 107:17 says, "Fools, because of their transgressions, and because of their iniquities, are afflicted." Our sins cause us pain and trouble. Proverbs 28:13 says, "He who covers his sins will not prosper, but whoever confesses and forsakes them will have mercy." If we confess our sin to the Lord and turn from it, we immediately receive His forgiveness. (See 1 John 1:9.) James 5:16 continues with, "Confess your faults one to another, and pray one for another, that ye may be healed." (See also Jeremiah 26:3; John 5:14.)

UNFORGIVENESS

Another way that may give the enemy access to your life is unforgiveness. This includes unforgiveness toward others, ourselves, or God. Second Corinthians 2:10–11 says, "Now whom you forgive anything…lest Satan should take advantage of us." In other words, if we don't forgive, we can be taken advantage of by the devil. There are many people who never really forgive the person who has done them wrong. They will say, "I forgave, but I'll never forget." That is not true forgiveness. Hebrews 10:17 tells us that once God forgives us, He will remember our sins no more. We must do the same. If we don't forgive, we will open a big door to the enemy to enter in and cause destruction in our lives. In Matthew 6:14–15, Jesus says, "For if you forgive men their trespasses, your heavenly Father will also forgive you. But if you do not forgive men their trespasses, neither will your Father forgive your trespasses." I don't think we want to be without the Father's forgiveness.

HONORING YOUR PARENTS

Honoring your parents is another way to prevent the enemy from causing mayhem and cutting your life short. Ephesians 6:2–3 says, "Honor thy father and mother; (which is the first commandment with promise;) that it may be well with thee, and thou mayest live long on the earth" (KJV). This verse presents one reason why some die young. They don't honor their parents.

FEARING GOD

Another principle to preserve the length of your life is having a holy fear of God. "The fear of the LORD prolongeth days..." (Prov. 10:27, KJV). Proverbs 19:23 also says, "Fear of the Lord gives life, security, and protection from harm" (NLT). Fearing God does not mean that if we do something wrong He is going to strike us down, so we better shape up! God is not looking for ways to harm us, but rather to help us and bless us. The fear that I am speaking of is the kind of fear that possesses an honest reverence for who He is. He is the one and only Almighty God. We honor and acknowledge Him as the Supreme Being with infinite power and authority. Along with understanding this, we are to receive His love, trust Him, and approach Him as our dear Father.

UNGODLY ASSOCIATIONS

We are influenced by those we spend time with. What values, beliefs, or attitudes do our friends live by? What effect is it having on us? "He that walks with wise men shall be wise: but a companion of fools shall be destroyed" (Prov. 13:20). Proverbs 12:15 says, "The way of a fool is right in his own eyes, but he who heeds counsel is wise." This implies that a fool thinks he knows it all. According to Scripture, a fool is also someone who mocks sin and someone who says in his heart, "There is no God." (See Proverbs 14:1, 9.) Do we associate and spend time with those who mock God and His people?

Proverbs continues to warn us against entering partnership with a thief, not to associate with people who flatter with their tongue, and stay away from someone who is a talebearer because they cause strife. (See Proverbs 20:19; 26:20; 29:24.)

There are many verses I could point out that show where we may be in error. There are things we can do, or not do, that will leave us vulnerable. So again, it is not God's fault but ours. You may be thinking, "What about God's grace?" Grace is not a cover-up for our ignorance or an excuse for our sin. Grace is an empowerment to live in obedience to His Word. We, as Christians, are held accountable to do just that—obey His Word. This is not legalism; this is simply obedience. And besides, when you really know

God, you want to spend time with Him and learn His ways. Otherwise, we are taking a spiritually lazy and irresponsible position. This attitude says, "When bad things happen, blame God." It also says, "Why, it couldn't be *my* fault. I couldn't possibly be to blame!"

Sometimes we experience unpleasant situations because we are in a hurry. Have you ever driven your vehicle in that manner? I have. Accidents can happen simply because we are hasty and we're not taking the time to acknowledge the Lord. Proverbs 3:5–6 instructs us to acknowledge the Lord *in all our ways*. If a tragic accident occurs, we shouldn't blame God and question, "Why did God allow that?" We don't have all the information. We don't know the details surrounding the person's life, their relationship with God, how they were driving, their prayer life, if they ignored the Holy Spirit's inner witness warning them not to go somewhere, and so on.

Shortly after 9/11, I heard a program where numerous people were sharing how God was speaking to them that morning. Some shared that they just didn't have a peace to go to work that day. Others were distracted by doing errands before work—or so they thought. One little girl insisted that her father spend time with her before he went to work that day. Her persistence made him late for work. By hearing God's warnings that day, many people's lives were spared. It was so very terrible with that many lost, but it would have been worse without God's intervention.

Sometimes, we are so distracted through busyness, daily pressures, and deadlines that we can ignore a message from God. He will lead us, but He'll never force us to seek Him or to yield to His direction. It's not His will that someone drives carelessly and harms another. Yet, many people will claim that whatever happens is God's will. If that is true, why wouldn't we say, "Well, if he dies and goes to hell, then it must be God's will. And, if he receives Jesus and goes to heaven then that's God's will." No. The scripture is clear that it isn't God's will for any to perish (2 Pet. 3:9). Why did Jesus tell us to pray for God's will to be done on Earth as it is in heaven (Matt. 6:10)? He wouldn't tell us to pray for this if God's will was automatically done all the time. However, many of us take a spiritually irresponsible stance when bad things happen in our lives. We think everything is God's will. Thankfully, God is good and very gracious so He can make good come out of a bad situation, but that doesn't mean it was His will for it to happen in the first place. Ephesians 5:17 says, "Therefore do not be unwise, but understand what the will of the Lord is." How will we learn, mature, and recognize what is a test from God, an attack from the enemy, or a failure to obey His Word? We must get our answers from His Word, not from our experience or from the experience of others.

GOD WANTS TO BLESS US

Every day we have a choice to love people, forgive, and show kindness. Luke 6:35 declares, "But love your enemies, and do good…for He [the Father] is kind unto the unthankful and to the evil." Our Father God is our example, and we are also to show the same love and kindness to all. Here's an example of how showing kindness results in a benefit even years later.

During my real estate career, I remember a time when a nice, older couple came to an open house I was hosting. They were so pleasant, kind, and well dressed. They wanted to lease a home rather than purchase the one I had for sale. So I told them about a home I had seen in the neighborhood that had a "For Lease By Owner" sign in the window. We decided to walk over together to find out more information.

When we got to the house, I knocked on the door and asked the owner if she was still looking to lease her home. She immediately screamed at me and told me how she hated real estate agents and would never work with one. I said, "I understand, and I know some agents can be difficult, but you can just work with this couple directly. I don't need to be involved in any way. I don't want any money. They really need a place, and I am sure they would be just what you are looking for."

Well, she slammed the door in my face. I asked the nice couple to go back to her later and see if she would talk to them without me there. They did, and she leased it to them. After I learned that everything had worked out very well, I sent a thank you note to the owner, who had slammed the door, thanking her for taking care of them. As time went on, I would occasionally run into the nice couple.

Six years went by, and at this time I was the president of the homeowners association. The entire complex needed to be painted. We were going to have it changed from the plain 1970s' beige color and have it professionally coordinated with a variety of colors. We needed a majority vote. It came to the final night for the vote, and we were one vote short. At the meeting, the homeowner who slammed the door in my face stood up in the meeting and said, "I'm going to vote for the painting and go along with Bill Wiese's recommendation to change the colors. He looked out for a nice elderly couple once, so I'm sure he is looking out for us now. So he has my vote." With that we had our ninety-three votes.

This story shows that if we demonstrate the love of God toward people, even when they treat us poorly, it will always come back to bless us later. By the way, the people in the neighborhood ended up loving all the color changes.

I would like to share another story of how God desires to bless us. Again, the reward came by seeking Him (Heb. 11:6). I had been rising up early and praying each day, but this one particular day I felt strongly impressed to get up and pray. (Of course, time with the Lord is always the best way to start every day.) I rose up, and while praying, I again felt impressed to study all the facts and figures of our neighborhood. As a real estate broker, I sold the homes in the neighborhood where I lived. So after my time in prayer, I began to do research to obtain these facts. By that afternoon, I had memorized all the information. Well, later that evening, I received a call from a homeowner who wanted to sell his property. He said that he wanted to interview me and then two other agents afterward. He would then make his decision and list his home with the agent he thought was best for the job. I told him that would be fine.

During my interview, he began asking a series of questions having to do with various facts and figures about the neighborhood. He asked, "How many models of my home are there?"

I responded, "Forty-one."

He then asked, "How many have sold this year?"

I replied, "Four."

He continued, "How many last year?"

I said, "Seven."

"How many total models are there?"

I said, "Six."

He asked, "How many of the other five are there of each?"

I said, "Thirty-five model plan 303; thirty plan 300; twenty-seven plan 301; twenty-six plan 302; and twenty-three plan 304."

He then asked, "How many acres is the complex?"

I said, "Thirty-three."

"How many acres is our lake?"

I replied, "One and one-half."

He then shook his head, as if in amazement, and said, "How could you remember so many figures?"

I said, "It's part of my job to know them." Of course, I just learned all of this information that very morning.

He then said, "You got the job!"

He didn't bother to interview the other two agents. I listed the home, thanked him, and left as it was getting late. As I was walking away, a neighbor stopped me and asked me if I had any homes for sale. I told them I just listed one thirty seconds ago. They asked if they could see it. I turned around and went right back and knocked on his door. I asked him if I could show it to this couple. He said, "You certainly do work fast." We came in and they looked at the home and bought it right then. It was the quickest sale I ever made.

My point is this: Most likely, I would not have been given the listing if I didn't get up that morning to pray and heard God's voice to look over the neighborhood facts, because I would not have been able to answer the man's questions. Psalm 57:8–9 says, "I myself will awake *early*. I will praise thee." In Proverbs 8:17, it says "Those that seek me *early* shall find Me." In addition, Psalm 90:14 says, "O satisfy us *early* with thy mercy." I am not saying that you're in disobedience if you don't wake up early and pray. I'm saying there is a special blessing for us when we follow the leading of God and seek Him early!

God is always looking for ways to bless His people. We are the ones who hinder those blessings. Many of us don't spend enough time in prayer, and thereby we miss hearing His voice.

WHY WE REJECT GOD

God is kind to all (Luke 6:35), and everything we have that is good is from Him (James 1:17). His desire is to see every person saved (Acts 2:21; 1 Tim. 2:4). So why do people resist such a kind and loving God? What is the problem?

The bottom line is that mankind doesn't want to let go of their sin. When we are confronted by the light of God's Word, our sin is exposed. We would rather hide in the darkness and not face it. But if we will simply come to God, He will help us get rid of the sin that enslaves us. Instead of running *from* God, we should run *to* Him.

Often man chooses to go against the ways of God, thereby stepping outside of God's protection. If we reject His way, then just as God said, we will end up in hell. We choose to go there by our own stubborn will, rejecting the way God has provided us for escape. A. W. Pink said:

> The sinner is bidden to "taste and see that the Lord is good." He is freely invited to be a guest at the Gospel feast. The promise is wide and plain—"Him that cometh to me I will in no wise cast out." But if the sinner will not come to Christ that he may have life, then his blood is upon his own head. If he will not believe, then it is his own will which damns him.[5]

Why do we think we know better? I believe one reason is because of pride. It takes humility to admit we don't know it all and that we are sinners. I definitely do not know it all. That is why I want to be careful to point you to what the Scriptures say.

There was a Harris Poll done several years ago, and it revealed that 73 percent of Americans believe in hell. However, it also revealed that only 2 percent believe they will go there.[6] Dr. Erwin W. Lutzer said, "Genuine fear of suffering in hell has vanished from the mainstream of Western thought. Few, if any, give prolonged thought to the prospect that some people will be in hell. Fewer yet believe they themselves will be among that unfortunate number."[7]

Jesus didn't come into this world to condemn it; quite the contrary. He came to save it (John 3:17). What people need to be aware of is that the world was already condemned because of Adam's sin (Rom. 5:15–19). Adam sold us over to the devil. God doesn't have to send anyone to hell. We are *all* already on our way there. Jesus came to redeem us (Titus 2:14; 1 Pet. 1:18–19) and save us *from* hell, not send us there! Heed His call:

> Enter ye in at the strait gate: for wide is the gate, and broad is the way, that leadeth to destruction, and many there be which go in thereat: Because strait is the gate, and narrow is the way, which leadeth unto life, and few there be that find it.
>
> —Matthew 7:13–14, KJV

Jesus said that most are going to hell. Therefore, people's opinions about their eternal destinies are seriously out of line with the truth. Dr. Chuck Missler said, "The bottom line is, God does not send people to hell. People wind up in hell because they refuse to turn to Him for the forgiveness and the love provided them through the shed blood of His Son, Jesus."[8]

Secondly, some people have a warped view of God because of their relationship with their earthly father. This, in turn, causes us to reject a heavenly Father. We may have experienced abuse, pain, and abandonment from our father. Because of our experience, we view God and His commandments as harsh, oppressive, burdensome, and demanding. We hear biblical terms such as *serve* and *obey*, and they make us angry. For many, to serve and obey anyone comes across with a negative connotation akin to slavery and tyranny! God looks mean and unfair, ready to hit us over the head the moment we displease Him. Yet they don't realize that the reason God wants us to serve and obey Him is so He can protect us from harm. In addition, this is the means by which He rewards us (Job 36:11; Heb. 11:6). So instead, we steer clear of anything to do with God, church, or Christians. Because of our damaged soul, we refuse God's love and reject Him.

If our earthly father didn't give us a twisted view of God, religion may have done so. Religion represents the father whose approval you strive for but will never receive. You're never *good enough* to receive God's love and acceptance. You're taught to keep countless rules, but you never know why. You also never know God personally, and He really doesn't sound like someone you'd want to spend time with because He is too demanding.

This is not the God of the Bible. He has been extremely misrepresented over the centuries. To a large degree, man's tradition has been taught, not God's Word. And those outside church walls claim that the Bible is a fairy-tale book for the weak and uninformed. If it is simply a fairy-tale book, why do these same people get so angry when you warn them that their choice sends them to hell?

I know there are also many who deny God even exists. One atheist asked me, "If there is a God, then why is there so much evil in the world?" I responded with a question, asking, "If there is no God, then why is there so much good in the world?" He couldn't answer. I heard another minister say that he was confronted in one of his meetings by an atheist who said, "I don't believe there is a God, and I think you are wrong to teach that there is." He responded to the atheist with this question: "Do you think you know all there is to know in life?" The atheist said, "No, I don't know everything." The minister said, "Well, let's say you are an exceptionally bright man, one of the smartest people in the world, and you know half of everything there is to know. Do you think God could be in that other half?" Something to consider!

So as I have pointed out, God doesn't send anyone to hell. We send ourselves. By rejecting His provision of redemption from our sins (Jesus), we are saying to God, "I think You are wrong. I think there is another way to get to heaven." This leads us to the next question in chapter 3, "Don't All Roads Lead to God?" Some people believe that whatever one believes may be right for that person yet not for another. Will everyone's belief turn out to be true? They say, "We all will end up in heaven if we do good things in life." We will find out if this is the case in the following chapters.

CHAPTER 3

DON'T ALL ROADS LEAD TO GOD?

SUPPOSE YOU INVITE ME OVER TO DINNER, BUT I NEED DIRECTIONS to get to your place. You tell me to take Highway 95 South to Main Street. Turn right, go up the hill, then turn left, and your house will be at the top of the hill. I say to you, "Well, I think I'm going to go north on Highway 95 and get off at Beach Boulevard, because I think all roads lead to your house." You inform me, "You will not get to my house traveling that way; this is the only way to my house. Please follow my directions if you want to see me and enjoy a nice dinner." In the same way, God gives us clear directions to His house. I think God knows where He lives! If we choose to follow His directions, we will arrive at His house; if we don't, we won't. It's that simple.

People want to hear that many roads lead to heaven, and if we are good enough, we will all arrive there. They ask, "What about all those other religions? Isn't that narrow-minded to think Christianity is the 'only way' to get to heaven?" No, it is not narrow-minded; it is specific. There may be some beliefs you were raised with and never questioned, but the fact is your belief may not be leading you in the direction you want to go. Jesus said in Luke 11:35, "Make sure that the light you think you have is not actually darkness" (NLT).

If we can all believe whatever we want to, yet be "good enough" to be accepted, then why did Jesus need to suffer and die for us? Why did He

29

have to come? If we can make it on our own, then we don't need Jesus. That is definitely not what the Bible teaches, as we will see later. I know many don't like being told there is only one choice. But let me give you another analogy.

Suppose you had a terminal illness and there was no cure that anyone knew of. You finally come across one doctor who says to you, "I have found medicine that will cure you completely. This is the only cure available." Would you say to him, "Hey, Doc, I don't like that this is the only cure. I would like to see some other choices; otherwise, I'm not going to take the medicine." I don't think that is what you would say. It would be considered foolish to turn down the only known cure just because there is no other. You would most certainly be very happy that there is a cure.

In this life, there is only one way to avoid hell and spend eternity with God, but you must take the prescribed medicine. You do have the choice, however, to refuse it and spend eternity in hell. It doesn't seem too bright to me to turn down the only known cure for eternal damnation, but it's your life. Please understand that there are no other options. First John 5:12 says, "He that hath the Son hath life; and he that hath not the Son of God hath not life" (KJV). Only through Jesus can we find our way out of hell's fire. He is "the way, the truth, and the life: no man cometh unto the Father, but by me [Jesus]" (John 14:6, KJV). That's as direct and as clear as you can get.

Dr. Erwin Lutzer gives an excellent correlation:

> After the news of the *Titanic's* tragedy reached the world, the challenge was how to inform the relatives whether their loved ones were among the dead or the living. At the White Star Line's office in Liverpool, England, a huge board was set up; on one side was a cardboard sign: *Known to be Saved*, and on the other, a cardboard sign with the words, *Known to Be Lost*. Hundreds of people gathered to intently watch the updates. When a messenger brought new information, those waiting held their breath, wondering to which side he would go and whose name would be added to the list.

Although the travelers on the *Titanic* were either first-, second-, or third-class passengers, after the ship went down there were only two categories: the saved and the drowned. Just so, we can divide people into many different classes based on geography, race, education, and wealth. But on the final Day of Judgment, there will be only two classes: the saved and the lost. There is only heaven and hell.[1]

God told us the way, so why do so many want to change what He said and make it their way? God makes the rules, not us.

Dr. Chuck Missler says, " Yet for many, the preaching of the cross is foolishness. That's exactly what the apostle Paul pointed out: 'For the preaching of the cross is to them that perish foolishness; but unto us which are saved it is the power of God' (1 Cor. 1:18). Notice that there are only two categories: those that perish, and those that are saved. Which are you? How do you know? There should not be the slightest doubt in your mind. It is far too important to be left to guesswork or an unfounded hope."[2]

Please take to heart the truth of God's Word. You don't want to leave your eternity to "guesswork." If you are one who thinks that if you lead a good life in general and do some good works, you will end up in heaven, are you certain about your decision? If so, what do you base your certainty on?

CHAPTER 4

AM I GOOD ENOUGH
TO ENTER HEAVEN?

A 2007 Barna Research survey showed that 54 percent of all adults believe that if a person is generally good, or does enough good things for others during their life, they will earn a place in heaven.[1] Well, does that coincide with what the Bible teaches? Is it "good works" that grant us entrance into paradise? First, let me ask you a question: Whose standard of "good" do we go by? Yours and mine may differ. We tend to think, because we are just "human" (and humans make mistakes), that a reasonable and loving God would understand and overlook our faults. We assume God has that same line of reasoning, that He will surely not count our shortcomings serious enough to warrant hell as our final abode. However, our premise is mistaken. This is the most common misconception among people. Our concept of "being good" is not what grants us entrance; our entrance into heaven is based on relationship.

Many think that they can just show up at heaven's gates and say, "I'm here. Let me in. I'm a good person!" One must think fairly highly of himself to think he will just stroll right into heaven because he is a "good person." We wouldn't even expect to gain entrance into another country like that, much less heaven. Try saying that to the border patrol personnel in another country: "Let me in; I'm a good person!" I don't think that would work. They would want to see your passport and visa. In the same way, Jesus will be the judge on Judgment Day, and He will ask us why He should let us in.

If we respond with, "I'm a good person," He will show us just how "good" we really are.

Do you truly believe your life would look all that good if fully exposed to a holy God who knows every action, thought, and intent of our heart? Be completely honest; God knows the good, the bad, and the ugly we have all done. I know I wouldn't look too good. As a matter of fact, the Bible says that even if we did do a whole lot of good, our good works are as filthy rags to God (Isa. 64:6). It also says in Job 15:16, "How much more abominable and filthy is man, which drinketh iniquity like water?" (KJV).

There is not one of us who is good enough to qualify for entrance into a place as perfect as heaven (Rom. 3:12). First of all, we are born into sin (Rom. 5:14, 17–18, 21). We inherit sin just as our personalities, traits, and features are inherited from our parents. In addition, we commit sin every day, and if we commit only one sin in our entire lives, we wouldn't make it (James 2:10). Placing trust in our own good works will most certainly leave us out. Titus 3:5 states, "Not by works of righteousness which we have done, but according to His mercy He saved us." (See also Romans 3:12, 20, 28; Ephesians 2:8–9.) To give us an idea of how far short we all are from God's standard of good, I would like to share with you an analogy.

There were two men standing on the beach in California. One man was quite sickly, skinny, and weak. He appeared so frail and was barely able to stand. He was asked to jump as far as he could. In his condition, he could only jump one foot. Very sad! The other man was standing strong and tall. He was the epitome of health. He had long legs, and every muscle was developed to perfection. Now he also was asked to jump as far as he could. From a still position, with one leap, he flew through the air and traveled over fifty feet. Amazing! Who could do that from a standstill? He was obviously far superior to the other man. However, the goal for both men is to now take a leap, but they must both land on the beach in Hawaii. Well, you can see that the shape of the two men will have no bearing on the success of that endeavor. They will both need a boat. And so it is with our "good works." No matter how good we think we are, compared to God's standard, we are all in serious trouble (Rom. 3:12). We are sinking in the ocean of sin, and Jesus pulls up alongside with an extreme desire to lift us on board into His ship. Yet many shout, "No, I don't need Your help." The fact is, not one of us could ever be good enough to meet His standards. His standard is far too high.

We all can relate to standards as most of us live by them. For instance, in our own homes some of us require people to take off their shoes, some will not allow smoking or a pet in the house, and so forth. What about the workplace? Let's take NASA, for example. If you sought employment there, you would need a very specific and high degree. You would need to be in excellent health, have a clean background, and so on. Well, if we don't expect to just stroll into NASA and be hired without the proper education, then why do we assume we can just show up at heaven's gates and meet its requirements by just being good?

Many of us don't even meet up to our own standards, much less God's—and His standard is perfection! (See 2 Samuel 22:31; Psalm 18:30; 19:7; Matthew 5:48; Hebrews 5:9.) We want to compare ourselves to others, and in that comparison, we look pretty good. However, if we are talking about avoiding hell and going to heaven, then we need to compare ourselves with God's standard.

A LITTLE TEST

When people mention to me that they are good people and don't deserve hell, I ask them if they have ever told a lie, even one. Most will admit, "Yes." I then ask them, "What does that make you? Their answer should obviously be, "A liar." But you won't hear that out of their mouths. They will say, "Well, that makes me human." The same goes with stealing. There will be no admittance of being called "a thief." Why is there a reluctance to call sin what it is? Imagine that you are caught stealing a car and brought before the judge. You say, "Judge, I'm not a thief; I'm only human." He would say, "You're a thief; off to jail with you." This "human" business would not cut it in a courtroom, so why do many think it will cut it with God? And where did that come from anyway? To be politically correct today, we don't say the "sin" word. Besides, there has been such an acceptance of a sinful lifestyle that few even recognize what sin is when it is staring them in the face.

Let me give you an idea of God's standard of good with this little test, and let's see just how good we all are!

The "AM I GOOD ENOUGH FOR HEAVEN?" Test

Please answer YES or NO for each of the following questions.

- **Have you ever lied?**

YES ☐ or NO ☐

If yes, Revelation 21:8 says, "All liars shall have their part in the lake which burns with fire." If we lie just once in our lives, even a small lie, it disqualifies us from entrance. James 2:10 says, "For whosoever shall keep the whole law, and yet offend in *one point*, he is guilty of all" (KJV).

- **Have you ever stolen anything?**

YES ☐ or NO ☐

If yes, the Bible declares that if we steal even one thing, we are considered a thief, and no thief will enter heaven (1 Cor. 6:10; Eph. 5:5). You claim, "Well, I don't steal." Oh, really? Have you ever taken five minutes extra from a break at work or made personal calls on your boss's time? Have you ever written off a dinner on your tax return that was really with a friend and not a business dinner? Have you ever not claimed some income on your tax return? Jesus said to "render therefore unto Caesar the things which are Caesar's, and unto God the things that are God's" (Matt. 22:21, KJV).

- **Have you ever lusted after any other person?**

YES ☐ or NO ☐

If yes, Jesus said that you have committed adultery in your heart already if you have lust (Matt. 5:28).

If we lie, steal, or lust only once in our entire lives, we would fail God's standard—and that's just three of the Ten Commandments. Do we still have any players?

Some have actually said that they have never lied in their entire lives (they would be lying right there). This is easily proven by asking a few basic questions. First, when the phone rings, have you ever told your wife to tell the caller, "I'm not here"? Now, most of us have done that before. Guess what you call that? Or what about if you were asked to attend a meeting and your reply was, "I'll be there"—and then you don't show up. You have not kept your word. Or perhaps you were late for work and said that you were stuck in traffic when, in fact, you ran a personal errand. What about being angry without a cause (Matt. 5:22) or having an evil intent or thought? I could go on, and these are just a few of the Ten Commandments!

The Ten Commandments, found in Exodus 20, were given to man as God's standard of behavior for our lives. Many are familiar with all of them in one way or another:

1. Do not worship or give allegiance to anyone or anything other than God.

2. Do not make any idols.

3. Do not take the name of the Lord in vain.

4. Keep the Sabbath holy.

5. Honor your parents.

6. Do not kill.

7. Do not commit adultery.

8. Do not steal.

9. Do not bear false witness.

10. Do not covet.

The Ten Commandments are so simple that they have been a constant source of debate. But simply stated, they help us to know when we have done wrong (Rom. 4:15). They are also not to be taken one over the other. They all must be kept to meet God's standard. According to James 2:10, "Whoever keeps the whole law and yet stumbles at just one point is guilty of breaking all of it" (NIV).

GUILTY AS CHARGED

As you can see, we all have done these things. This is considered sin to God and keeps us from receiving access to heaven. The Bible says in 1 John 1:8, "If we say that we have no sin, we deceive ourselves, and the truth is not in us." Again, Romans 3:10 says, "There is none righteous, no, not one." The reason I am pointing out these small things is to show us how far short we all are from God's standard of perfection. And that is just the tip of the iceberg of sin in our lives.

Ray Comfort quotes Charles Finney in his book *Hell's Best Kept Secret*, saying, "It is of great importance that the sinner should be made to feel his guilt, and not left to the impression that he is unfortunate. Do not be afraid, but show him the breadth of the Divine Law, and the exceeding strictness of its precepts. Make him see how it condemns his thoughts and life."[2] Ray Comfort and Kirk Cameron say in another book, "Jesus had said, 'Be perfect, just as your Father in Heaven is perfect' (Matthew 5:48.) This statement must have left His hearers speechless—which is likely what Jesus intended, because the function of the Law is 'that every mouth may be stopped, and all the world may become guilty before God' (Romans 3:19). Who can justify themselves in God's sight if we are commanded to be perfect? *No one*. Our mouths are stopped and we see our guilt."[3]

So if you were to be judged by God's standard, would you be guilty or innocent? Guilty, of course! All of us would be. If we try to justify ourselves by our works, we are under a curse. Galatians 3:10 says, "For as many as are of the works of the law are under the curse." Galatians 2:16 says it plainly, "Knowing that a man is not justified by the works of the law, but by the faith of Jesus Christ" (KJV). And again in Titus 3:5 it says,

"Not by works of righteousness which we have done, but according to His mercy He saved us." Paul wrote to the Romans, "There is none who does good, no, not one" (Rom. 3:12). Heaven, therefore, is not attainable by man. Therefore, this idea of "good works" getting us into heaven is far from reality.

Billy Graham said, "Only when we turn to Christ in faith and trust, confessing our sins to Him and seeking His forgiveness, can we be assured of our salvation. Satan will do all in his power to make us trust ourselves instead of Christ."[4]

In the Bible times, scribes and Pharisees were men who were considered the experts of the Law. In Matthew 5:20, Jesus said, "For I say unto you, That except your righteousness shall exceed the righteousness of the scribes and Pharisees, ye shall in no case enter into the kingdom of heaven" (KJV). The scribes and Pharisees spent their entire lives trying to keep the Law and couldn't come close. As a matter of fact, this is the group whom Jesus had some strong words against and found the most fault with. With all their attempts to perform and keep the Law, they couldn't. They placed burdens on people that they themselves were not able to bear. They prided themselves on how righteous they were, when, in fact, their pride caused them to be worse than the others.

Thinking we are so very righteous is a deception. We all want people to think we are better than we really are. But God knows our heart, and He said it plainly, "The heart is deceitful above all things, and desperately wicked; who can know it?" (Jer. 17:9). Our own heart is not as good as we all would like to think it is.

LOVE VS. PUNISHMENT

Many also believe that since God is love, He is not a God who punishes sin. By believing this lie, they sit rather comfortably and oblivious to the fate that awaits them. Our sins are justifiable in our eyes, partially because of today's permissive society. Society in general, particularly our Western culture, has watered down sin to such a degree that the word *sin* is nonexistent in our vocabulary. This mentality has even invaded our pulpits. We now have "issues" or "challenges" or "problems" to deal with, but please don't use that dreaded, offensive, archaic "s" word. In the name of being politically correct and tolerant, we have abandoned the "judgmental" God of the Bible and replaced Him with a false god to suit our ideas, opinions, lifestyle, and, yes, our "sin." Perhaps idolatry (worshiping a false god) is the fastest-growing sin among Christians and non-Christians alike.

The late Dr. Walter Martin summed up this complacent attitude toward sin in his book *The Kingdom of the Cults*:

> The human soul, marred and stained as it is by the burden of personal sin, seeks constant escape from the reality of that sin and the sure penalty due because of it. Once the reality of eternal punishment is clouded by idealistic concepts of everlasting bliss without the fear of personal reckoning, the soul can relax, so to speak, and the sinner, unconscious of the impending doom, which is God's justice, rests secure in the persuasion that "God is love."[5]

Some are able to grasp the idea of punishment for sin, but it is usually only for those vile crimes against society such as murder, rape, child abuse, and the like. But the Bible says that all lying, stealing, lust, unforgiveness, the fearful, unbelieving, idolaters, fornicators, and so forth, no matter how minor they feel their sin is, shall not inherit the kingdom of heaven. (See 1 Corinthians 6:9–10; Ephesians 5:5; Revelation 21:8, 27.) If you start telling people that the sweet, loving Jesus whom we know does also state in His Word that we will go to hell if we don't trust in Him and repent of our sins (Luke 13:3; John 11:25; Acts 4:12), they will become quickly offended. As long as we preach, "Jesus loves you," we won't ruffle anyone's feathers. But the moment we preach repentance, we anger many.

Some get angry for even mentioning the possibility of them going to hell. They have commented to us that it is mean to even suggest such a thing. Let's say your doctor tells you that you have an infection, and unless you take a certain antibiotic, you will die. Would you say that the doctor is being mean by telling you death is certain unless you take the pills? No, of course not! You would be grateful for the warning and especially for the antidote. In the same way, God tells us we are going to die because we all have a disease. It's called sin. He then provides the antidote for our sin, which is His Son Jesus dying in our place on the cross. What we are to do is repent and receive the antidote, Jesus. Why, then, should we be angry with God for warning us of our condition? We should be grateful for the warning, and again, especially for the antidote.

The reason for this is because of the belief that they are basically good people, and they feel offended with the inference that worthiness of hell is deserved. Those offended feelings cause them to have a strong resistance to Christians and an even stronger dislike for the Bible. Jesus said in John 7:7, "The world…hates Me because I testify of it that its works are evil." If they hated Jesus, they will hate the Christians also. John 15:18 states, "If the world hates you, you know that it hated Me before it hated you." They don't realize that it has nothing to do with being "good" or "bad." Their offense is unfounded. A Christian's warning is taken to be hateful instead of simply being a "heads up."

Once a person has understanding, he can then be appreciative of what God has done for him. Understanding is what is needed for the possibility of going to hell to make sense to anyone. Our good works will not save us from that dreaded place.

You might be wondering, "Well, can't God overlook my sins, especially since they are only minor? Since He is a loving God, I'm sure He understands me." Read on and you will find out.

CHAPTER 5

CAN'T GOD JUST OVERLOOK MY SINS?

GOD LOVES US VERY MUCH, AND HIM OVERLOOKING OUR SINS MAY sound like a reasonable request, but there are two very good reasons why He cannot do this. First of all, God's nature is unlike ours. He is holy, and His holiness will not allow sin to survive in His presence. Sin is something we all commit on a regular basis; therefore, we cannot be allowed in the presence of God's holiness. The Bible says that we are born and shaped in sin (Ps. 51:5). So the problem is that even the smallest sin excludes us from Him (James 2:10). Our very nature is sin, and His nature is absolutely pure, holy, and perfect. (See Leviticus 19:2; 20:26; Psalm 18:30; 19:7; Matthew 5:48; Revelation 15:4.) He cannot even look upon sin, or evil, as we can (Hab. 1:13).

Hebrews 12:29 states, "God is a consuming fire." What does that mean? Charles Stanley said this about fire:

> Fire is hot by nature. Fire doesn't make itself hot; it is hot. That is the nature of fire. If you stuck your hand in a campfire to retrieve a hot dog that fell off your stick, you would be burned. You wouldn't get mad at the fire. You wouldn't say, "I can't believe that fire burned me. I never did anything to the fire! Why would it treat me like that?" Fire and your hand are incompatible. They don't do well together.[1]

The nature of fire is to burn. In the same way, the nature of God is to consume sin. Therefore, since man is sinful, man has a problem. It is not a matter of our sins being minor and thereby being overlooked. It is because any sin, even minor, cannot exist in His presence. It is utterly destroyed. This is why Romans 6:23 says that the penalty for our sin is death. Why the severity? Because sin to God is "exceedingly sinful" (Rom. 7:13).

So how does a loving God solve the problem of man being able to coexist with Him in heaven? By making man appear sinless before Him. The only way this can happen is if someone sinless takes man's sins away. Jesus is the only person who could fulfill and did fulfill that requirement. He took our sins and died in our place on the cross at Calvary (Rom. 5:8–9). If we acknowledge that Jesus is God, died for our sins, and rose from the dead, and if we repent (Luke 13:3) and receive Jesus as our Lord and Savior, our sin will be erased and Jesus's record of perfectly keeping God's standards will be put in the place of our imperfections. Now we can stand in God's presence *as if* we had never sinned, because our sins are washed away by the blood He shed (Eph. 1:7; Col. 1:14; Heb. 9:12; 1 Pet. 1:19; 1 John 1:7).

We then appear before God with the righteousness, or right standing, of Jesus (Rom. 5:17–18; 2 Cor. 5:21). We don't stand on our own righteousness, because it is as filthy rags in comparison to His (Job 15:16; Isa. 64:6; Titus 3:5). No one can keep the Law, stand before God, and say, "I have kept every word and obeyed Your law without compromise." No, Romans 3:19–20 says, "Now we know that what things soever the law saith, it saith to them who are under the law: that every mouth may be stopped, and all the world may become guilty before God. Therefore by the deeds of the law there shall no flesh be justified in his sight" (KJV).

In his book *Planet Earth—2000 AD*, Hal Lindsey said, "The Law was given to drive us to despair of self effort as we try to keep it. It leads us to accept grace as the only means of pleasing God."[2]

The second reason that God cannot overlook our sins is this: He is a just God and must punish sin. The Bible says in Deuteronomy 32:4, "He is the Rock, His work is perfect; for all His ways are justice, a God of truth and without injustice; righteous and upright is He." Psalm 96:13

says, "He shall judge the world with righteousness, and the peoples with His truth."

A judge in our courts would not be considered good if he just let all the criminals go free. No one would say, "That judge is a good judge because he lets everyone off." No. That judge would not be considered good if he didn't punish the guilty. So why do we think God should just excuse our sin?

In our eyes, minor sin should be overlooked, and most think their sins are minor. But all sin is serious to God. It is all evil, no matter how minor. For the most part, we humans don't think sin is any big deal. So we tend to think God is unreasonable to punish so severely for something seemingly so trivial. Yet we deserve to be punished, and it is not unreasonable. We willfully disobey God, and He told us the consequences of our sin. However, God took out His anger for our sin on Jesus. Jesus took our punishment. We don't have to be punished if we accept the sacrifice He made for us and put our trust in Him. If we truly understood the holy nature of God and how offensive sin is in His sight, we would be grieved in our hearts for the offenses we commit against Him. But many are not grieved and don't realize that we all need a Savior. These next verses state clearly why we need a Savior and what Jesus has done for us.

I ask you to please read these scriptures carefully, as this should be ample enough to open your eyes of understanding and see His plan for us.

> All people, whether Jews or Gentiles, are under the power of sin. As the scriptures say, "No one is good—not even one. No one has real understanding; no one is seeking God....No one does good, not even one." "Their talk is foul...their speech is filled with lies...." "Their mouths are full of cursing...." "They have no fear of God...."
>
> Obviously, the law applies to those to whom it was given, for its purpose is to keep people from having excuses and to bring the entire world into judgment before God. For no one can ever be made right in God's sight by doing what his law commands.

For the more we know God's law, the clearer it becomes that we aren't obeying it....

We are made right in God's sight when we trust in Jesus Christ to take away our sins. And we all can be saved in this same way, no matter who we are or what we have done.

For all have sinned; all fall short of God's glorious standard. Yet now God in his gracious kindness declares us not guilty. He has done this through Christ Jesus, who has freed us by taking away our sins. For God sent Jesus to take the punishment for our sins and to satisfy God's anger against us. We are made right with God when we believe that Jesus shed his blood, sacrificing his life for us....

Can we boast, then, that we have done anything to be accepted by God? No, because our acquittal is not based on our good deeds. It is based on our faith. So we are made right with God through faith and not by obeying the law.

—Romans 3:9–28, NLT

I hope you can grasp what was just said. That is God's Word, not mine. He said it so plainly that I don't know how anyone could miss it.

Billy Graham explains this clearly: "Repentance is one of the two vital elements in conversion and simply means recognition of what we are, and a willingness to change our minds toward sin, self, and God. Repentance involves first of all an acknowledgement of our sin. When we repent, we are saying that we recognize that we are sinners and that our sin involves us in personal guilt before God. This type of guilt does not mean incriminating self-contempt; it means seeing ourselves as God sees us, and saying, 'God be merciful to me a sinner' (Luke 18:13, KJV)."[3]

The other "vital element" as Billy calls it is this: to acknowledge that Jesus is the Son of God, He shed His blood in our place, was crucified on a cross, died, and rose again the third day (John 14:6; Acts 4:12; Rom. 6:23; 10:9–10; 1 Cor. 15:3–4). These are the two elements that make up salvation. If we can truly grasp the fact that God's nature is holy, then perhaps we can understand why He cannot look upon sin.

You may think that God should look at your good heart and consider that. Well, is our heart really all that good? Would we really want God to examine our hearts?

CHAPTER 6

BUT GOD KNOWS MY HEART!

THERE ARE MANY WHO LOVE TO USE THE VERSE IN 1 SAMUEL 16:7, "FOR the LORD does not see as man sees; for man looks at the outward appearance, but the LORD looks at the heart." They have taken this concept far beyond its intent and way out of context. Based on the misunderstanding of this scripture, they say things like, "But God knows my heart. Surely, since He is a loving God, He knows I meant well." Yes, He does know our hearts. And that makes it even worse! Let us look at what our hearts are really like for a moment. The Bible says in Jeremiah 17:9, "The heart is deceitful above all things, and desperately wicked; who can know it?" Proverbs 28:26 says, "He that trusteth in his own heart is a fool" (KJV).

God knowing our heart won't help us. The Bible also mentions that we can have a heart that is froward (Ps. 101:4), that errors (Ps. 95:10), that imagines mischief (Ps. 14:2), that is proud (Ps. 101:5), that utters perverse things (Prov. 23:33), that is desolate (Ps. 143:4), that holds within it the seven abominations (Prov. 26:25), that devises wicked imaginations (Prov. 14:10), that carries reproach (Job 27:6), that is evil (Jer. 3:17), that Satan can fill (Acts 5:3), that is secretly enticed (Job 31:27), and that can walk after our eyes (Job 31:7).

So in stating, "God knows my heart," we infer that it should help our case. But as you can see from the above verses, if God were to go by our hearts, we would all be in deep yogurt. However, He still loves us and is always seeking to reveal Himself to us in spite of knowing our hearts.

David said in Psalm 51:10, "Create in me a clean heart, O God."

Knowing God is the only way we can have a pure heart. He will give us that heart that seeks after Him. Through the reading of His Word, our minds are renewed and we become more like Jesus. Our foolish concepts begin to fall away. Many Christians don't read the Bible, and their thoughts and hearts can also be deceived. Learning His Word in order to become more like Him is a lifelong process. The more of His Word we get down into our hearts, the more loving, compassionate, and forgiving we become. Psalm 119:10–11 says, "With my whole heart have I sought thee: O let me not wander from thy commandments. Thy word have I hid in mine heart, that I might not sin against thee" (KJV). A godly heart is a heart that desires to serve Him and that loves Him (Ps. 119:67; Prov. 3:1–5; 6:21).

CHAPTER 7

WHY DID GOD CREATE SUCH A HORRIBLE PLACE?

THE BIBLE TELLS US VERY CLEARLY WHY HELL EXISTS. JESUS SAID HE prepared it for the devil and his angels (Matt. 25:41). He didn't make it for man. Man was created to live forever with God with unlimited access to heaven. However, man can choose his own way. If he makes the wrong choice, it is man's fault, not God's. Here is the situation:

Man is a spirit, he possesses a soul (mind, will, and emotions), and he lives in a body. For the ease of discussion, I will use the word *soul* to represent both soul and spirit. The soul cannot die, in the way we think of death. Death to the soul means to be separated from God. It does not mean to cease to exist. If man rejects the only way provided for entrance into heaven, then there is no other place for the soul to go. Our physical bodies can only exist on this earth. They cannot exist in outer space or under the water. In the same way, our soul was built to exist in one of two places—heaven or hell.

Imagine a place completely void of all good. If we understand that God is good (Ps. 25:8; 34:8; 100:5) and God is love (1 John 4:16) and that every good thing comes from Him, we will therefore understand that when God, His influence, His attributes, and His goodness are totally and completely removed from a place—all that is left is utter evil, chaos, corruption, death, torment, misery, fear, despair, and destruction. When God is removed from the equation, *all* the good goes with Him. So God didn't have to "make" hell so horrible. It was inevitable because all of His mercy, goodness, and love is removed far from hell.

Henry M. Morris, PhD, a highly respected scientist, and Martin E. Clark state, "Essentially, hell is the place where all aspects of the presence of God will be completely withdrawn forever…Thus, in hell there will be no love, for 'God is love.' There will be no light, for 'God is light and in Him is no darkness at all.' There will be no peace, or rest, or joy, since these are all attributes of God. On the contrary, there will be eternal corruption, strife, rebellion and hatred."[1]

Without God's influence, any place would automatically be horrible. In addition, hell is where God's wrath is poured out.

Hell is first meant for the devil and, then, a place to punish the disobedient. But you don't have to go there. People are only there by their own choosing. God has given us the warning that He will punish sin and that there is a wrath to come (Rom. 1:18; 6:23; Eph. 5:6; 2 Thess. 1:8–9; Rev. 20:15).

Try to see it this way: It is just like having prisons in our country. You wouldn't say that our nation's leaders are mean for building prisons. No, prisons are built to protect the innocent from the criminal. When man first came to this country, he didn't look around and say, "Well, let's see how many prisons we can build here." No, he looked at all the beauty and saw the potential for growth and production, right? In the same way, God made the earth with all of its beauty and had only the best plans for mankind in mind.

The point is, prisons were not in mind when men came to this country, and hell wasn't God's first intent when He made the earth and man. Even so, it is by our choice that we end up in hell. If we steal a car and end up in prison, can we blame our nation's leaders? Even if we were ignorant of the law, there would be no excuse. We would still be responsible for our actions. Charles Spurgeon said, "If the thing is untrue, it is with you to reject it; if it be true, at your own peril reject what God stamps with divine authority."[2]

CHAPTER 8

DOES THE CRIME FIT THE PUNISHMENT?

SEVENTY YEARS OR SO OF SIN, WHICH IS THE AVERAGE SPAN OF A human's life, doesn't warrant an eternity of punishment, right? That wouldn't seem logical. In our world, a time of confinement is usually adequate payment for the crime committed. However, that is not how God's kingdom works. The problem is, we are so used to living by a certain time schedule, yet in God's kingdom time is not the issue. Our problem with sin has nothing to do with time. Time could never resolve the problem. Our problem with sin has to do with relationship. Say we served a hundred years or so of punishment. At the end, we would still be sinners. Time wouldn't fix that.

Eternity could never even pay off one sin. If we could "do our time" and pay off our sins, so to speak, it would be like saying, "God, I paid the price, I did my time, and I am now justified to stand in Your presence." Well, that is not ever going to be the case, because no matter how long a person was in hell, it would never make a sinful man righteous. Man will always be sinful and cannot ever be justified on his own. Job 15:16 states, "...man, who is abominable and filthy, who drinks iniquity like water!" Isaiah 64:6 says, "All our righteousness are like filthy rags." Romans 3:23 says, "For all have sinned and fall short of the glory of God."

The consequences of our sins are eternal, so it took an eternal God to pay for them. Dr. Erwin W. Lutzer said, "The powerful lesson to be learned is that no human being's suffering can ever be a payment for sin."[1] He goes on to say,

> What if, from God's viewpoint, the greatness of sin is determined by the greatness of the One against whom it is committed? Then the guilt of sin is infinite because it is a violation of the character of an infinite being. What if, in the nature of God, it is deemed that such infinite sins deserve an infinite penalty, a penalty that no one can ever repay.... The Bible tells of the love and mercy of God.... But it also has much to say about His justice.... To put it clearly, we must accept God as He is revealed in the Bible, whether He suits our preferences or not.[2]

In the book *Hell Under Fire*, Sinclair B. Ferguson states:

> Scripture frequently illustrates that the punishment "fits"—that is, it is utterly consistent with—the crime. Paul gave striking illustration of that in Romans 1:21–32. Those who claim to be wise became fools and exchanged God's truth for the lie. Even while flouting themselves against God's law and believing his wrath to be powerless, they "receive in themselves the due penalty for their perversion."[3]

You can either let Him pay for it, or you can pay for it for all of eternity. Which is it going to be? Either way, God's punishment fits our crime of sin and rebellion. In his book *Out of Your Comfort Zone*, R. T. Kendall writes, "There are two ways by which God ultimately punishes sin; either by the sacrifice of His Son, whose blood completely and eternally satisfies His justice, or by the fires of hell, which never completely satisfy His justice, which is why hell is unending."[4] The Bible says that "the ungodly shall not stand in the judgment" (Ps. 1:5). It doesn't matter if our sins are many or few. For those who don't care about the things of God, the Bible states, "And even as they did not like to retain God in their knowledge, God gave them over to a reprobate mind" (Rom. 1:28, KJV). Since they didn't want anything to do with God, they will have their request granted for all eternity (Rom. 1:18; Eph. 5:6; 2 Thess. 1:9; Rev. 14:11). Just as those in heaven will not be dismissed after a short while, neither will those in hell ever be released. Both heaven and hell are eternal (Job 18:15, 21; Isa. 66:24; Dan. 12:2; Matt. 13:49–50; 25:41, 46; Mark 9:43–49; Luke 3:17; 2 Thess. 1:9–10; Heb. 6:2; Jude 7, 13; Rev. 14:11; 20:10–15).

Also, if man was finally let out of hell and then taken to heaven, his sinful nature would still be present. He would only be grateful that he was let out. He didn't come to God by free will, but only to escape the suffering of hell. He would defile heaven. Revelation 21:27 states, "But there shall by no means enter it anything that defiles."

There will be no one in hell unjustly. Every single person there will deserve to be there because they rejected God's dying on a cross for them— His eternal act of love. Many mock God their entire lives and think they can sin and get away with it. The fact is, you can't. No one can.

> For if we sin willfully after we have received the knowledge of the truth, there no longer remains a sacrifice for sins, but a certain fearful expectation of judgment, and fiery indignation which will devour the adversaries. Anyone who has rejected Moses' law dies without mercy on the testimony of two or three witnesses. Of how much worse punishment, do you suppose, will he be thought worthy who has trampled the Son of God underfoot, counted the blood of the covenant by which he was sanctified a common thing, and insulted the Spirit of grace? For we know Him who said, "Vengeance is Mine; I will repay," says the Lord. And again, "The LORD will judge His people."
> —Hebrews 10:26–30

We are much better off meeting the loving Jesus now, while we have the opportunity, instead of the insulted Holy Spirit and Jesus, who declares, in Hebrews 10:30, "Vengeance belongeth unto me, I will recompense" (KJV). "It is a fearful thing to fall into the hands of the living God" (Heb. 10:31). All who don't know Him will face Him on Judgment Day.

Time could never suffice to justify man before God. Payment of time is the wrong premise. It took His shed blood. It took an eternal, sinless God to pay for our eternal sins. Deuteronomy 30:19 says to "choose life"; why wouldn't you?

CHAPTER 9

HELL BY DEFAULT

MANY BELIEVE THAT BY REMAINING NEUTRAL IN REGARD TO A decision for Christ, one would still be in safe harbor. Since they haven't rejected the idea of the acceptance of Jesus, they feel a decision has not been made, and heaven would still be their destination. However, that is not the case. John 3:18 says, "He who does not believe is condemned already, because he has not believed in the name of the only begotten Son of God." By not choosing life, we are already on the road that leads to destruction (Matt. 7:13–14). A lack of a decision is in fact a decision. We are all on our way to hell until we choose to follow Jesus. It is only then that we get off that road to destruction. God is warning us and giving us clear instructions on how to get off that road (Prov. 14:12; Ezek. 3:17; Luke 13:3; John 3:36; Rom. 10:9–10; 2 Thess. 1:9). In other words, there are no "fence" positions. Hell by default is a result of no choice.

In some court cases, if one of the parties doesn't show up, they lose by default, or the other party wins by default. The definition of *default* in the *New American Heritage Dictionary* is "the failure of one or more competitors or teams to participate in a contest—win by default. Or, to lose a case by not appearing." Default can also mean, "failure to act, or neglect."

The lack of a decision can bring about painful results. What about an investment you knew you should sell, or a property you should have accepted the offer on? Or say you wanted to see someone who was dying in the hospital and share with them that you love him or her, but you procrastinated and suddenly that person died. Your lack of a decision to go, or hesitation, resulted in a lifetime of regret. In the same way, the lack of a decision or no decision in regard to our souls will result in an eternity of regret. Jesus said that we are either with Him or against Him (Matt. 12:30).

It is so very important to make a decision while we have the chance. Those in hell have an eternity to regret their hesitation as they too thought they would have more time in this life to think about it. They thought they were still safe. They were wrong, and only one second after they were dead it was too late.

Many live their entire lives wanting nothing to do with God. They don't acknowledge that Jesus is God, and they don't ever pray or read the Bible. Yet they believe they are going to heaven when they die. Why would they even want to live with Him for all eternity when they didn't want to even spend a Sunday morning at church with Him? The point is, if you are one who doesn't care about the things of God, then most likely you wouldn't like being around all those godly people and the Lord Himself. In their book *The Bible Has the Answer*, Dr. Henry Morris and Martin Clark state, "...If a person either rejects or ignores the love of God in Christ, thereby choosing to remain independent of God...Such a person would also be utterly miserable in heaven, with his pride and sinful nature and his desire to remain independent of God."[1] I think many do not think about actually being around God, but more simply, just being in a pleasant place such as heaven. But heaven is not some ethereal state that our spirit and soul exists in while floating on a cloud. In speaking to believers, 2 Peter 1:11 says, "And God will open wide the gates of *heaven* for you to enter into the *eternal kingdom of our Lord and Savior Jesus Christ.*" In this verse, it is clear that heaven is not only a place but the kingdom of the Lord Jesus Christ. It also states that we enter heaven because He is *our Lord and Savior.* If Jesus is not our Lord and Savior, why would we be a citizen living in His kingdom? What many need to reevaluate is that God lives there, and they will be in His environment. If someone doesn't desire the Lord's presence here on Earth, then heaven isn't the place for them. Some think that they will be able to enjoy the same comforts in the afterlife that they had in their life on the earth, yet keep God out of it. But the fact of the matter is, there is no place where good exists without God. A place without God is void of all good. James 1:17 says, "Whatever is good and perfect comes down to us from God" (NLT). You can't have the good without God. All "good" goes with God.

CHAPTER 10

HOW DOES GOD WARN US?

THERE ARE THOSE WHO WOULD STILL ACCUSE GOD OF NOT BEING fair. They would also bring up a man who lives in the remote part of the jungle who never heard of Jesus. "Will God send him to hell too?" they sharply ask. Below I have listed some of the ways God reveals Himself to us so that man is without excuse. God's continual warnings show us how long-suffering, patient, and kind He is to us all. His love is infinite. No one will be able to stand there on Judgment Day and point the finger in God's face and accuse Him of being unfair.

FIVE DIFFERENT WAYS GOD WARNS US

Throughout our lives He tries to get our attention and give us warnings about our impending judgment if we don't repent. Ezekiel 3:17 says, "Hear a word from My mouth and give them warning from Me." Isaiah 45:22 says, "Look unto me, and be ye saved, all the ends of the earth: for I am God, and there is none else" (KJV). There are at least five methods that God uses to get people's attention.

1. CREATION

Creation shows us evidence of design everywhere, which points to a designer. When we see such intricacies in the balance of life, the harmony and order in creation, the design in every aspect of life, it should be over-whelmingly evident that there must be a Creator, a designer. Romans 1:20 says, "For since the creation of the world His invisible attributes are clearly seen, being understood by the things that are made, even His eternal power and Godhead, so that they are without excuse." Just look at birth. The growth stages of a baby in the mother's womb are staggering. To learn what takes place and how everything is developed in its proper place and at the right time is nothing short of a miracle. How the symmetry of a human being is so perfectly designed!

There are countless other things we could examine that also bear clear evidence of design. If we came across a beautifully made watch lying in the sand on the beach, we would not think that over the eons of time, the sands blew, the rain fell, and one day, this beautiful watch formed. No! Of course not! That would be foolish. Yet, the wrist that wears the watch is far more complex than the watch. Still, many believe that we humans have developed through an evolutionary process. Are you going to tell me that all of that intricate design just happened by accident? I don't think so.

Dr. Edwin W. Lutzer said:

> Those who live without specific knowledge about Christ will be judged by the light of nature and their own conscience (Romans 1:20; 2:14–16)....Each day of every life will be analyzed in minute detail. The hidden thoughts and motives of each hour will be replayed, along with all the actions and attitudes. The words spoken in secret will be made public, the intentions of the heart displayed for all to see.[1]

Our lives will look quite dismal if viewed in that manner, and they will be on display for all to see. Everyone will know just how good we were. If you are one who thinks you are "pretty good folk," your life along with everyone else's will be under the microscope. God will reveal everything there is to know about you. Since you are claiming you are "good enough" to be allowed in, He will show you your true self. I know I wouldn't want to be judged in that manner, on my every thought and action, and subjected to that amount of scrutiny.

No matter what you believe, it is going to take some faith. If you believe in the Bible, there is more than enough proof for its accuracy, validity, and its authenticity, but it still takes faith. However, if you are going to believe in evolution, that also is going to take faith. And it takes a lot more faith to believe that all this order we see came out of an explosion. The other point is that evolution is still only a theory, and no one has ever proven one thing. The Bible says, "The fool has said in his heart, 'There is no God'" (Ps. 14:1; Ps. 53:1).

The evolutionist will declare that his belief is rational and scientific. Well, how rational is a statement such as, "First there was nothing; then, it exploded."[2] That is the essence of the big bang theory. That doesn't sound too scientific to me! Where did the "nothing" come from to explode? Dr. Jonathan Henry said in *The Astronomy Book*, "But when has an explosion led to more order and structure than there was before? Such a thing has never been observed. Since science has never observed it, the big bang is only a belief, not science."[3] (There are some great books to read on the creation and all the scientific, historical, archeological, and geographical proofs of the Bible; a few are listed in the bibliography.)

As you can see, it takes faith to believe that a universe came out of nothing. Evolution is not a science, but a religion, a belief. I can tell you for certain, that if an atheist is left swimming in the ocean with sharks all around him, as I was, we would see just how long he clings to his beliefs. It wouldn't be long until the words, "God, help me" rolled off his lips!

2. OUR CONSCIENCE

God gave us a conscience to know right from wrong and to know that He exists. The Bible says that "the truth about God is known to us instinctively because God has put this knowledge into our hearts" (Rom. 1:19, NLT). Even a child knows when he or she has done wrong. Our conscience is like a navigation device within us. This device helps guide us into decisions that protect us from harm. Sadly, many people ignore their conscience. Over time, the Bible says it becomes seared as by a hot iron (1 Tim. 4:2). The only way to "unsear" our conscience is by turning away from our sin and disobedience to God and asking for His forgiveness. Even as believers, being quick to repent for disobedience is key to maintaining a tender conscience.

Let me ask you a question: Why does man have a conscience in the first place? If we came from an animal, why is it that the animals don't have a conscience also? Animals are very sensitive and can show love and companionship, especially a dog, but even a dog cannot display a conscience. If all that exists are laws of nature to govern the universe, then where did a conscience come from? John Bunyan states in his book *Visions of Heaven and Hell*, "Every creature testifies to the existence of its Creator, and man's own conscience, more than a thousand witnesses, cannot help but dictate the reality of God to him."[4] According to the *MacArthur Bible Commentary*, "The conscience is a divinely given warning device that reacts to sin and produces accusation and guilt."[5]

If a man falls from a building to the ground, does the law of gravity say, "I feel terrible because I pulled that nice man down to the ground and killed him"? I think not! So it is obvious that the laws of nature do not possess a conscience. A conscience only exists in man and comes from a loving and caring Being—and that Being is the God of the Bible, the God of the universe. He placed His nature in us. Knowing there is a God should cause us to seek Him. If we truly seek Him, He will reveal Himself to us. First Chronicles 28:9 says, "If thou seek him, he will be found of thee" (KJV). Jesus said in Matthew 7:7, "Seek, and ye shall find" (KJV).

3. THE BIBLE

God has given us the Bible, which is His Word *in writing* with clear directions and instructions. I am in the real estate business, and when selling or purchasing a property, everyone wants the agreement to be spelled out clearly in writing. The first thing an attorney would ask is, "Is it all in writing?" If so, then it is enforceable (all things being equal). If we all can expect to rely on things in writing as being legal and that we will get what has been agreed upon, then why do we not equally value God's Word, which is spelled out and in writing?

There are many times in business when just because something is in writing, it doesn't mean we will get what is agreed upon. It also depends on the character of the individual. Yet, here we have God putting it in writing. How much stronger can it get? He cannot lie, and He will easily and most assuredly do what He has said. The Bible says that the Lord never changes (Mal. 3:6). The Bible has been scrutinized by literally thousands of scholars, historians, archeologists, and the like, and they have dissected every word, and even every syllable, and have not found one discrepancy. You can read about proof of this in some books listed in the bibliography.

4. OTHER PEOPLE

God sends people across our path to tell us about Himself and how to get to heaven. If you think about it, how many times have you been approached by someone and told about Jesus? Many times! He also has preachers all over the world and churches on almost every corner. There are so many ministries that reach out to all parts of the earth and have done so for hundreds of years. There are television shows, CDs, DVDs, radio programs, magazines, the Internet, and so on, and each is filled with information about the gospel.

5. DREAMS AND VISIONS

God gives man dreams and visions to "keep back his soul from the pit" (Job 33:14–24). So God has a way of even reaching the person in the most remote mountainous area. There have been many documented cases of these occurrences in books that have been written. As a matter of fact, my wife knows of a true story from a very reliable, dear friend of hers. There was a tribe who had never been reached with the good news about Jesus. The area they lived in was so remote. When missionaries arrived, they were asked by one of the tribal leaders, "Are you the one who was to come to us to tell us about the Golden Book and the Savior?" This tribe had never been contacted by anyone from the outside, to anyone's knowledge, yet they had heard that there was a special book about a Savior. How did they know that?

God gives everyone all throughout their lives opportunity after opportunity to be warned about hell. There are signposts of warning about the bridge being out, so to speak, all along our road of life. I have heard that there are two hundred sixty-four warnings in the New Testament about hell and judgment. That is in just twenty-seven books, which contain two hundred sixty chapters. That means that there is approximately one warning for each chapter. If you equated the warnings to actual signs on the highway and equated the twenty-seven books to twenty-seven miles, there would be a signpost every five hundred feet or every six seconds if you were traveling sixty miles per hour. Seeing that many signs would get anyone's attention. If we decide to drive off the bridge and ignore all those signs, it is our own fault, not God's.

A few preachers have portrayed God as one holding the hammer just waiting for you to blow it so He can strike you over the head. This is not God. Even in the Old Testament when God had to execute judgment, He gave warning after warning to the people and had no delight in their punishment. He even warned Judas. In Matthew 26:21, Jesus said, "Verily I say unto you, that one of you shall betray me" (KJV). Then in verses 23–25, He said, "He that dippeth his hand with me in the dish, the same shall betray me. The Son of man goeth as it is written of him: but woe unto that man by whom the Son of man is betrayed! It had been good for that man if he had not been born. Then Judas, which betrayed him, answered and said, Master, is it I? He said unto him, Thou hast said" (KJV). Then in John 6:70 Jesus said, "Have not I chosen you twelve, and one of you is a devil?" (KJV). In Luke 22:3, "Then entered Satan into Judas" (KJV).

Jesus told Judas it was him and that whoever betrayed the Son of Man would have been better off never having been born. So you see, Judas was warned and could have stopped what he was doing, confessed to Jesus, and asked for forgiveness. But since he didn't heed the warning, he basically sent himself to hell. You might say, "Judas couldn't have stopped himself or been forgiven because it was ordained in Scripture." It was in the Scriptures because God knew he wouldn't repent. But God would not force someone to sin and go to hell to fulfill Scripture. Man, even Judas, had a free will and could have repented. Judas chose to disobey, even after the warning. He wasn't forced to sin.

Consider the following scriptures, and you will see God's heart revealed:

But you have prostituted yourself with many lovers, says the LORD. *Yet I am still calling you* to come back to me.

—Jeremiah 3:1, NLT

Come home to me again, *for I am merciful....* Only acknowledge your guilt. Admit that you rebelled against the Lord your God.

—Jeremiah 3:12–13, NLT

Come back to me, and I will heal your wayward hearts.

—Jeremiah 3:22, NLT

"Run up and down every street," says the LORD. "Look high and low; search throughout the city! If you can find *even one person* who is just and honest, *I will not destroy the city.*" [Can you see the Lord's heart here? He desperately does not want to administer punishment, but mercy!]

—Jeremiah 5:1, NLT

I spoke to you about it *repeatedly*, but *you would not listen.* I called out to you, but *you refused* to answer.

—Jeremiah 7:13, NLT

When people fall down, don't they get up again? When they discover they're on the wrong road, don't they turn back? Then why do these *people stay on their self-destructive path?* Why do the people...*refuse to turn back, even though I have warned them?*

—Jeremiah 8:4–5, NLT

Perhaps they will *listen and turn from their evil ways.* Then I will change my mind about the disaster I am ready to pour out on them *because of their sins.*

—Jeremiah 26:3, NLT

If you will not listen to me and obey my word I have given you, and if you will not listen to my servants, the prophets—*for I sent them again and again to warn you, but you would not listen to them*—then I will destroy this Temple.

—Jeremiah 26:4–6, NLT

...for they *would not listen* to my warnings.

—Jeremiah 36:31, NLT

Again and again I sent my servants, the prophets, *to plead with them*, "Don't do these horrible things that I hate so much." But my people *would not listen* or turn back from their wicked ways.

—Jeremiah 44:4–5, NLT

For he does not enjoy hurting people or causing them sorrow. (The Lord has no pleasure in allowing punishment. He does not afflict from His heart—He doesn't want to, but He is perfectly just. The Lord over and over pleads for people to simply turn back to Him for He delights in showing mercy.)

—Lamentations 3:33, NLT

You must give them my messages *whether they listen or not*. (God always warns because He is perfectly fair and just. It is our choice whether we listen.)

—Ezekiel 2:7, NLT

Don't you realize how *kind, tolerant,* and *patient* God is with you? Or don't you care? Can't you see how kind he has been in giving you time to turn from your sin? But no, you won't listen. So you are storing up terrible punishment for yourself because of your stubbornness in refusing to turn from your sin.

—Romans 2:4–5, NLT

He is continually seeking the best for us and wants to bless us. He is always warning us and is patient. You can see by the above verse that it is man's desire to hold on to his sin that sends him to hell. I could speak a thousand scriptures, but it is up to the hearer to open his heart. Remember that old saying, "You can lead a horse to water..."?

CHAPTER 11

WE WOULDN'T WANT TO OFFEND ANYONE

IN TODAY'S SOCIETY, THERE IS AN ACCEPTANCE OF JUST ABOUT everyone's beliefs to the point where many espouse to the opinion that there is no longer a right or wrong. "All things are relative," our society declares. This acceptance seems, on the surface, to be much more "understanding" and "open-minded." However, is this embracing of everyone's beliefs being open-minded, or is it helping to promote a moral decay in our culture? The lie of relativism has been packaged as consideration for others. Yet, it is not really consideration for others, but rather, toleration of others' moral depravity. I believe one reason for this acceptance is so that we can feel comfortable in our own compromised lifestyles.

Most do not want their sins exposed, so they accuse Christians and the Bible of being judgmental and narrow-minded. Christians are then perceived as being intolerant. There is then a fear that the moral convictions of others might be forced on them, thereby causing a disdain for Christians. An example of this perceived narrow-mindedness would be something like this scenario: For many, to live with a person before marriage seems wise. By doing so, one can discover the things about the other that a person would want to know before a commitment. So a "trial period" is preferred rather than a commitment of marriage. This seems rational and prudent to many.

The Christian belief would not agree with that scenario and would thereby be viewed as narrow-minded and judgmental. The Christian is not going to threaten that individual's lifestyle whatsoever. That person's fear of a threat is totally unjustified. They are completely free to do as they please, without opposition from anyone. In addition, Christians are seen as being "out of touch" with today's culture. Most of Hollywood and the movie industry support this lifestyle, and whoever doesn't is considered intolerant and judgmental.

In her book *Death by Entertainment*, Holly McClure said:

> Among the latest political messages coming out of Hollywood these days is the message of "tolerance" and anything having to do with "hate crimes."...By the mid '90s it became clear to anyone who watched television that sexual material, foul language, and violence were becoming increasingly prevalent....The family audience found it increasingly hard to watch programming without questionable filth in it. A tolerant mentality has introduced an open mind-set to accept whatever we see on TV as OK....What would have been considered intolerable at one point is now routinely found in sitcom scripts.[1]

Tolerance has then become the high moral ground instead of truth. Franklin Graham writes:

> Tolerance has become the new watchword of our times. It is heralded as perhaps the highest virtue in Western culture that glues people of differing backgrounds and ideologies together for the sake of promoting cultural unity. And why shouldn't it be? It sounds good, right? In fact, it sounds so good that anyone who would dare talk negatively about this sacred cow of civility would almost be considered immoral. But that's just the point. The media and the governmental bureaucrats tell us to be tolerant of everything and anything except the Gospel of salvation, all in the name of political correctness. It seems almost ironic that Christians are not being tolerated by such a "tolerant" society....America is

infatuated with the false understanding of tolerance. To be truly tolerant is not to give every idea equal standing or to compromise the Truth in the interest of keeping the peace and making everyone happy. Being tolerant does mean accepting the fact that every person is created in the image of Almighty God and that we each have a soul that will live for eternity. Jesus Christ paid the price for our eternal salvation through the shedding of His blood on Calvary's cross for all men equally.[2]

Many do not want to be told by God or anyone else how they should live their lives. To say that someone's belief is right or wrong is to say there are absolute truths, and that doesn't sit "politically correct" with some. Many today are conditioned by our media that no one has the absolute truth. Dr. Chuck Missler said, "The denial of the very existence of absolute Truth is the characteristic of our current culture."[3] If absolute truths don't exist, then how could men ever form a judgment or make a law? C. S. Lewis said, "A man does not call a line crooked unless he has some idea of a straight line."[4]

To say that there are no absolutes because "truth to one is not truth to another" is not only untrue, but it is also illogical thinking. I pose the question to those who believe in no absolutes: How would you be able to come up with a comment that someone is prejudiced when you, by your own standards of relativism, declare there is no right or wrong? Your own condemnation of absolute truths won't allow you the freedom to state anything definitive. You would thereby require some standard of right or wrong in order to come to the conclusion that someone is prejudiced. There obviously must be, indeed, some sort of "straight line" somewhere in your thinking. Where did you acquire that straight line? If it's from your own concepts, then that is the very thing you try to oppose. If you state someone is "judgmental," you yourself had to make that determination, which means you judged that person. How can anything ever be formulated in one's mind of a right or wrong since relativism doesn't allow someone to be right or wrong? You would then have to admit that it would come from your own conscience. And, of course, we all do have a conscience.

God gave us this conscience to know right from wrong, which leaves us without excuse. We are to rely partially on this conscience to help us formulate and monitor our decisions. The problem is that it can easily become clouded with our own misconceptions and presuppositions. Our hearts can deceive us. The Bible says in Jeremiah 17:9, "The heart is deceitful above all things, and desperately wicked: who can know it?" Therefore, we need to rely on something in addition to our conscience, something more concrete and trustworthy. And that is the Bible!

God gave us His instruction manual for life's issues. That eliminates the vast array of opinions that will most definitely cloud an issue. It is wise to have input from others, as the Bible says in Proverbs 1:5, "A man of understanding shall attain unto wise counsels" (KJV), and again in Proverbs 13:20, "He that walketh with wise men shall be wise" (KJV). But to try to satisfy everyone, we would then compromise the truth.

Some are afraid of absolutes, as they think it will force another's beliefs on them and promote narrow-mindedness. But to have absolutes in your life does not mean that you become so rigid that you no longer see things on a case-by-case basis. As individuals, (we should always view things in light of all the relevant facts and display mercy along with truth.) Proverbs 20:28 says, "Mercy and truth preserve the king: and his throne is upholden by mercy" (KJV). (See also Proverbs 3:3.)

The right thing for us to do, in this society where it seems convenient to tolerate anything and everything, is to rely on what the Bible decrees, which then convicts our conscience and teaches us to establish moral truths. We then live by these truths and benefit in our spirit, soul, and body.

The Ten Commandments in the Bible are where we derive most of the laws of our society today. None of us would want someone to steal our property. Well, that law came from God. He established property rights and ownership in the Bible. We welcome many of God's laws and do not even realize that we are doing so. We welcome protection rights, discrimination laws, the sanctity of marriage, the right to raise our children, and so forth. These are all God-instituted laws and rights.

To believe in no absolutes is not at all the way we all operate in today's society. We have come to rely on all these laws, and these laws are considered absolutes. This "relativism" is a lie we have been sold. I have asked those who believe in no absolutes, "Are you absolutely certain there are no absolutes?" No matter how one answers that, you can see the fallacy in that line of thinking.

It seems that many people believe that to have no absolutes relieves them from the accountability the Bible brings with it. To think our actions and decisions could send us to hell is not a comforting thought. However, it has been found that belief in hell is actually good for a society. There was an article by MSNBC on July 27, 2004, titled, "Belief in Hell Boosts Economic Growth, Fed Says." "Fear of nether world is a disincentive to wrongdoing. Economists searching for reasons why some nations are richer than others have found that those with a wide belief in hell are less corrupt and more prosperous, according to a report by the Federal Reserve Bank of St. Louis."[5]

Whether some know it or not, belief in the Bible is good for our society and for us individually. It is unfortunate that many people don't read the Bible and are unaware that it is written for all our best interests. It gives us clear instructions for life's purposes, and it gives us clear directions to heaven. It gives us that "straight line" by which we can know right from wrong. It is a manual for life on Earth. We read manuals all the time for our computers, cars, appliances, and so forth, and learn how to operate them better. We can save time and avoid mistakes by simply reading the directions. Yet we avoid reading the one thing that will help us greatly. The Bible teaches us how to overcome and even avoid many of life's crises. But instead, we listen to people who don't read it. We could easily avoid some grim circumstances if we knew what it said for ourselves.

So why don't people want to read the Bible and learn from it? The problem seems to be twofold. First, most don't have a clue as to how much what the Bible teaches can benefit their lives; and second, there are many who don't want the Bible in their lives, as its teachings will hold them accountable for their actions. To justify their lifestyles, they condemn the Bible or brush it off as being a book of fairy tales or full of contradictions. An intelligent mind would at least inquire as to why the message of the Bible continues to spread and defy its critics throughout the centuries.

Since many are not reading the Bible, including Christians, we can see why there is not much of a stance against sin. We feel much more comfortable seeing others live a lifestyle more compromised than ours. We don't want to criticize someone's immoral behavior, and thereby we justify our own. The Bible, of course, convicts us of sin, and that is the main reason we don't want to hear it. Jesus said in John 7:7, "The world cannot hate you; but me it hateth, because I testify of it, that the works thereof are evil" (KJV).

Dr. Robert Jeffress writes, "In today's culture we think it is a virtue, not a vice, to be nonjudgmental and accepting of other people's flaws. So instead of turning away from immorality or violence, many of us turn toward it and tune into it via television, movies, and the Internet. But our willingness to tolerate evil is due not to our righteousness, but to our unrighteousness. Our ability to dismiss sin in others as well as ourselves is evidence of our unholiness, not our holiness."[6] He goes on to say, "Why is this reluctance to affirm absolute Truth a virtue? Why has the quest for tolerance replaced the quest for Truth as the highest ideal? Because of the unquestioned assumption that absolute Truth leads to hatred and oppression. That assumption is already widely accepted today in the academic world."[7]

Some are saying that Christians are prejudiced, judgmental, and actually a danger to society. Yet nothing could be further from the truth. It is all propagated by those who do not want to be held accountable for their lack of godliness. Dr. Henry Morris and Martin Clark said, "Men would like to believe that they are accountable only to themselves, therefore they seek either to reject God altogether or else to relegate Him to some intangible impersonal role in the cosmos, of no direct concern to themselves."[8] Keeping God out of their lives allows them the freedom to do as they choose: "Don't preach to me; I don't want to be told what to do." In hopes to silence the Christian, a label is placed on the believer as being narrow-minded.

A. W. Tozer said, "We allow what God hates because we want to be known to the world as good-natured agreeable Christians. Our stance indicates that the last thing we would want anyone to say about us is that we are narrow-minded."[9] This has caused many Christians to compromise and not voice a godly position on issues, but our silence speaks volumes.

As I mentioned, one of the lies that is promoted by some is that Christianity is a threat to society. However, to simply inform someone of a possible wrong path they may be on is not a threat but a warning. You can choose to reject the warning and do whatever you please. It's up to you. Why should being informed be considered threatening? The Christian's job is not to impose their beliefs but to deliver the message. Reinhard Bonnke said, "People who know the truth do not get into a demented rage. When critics arise, they let the truth prove itself. The very method for spreading Christian truth shows what kind of Gospel it is, no threats, no sword, nor intimidation."[10]

If a scientist had knowledge of an approaching asteroid that could potentially do severe damage to the earth, he would be jailed if he didn't inform us of the danger. Yet, when many people are warned that their action or lack of action may result in unfavorable consequences, they still want to label the message as threatening or blame someone else for their misfortune.

I was the president of a homeowners association for a number of years. There were those who sued the association for some accident that occurred or some damage that happened to their property, but it was usually a result of their own negligence or carelessness. They were quick to blame someone else; this is the norm in our society today.

This lack of absolutes and accountability results in an entitlement attitude. In the workplace, many people expect to be promoted or receive a large raise even before they have earned it. In some churches, those who contribute large donations feel entitled to tell the pastor how to run the church and what types of messages are "appropriate." Many teens feel entitled to a car upon their sixteenth birthday, even if they haven't earned it—and an expensive one at that. Many parents feel entitled to receive love and respect from their children, even if they were never around to love and nurture them. In addition, people live their lives with no regard for a relationship with God, but they demand to live in His house when they die. Perhaps this is the ultimate entitlement issue.

Without absolutes, we create our own god to suit our thinking. The god we create would never permit anyone that is good to be in hell. And, of course, we think we are one of the "good ones." But what can we consider good if we have no absolutes and tolerate any type of behavior? We can't judge ourselves by the Bible because we don't live at all by its standard. We don't even live up to our own standards. Even if we tried, none of us could ever achieve a perfect life. That's why the one true God does not require perfection—only repentance and trust in Him.

The difference in the way God thinks and the way we think is the following: If someone really hurts us, whether it be monetarily, emotionally, or physically, the typical response would be to demand payment or restitution, or we would harbor a hatred toward the individual. Yet God says to forgive them, pray for them, and even bless them; if they take your coat, give them your shirt also (Matt. 5:39–45). If they speak evil of you, speak well of them. Love your enemies, not just your friends. If you are broke and can't pay your bills, then give the little you have left to God (to a church or ministry that spreads the gospel) and to the poor. Give it away so you can get it back (Luke 6:35–38). If you are looking for a raise, never ask; only work harder or smarter. It works in reverse of the natural mind's rationale. These principles take into account the spiritual aspects of life, which have eternal consequences.

There are those who do not want God in their lives. His ways convict us of our selfishness and sin. R. T. Kendall said, "The God of the Bible is either too holy or too terrible for us, so we have come up with a God we are at home with.... The teaching of Jesus regarding hell was not meant to make us comfortable."[11]

Many reject the Bible and believe in whatever is convenient and non-convicting. By contrast, the Christian believes in a God who has spoken and who has revealed an absolute and unchanging standard of right and wrong, based ultimately on His own holy character. These differing beliefs have basically split our society right down the middle. There are the God-fearing people, and there are those who want to get God out of everything and believe that in the end there is no one to answer to. So we all have the choice in life—to follow our own desires or to follow God's desires. God forewarns us what lies ahead if we choose to go our own way. He tells us clearly, so we are without excuse. It is our choice, our eternal destiny!

CHAPTER 12

WHAT MAKES CHRISTIANITY UNIQUE?

PEOPLE ASK ME, "WHAT ABOUT ALL THE OTHER RELIGIONS IN THE world? Why do I have to be a Christian to stay out of hell?" I can tell you that there are distinct differences between them. For one, Christianity is the only belief that claims someone died for them and rose again. (See John 3:16; 4:42; Acts 4:12; Romans 5:8; 1 Corinthians 15:3–4; Colossians 1:14; 1 John 1:7.) Christianity is not a religion but a relationship. Billy Graham says, "Most of the world religions are based upon philosophical thought, except for Judaism, Buddhism, Islam, and Christianity. These four are based upon personalities. Only Christianity claims resurrection for its founder."[1] That claim is certain and proven to be true.

Christianity is the only "religion" that has solved the issue with sin. Sin is what sentences people to hell, and the only way you can stay out of hell is if you can appear perfect before God in judgment. The only way this is humanly possible is for us to accept that God the Son, Jesus, came to Earth and lived a perfect life as a man, took the punishment for our sins by dying on the cross, and rose again. We can then be covered by Jesus's perfection and stand before God blameless and avoid hell. What resolution for sin does any other religion give? None. John G. Lake said, "No religion among the religions of the world has ever offered a solution for the sin problem. Jesus Christ alone has brought the solution."[2]

Some of the other so-called gods demand that people must make sacrifices to them, and there is still never any assurance of going to a place of everlasting bliss after death. That's the best you are going to hear. Billy Graham tells about the beliefs of various other religions:

> In China when my wife was growing up, frequently babies who died before cutting their teeth were thrown out to be eaten by pariah dogs. The people feared that if evil spirits thought they cared too much for the children they would come and take another one. They tried to prove their indifference in this crude way. "Religion" impressed Ruth as being grim and joyless, and often cruel.... In some of the Pacific Islands, for instance, some of the islanders believe that the souls of their ancestors are in certain trees. Offerings are made to the tree, and they believe if any injury occurs to the tree, some misfortune will come upon the village.[3]

Billy goes on to say:

> In India a missionary who passed the banks of the Ganges noticed a mother sitting by the river bank with two of her children. On her lap was a beautiful new baby and whimpering beside her was a painfully retarded child of about three. On her return home that night, the missionary saw the young mother still sitting at the river bank, but the baby was gone and the mother was trying to comfort her little retarded child. Horrified at what she thought might be true, the missionary hesitated a moment and then walked over to the mother and asked her what had happened. With tears streaming down her cheeks, the mother looked up and said, "I don't know about the God in your country, but the god in mine demands the best." She had given her perfect baby to the god of Ganges. People have made human sacrifices in the name of religion.[4]

Does that sound like a god of love? The so-called gods of other religions are mean and never once mention love and forgiveness. The God of the Bible is a loving God and is always looking for ways to bless people.

You Don't Have to Earn It

Another point is that all other religions tell you what *you* must do to *earn* heaven. The Bible is the only authority that states we can do nothing to earn heaven. It is only what Jesus did *for* us that grants us entrance into heaven (Gal. 1:4). Again Billy Graham shares what other religions require of people: "I once saw a man in India lying on a bed of spikes. He had been there for many days, eating no food and drinking little water. He was attempting to atone for his sins. Another time in Africa I saw a man walk on coals of fire. Supposedly, if he came through unscathed, he was accepted by God; if he was burned, he was considered to be a sinner in need of more repentance."[5] Billy goes on to mention some of the false religious beliefs and how they cause people to do such harmful and evil things.

So many religions believe in all kinds of superstition and sacrificial ceremonies, all evil and damaging to the individual in some form. This is not the case in Christianity. Christians worship and serve the God of the Bible, who is loving, forgiving, and only asks for trust. He is the giver, and He is the one who suffered for us so that we wouldn't have to (Matt. 17:12; Mark 9:12; Luke 24:46; Acts 17:3; 1 Pet. 2:21; 3:18; 4:19). Other religions don't even talk of a loving God. Psalm 86:5 says, "For thou, Lord, art good, and ready to forgive; and plenteous in mercy unto all them that call upon thee" (KJV). God is love (1 John 4:16). His love is far beyond whatever we are capable of understanding (Eph. 3:19).

In Isaiah 45:21, God says, "There is no God else beside me: a just God and a Saviour; there is none beside me" (KJV). The God of the Bible, the only God, is telling you clearly that there are no other Gods. God loves us so much that He planned on becoming a man and dying in our place (Rom. 5:8). Can you comprehend such a loving act? The God of the universe became a man and endured the harshest punishment evil men could inflict, plus the effects of all the sins of the world!

Dr. Henry Morris said in his book *Defending the Faith*, "But God, knowing that man would choose to rebel against His will and would thereby deserve nothing but punishment and separation from Him, undertook also to work out a marvelous plan of salvation. It was agreed that God's eternal Son would become a man and would endure the punishment and separation from God which men deserved. He was 'foreordained before the foundation of the world' (1 Pet. 1:20) to be 'the Lamb slain from the foundation of the world' (Rev. 13:8)."[6]

The fact that God came up with such a plan to redeem us is completely amazing and is what makes Christianity unique. John G. Lake states, "Man, having fallen into that condition and being separated from God, needed a Redeemer. Redemption was a necessity because the Word says, 'Ye must be born again' (John 3:7). God had to provide a means of getting man back into the original condition in which he had once been."[7]

The Bible states that, "The Lord is gracious and full of compassion, slow to anger and abounding in mercy and loving-kindness. The Lord is good to all, and His tender mercies are over all His works" (Ps. 145:8–9, AMP). John 3:16 states, "For God so loved the world, that he gave his only begotten Son, that whosoever believeth in him should not perish, but have everlasting life" (KJV). All throughout the Old Testament, when the Israelites would be surrounded by their enemies, they would pray and cry out to God, and He would always help them. He would fight their battles and destroy their enemies, sometimes without Israel even firing a shot (2 Chron. 13:3–17; 20:15–23). They could come to Him, and He would be right there for them.

God is completely fair and just (Deut. 32:4; Ps. 96:13; Acts 17:31), and He will be on Judgment Day also. God is love (1 John 4:16), and the ultimate expression of love is to give unconditionally. God did this when He gave us His only Son (John 3:16). To accuse God of being mean is completely unjustified and is a gross misrepresentation. Let me ask you: Why should God have come down from His perfect place and suffer an excruciating death, just so we can mock Him and deny His free gift? Why should He even invite sinful man into His perfect home? What have we done for Him? The answer is…nothing.

WHY IS THE BIBLE MORE SIGNIFICANT THAN OTHER BOOKS OF BELIEFS?

Christianity is based on the Bible, God's Word. Through it we are able to know what God has planned for our lives and how He has made provision for us to spend eternity with Him. It is a book that carries the promises of God, yet it provokes controversy every place its contents are discussed. There is no other religious book that has undergone the scrutiny that the Bible has endured. People have tried for centuries to discredit its truths. Josh McDowell states in his book *Evidence That Demands A Verdict*, "The Bible has withstood vicious attacks of its enemies as no other book. Many have tried to burn it, ban it and 'outlaw it from the days of Roman emperors to present day Communist-dominated countries.'"[8] Dr. Bernard Ramm adds, "A thousand times over, the death knell of the Bible has been sounded, the funeral procession formed, the inscription cut on the tombstone, and committal read. But somehow the corpse never stays put."[9] It just continues to grow, and if the Bible were not the Word of God, it would have been destroyed years ago. Have you ever stopped to think, "Why is the Bible the only book that is continuously attacked?" No other religion is denigrated and mocked like the Bible.

There is overwhelming evidence and support for the Bible. It has been proven through history, archeology, geography, science, and so on, and no credible scholar has found even one discrepancy. Josh McDowell goes on to quote Dr. John Warwick Montgomery, saying, "To be skeptical of the resultant text of the New Testament books is to allow all of classical antiquity to slip into obscurity, for no documents of the ancient period are as well attested bibliographically as the New Testament."[10] He quotes Robert Dick Wilson as saying, "A man who was fluid in more than 45 languages and dialects concluded after a lifetime of study in the Old Testament: 'I may add that the result of my forty-five years of study of the Bible has led me all the time to a firmer faith that in the Old Testament we have a true historical account of the history of the Israelite people.'"[11]

Dr. Henry Morris and Martin Clark say in their book *The Bible Has the Answer*, "Dr. Nelson Glueck, probably the greatest modern authority on Israel's archeology, has said: 'No archeological discovery has ever controverted a biblical reference. Scores of archeological findings have been made which confirm in clear outline or in exact detail historical statements in the Bible. And, by the same token, proper evaluation of biblical descriptions has often led to amazing discoveries.'"[12]

Bernard Ramm said, "Jews preserved it as no other manuscript has ever been preserved. With their massora (parva, magna and finalis) [methods of counting] they kept tabs on every letter, syllable, word and paragraph. They had special classes of men within their culture whose sole duty was to preserve and transmit these documents with practically perfect fidelity-scribes, lawyers, massoretes. Who ever counted the letters, syllables and words of Plato or Aristotle? Cicero or Seneca?"[13]

There are hundreds of quotes I could give, but that is not the purpose of this book. There are several great books listed in the bibliography that have conclusive proof as to the validity of the Bible and its origins to eradicate all your doubts. Please read those mentioned if you are interested.

Christianity is unique in that it is the only belief that states you can do nothing to earn your way into heaven. It is what Jesus did for us. It is by His shed blood (1 John 1:7) only, and not by our boasting (Eph. 2:8–9; Titus 3:5) of good works that grants us entrance into heaven. No other religion claims resurrection from the dead for its founder.

CHAPTER 13

HOW CAN A CHRISTIAN SEE HELL?

SINCE THE RELEASE OF *23 MINUTES IN HELL*, I HAVE BEEN ASKED THIS question on numerous occasions. We know that dreams and visions were given to individuals throughout the Old and New Testament. Phil Pringle says, "Throughout Scripture, there are men who received visions beyond the natural world. They saw into the spiritual world. The visions seen by the apostle John on the Isle of Patmos, for example, left us with the amazing book of Revelation. There are 35 distinct visions and 34 dreams mentioned in Scripture. In all, 21 different men received visions. Some visions became the subject of entire books, such as Nahum and Obadiah. Much of Scripture is recorded from what the writer saw. Isaiah 2:1 'The word that Isaiah the son of Amoz saw concerning Judah and Jerusalem.' It is obvious that God employs spiritual sight to communicate messages to us."[1]

In a vision, a Christian can see hell, just as one can see heaven. Are there people today who have all kinds of "experiences" that are from the soulish realm or demonically induced? Yes. Are there people today who receive God-given dreams and visions? Yes.

Jesus said that you will know believers by their fruit (Matt. 12:33; Luke 6:44) just as we know an apple tree by its fruit. With all credit to the Lord, the fruit of sharing my experience has been many people committing their lives to God, and others have become passionate soul winners.

I know for myself that when I lack understanding about something that someone claims is scriptural, I must study it out in the Bible. If I dismiss the claim without investigation and study, I do so by ignorance or by my preconceived ideas. If my opinion (which may be based on limited knowledge or a lack of knowledge) prevents me from studying the Bible and humbly asking the Holy Spirit to teach me, I then reject because of my pride the claim that could be scriptural.

We worship a supernatural God. Yet when He chooses to do something supernatural in our lives, some of us have difficulty believing He would do such a thing—even though it lines up with Scripture. Before we take a look at some biblical examples, the first point I would like to address is that I did not die. This was not a near-death experience. This was an out-of-body experience that I believe comes under the classification of a vision. There are many other men in the Bible and in present times who have had visions. This is by no means to compare my experience with these and other great men but merely to give a scriptural basis for how I, or any Christian, could see hell.

The apostle Paul experienced heaven in his vision. He said in 2 Corinthians 12:2, "Whether I was in my body or out of my body, I don't know" (NLT). He didn't know if he left his physical body or not. The way that I know I left my body is that the Lord simply allowed me to see that I had left my body.

One of the great prophets, Ezekiel, was picked up by his hair and carried from Babylon to Jerusalem in his vision (Ezek. 8:3). Several verses throughout the Book of Ezekiel show that while the prophet had traveled in his vision, he had hair, a mouth, hands to dig, eyes to see, and a belly. In Ezekiel 8:8 he dug through a wall. Ezekiel 3:2 says, "So I opened my mouth." Verse 3 says, "...cause thy belly to eat..." As you read on, you can see that he could also taste, hear, and feel bitterness. "And it was in my mouth like honey in sweetness" (v. 3). Verse 13 says, "I also heard the noise of the wings of the living creatures..." In verse 14 Ezekiel "went in bitterness, in the heat of my spirit." In Ezekiel 11:1, "the Spirit lifted me up and brought me to the east gate." He had a spiritual body (1 Cor. 15:44) that could experience the same things you can in a physical body, such as eating.

In the Book of Revelation, John was "in the spirit" (Rev. 4:2, KJV). In Revelation 5:4, he said, "I wept much." In verse 5, "One of the elders said to me..." And in Revelation 10:10, John "ate it up; and it was in my mouth sweet as honey...my belly was bitter" (KJV). The point is, John wept, talked, ate, experienced bitterness in his belly, and had a mouth and a hand; therefore we can see that he had a body. His spirit body experienced everything you could in a physical body. Again, this is not to compare myself with these great men, but merely to explain my experience scripturally.

In Genesis 15:1–5, Abraham had a vision, and the Lord "brought him forth abroad" (v. 5, KJV). He traveled in his vision. Job 7:14 says, "Thou scarest me with dreams, and *terrifiest* me through visions" (KJV). In Isaiah 21:2, Isaiah was given a "*grievous* vision" (KJV). In Job 4:13–14, Eliphas was given a vision and said, "Fear came upon me, and trembling, which made all my *bones to shake*" (v. 15, KJV). It is then possible to have a terrifying, grievous, and bone-shaking vision. I would think that the experience I had would at least be considered one of those!

Even Dr. Erwin Lutzer said, "If Stephen saw our Lord before he died, and if Paul died and was caught up into paradise, it is just possible that other believers might also have such a vision.... We should not expect such experiences, but they could happen."[2] As for the Lord revealing Himself to me, look at Numbers 12:6. It states, "I the LORD will make myself known unto him in a vision, and will speak unto him in a dream" (KJV). Now, I know that this verse is in regard to a prophet, and I am not a prophet, but in the New Testament, because we have the Holy Spirit, I believe these blessings extend to us also and because of a better covenant (Heb. 8:6). All of us can get a dream or a vision from the Lord, if He so chooses to give us one. Joel 2:28 says, "Your old men shall dream dreams, your young men shall see visions." Habakkuk 2:2 says, "Then the LORD answered me and said: 'Write the vision and make it plain...'" So I have written the vision, and I believe it is made plain.

As I said before, I never sought for such a vision, or any vision for that matter, and never had any fascination with hell or the dark side. My wife and I never attend or view evil movies, and we hate every evil way. I am not an overly emotional person. As a matter of fact, I used to be called "Mr. Spock" when growing up. I was always very logical and reasonable and showed little emotion. I am certainly not given over to dramatics, and I am the least likely person to whom this could happen. I would almost be tempted to say that the Lord made a mistake in choosing me. But the word *mistake* and God do not go too well together. It is not important why He chose me, as we all have been given something to do for the Lord. What is important is that we all be obedient to whatever He calls us to do.

In a vision or in the spirit realm, you do have a body. My senses were keenly aware of my surroundings, and being in my spirit body was just as real as it would be in the physical body. Matthew 10:28 says, "Fear Him who is able to destroy both soul and *body* in hell." You do have a body in hell. This verse in the Gospel of Matthew is talking about the future hell, which is after Judgment Day (Gehenna), but I believe it is also representative of Sheol (which represents the hell that exists right now). In Luke 16, Jesus mentions the rich man who was contemporary to His time who died and was in Sheol. The rich man had eyes and a tongue in Sheol. He spoke, so he must have had a mouth. He must have had the rest of his body to support those parts. He thirsted and wanted water, so he could have drunk. He also saw Abraham and Lazarus, who also must have had bodies to be recognizable.

Erwin W. Lutzer states in *One Minute After You Die*, "The rich man who died and went to hades must have had a body, since he was able to use human speech and wanted his tongue cooled. He had eyes to see and ears to hear. His body, of whatever kind, was sensitive to pain and was recognizable to Lazarus, who was on the other side of the great divide."[3]

Proverbs 1:12 provides further proof and says, "Let us swallow them up alive as the grave [Sheol], and *whole*, as those who go down into the pit" (KJV). Ezekiel 32:27 says that the iniquities of those who have gone down into the pit "will be upon their *bones*." The word *bones* is the Hebrew word *esem*, which is the same word used in Exodus 13:19, 2 Samuel 19:12, 1 Kings 13:31, and many other places; it refers to actual bones that humans possess.[4] In the book *Hell Under Fire*, Dr. Daniel I. Block states, "That which survives of the deceased is not simply the spiritual component of the human being, but a shadowy image of the whole person, complete with *head and skeleton*."[5]

In their book *The Bible Has the Answer*, Dr. Henry Morris and Martin Clark state, "The temporary spiritual bodies of these dead men and women will not be consumed in the fires of Hades, since they are not physical bodies. Nevertheless, their spirits are real (in fact a man's spirit and soul are more real than his body, and will continue to exist in this real world even after this body is dead), and will undoubtedly be subject to intense suffering. The tremendous heat and pressure of such depths will serve as a fitting environment…which will continually torment the occupants of Hades."[6] You do have a body in hell, and it is possible to travel in a vision to hell in a spirit body (1 Cor. 15:44).

WHAT WAS THE PURPOSE OF THIS VISION?

Some have asked, "Why would God give you this vision. What is its purpose?"

The Lord told me on the return, "Many people do not believe that hell exists; even some of My own people do not believe that hell is real." Some Christians have said to me that Jesus would never call them "My own people," because they feel that it is a requirement for all Christians to believe in an eternal hell in order to be saved. However, where does it say in the Bible that in order to be saved you must believe in an eternal hell? Don't get me wrong; I am surprised that Christians don't all believe in an eternal hell, filled with suffering. We all should, as the Bible is very clear on that subject.

But my wife and I have met many professing Christians whom I believe are saved, yet they have been taught false doctrine in regard to hell. Some have been told that one ceases to exist when entering hell (annihilationist), or that you are eventually saved out of hell (universalism), or that hell is only a state of mind and not real physical torment. Their theology is simply wrong, but that doesn't mean they are not saved, as some have indicated. The Bible says, "Whosoever shall call upon the name of the

Lord shall be saved" (Rom. 10:13, KJV). It does not say, "Whosoever shall call upon the name of the Lord and has all their theology right about hell shall be saved." What about the thief on the cross? I am certain he did not have all his theology correct. He probably knew almost nothing but only to trust in the Lord as Savior and be sorry for his sins. In his book *A Ready Defense*, Josh McDowell writes:

> The Scriptures contain other examples of individuals who were accepted by God, even though their knowledge of Him was limited.
>
> 1. Rahab, the prostitute, had only the smallest amount of knowledge about God, but the Bible refers to her as a women of faith, and her actions were commended (Joshua 2:9; Hebrews 11:31).
>
> 2. Naaman, the Syrian, was granted peace with God because he exercised faith, even though he was living in the midst of a pagan culture (2 Kings 5:15–19).
>
> 3. Jonah, the prophet, was sent to Nineveh, a heathen society, and they repented at his preaching (Jonah 3:5).[7]

Soul sleep is another theological error concerning what happens after death. Some Christians believe this, as well as do those who are in religions that do not follow the fundamentals of Christian faith. Belief in soul sleep usually encompasses a disbelief in eternal torment, since the individual would be "sleeping," at least until Judgment Day. At that point, they believe the wicked person will be annihilated. This, of course, is completely unbiblical. However, in my opinion, if that is all a person is mistaken about (all other aspects of the faith being adhered to), then they would most likely still be saved. Dr. Walter Martin says, "The question of soul-sleep, however, should cause no serious division between Christians, since it does not affect the foundational doctrines of the Christian faith or the salvation of the soul. It is merely an area of theological debate and has no direct bearing upon any of the great doctrines of the Bible. The ground of fellowship is not the condition of man in death but faith in the Lord Jesus Christ and the love He commanded us to have one for another (John 13:34–35)."[8]

Belief in hell as a conscious, eternal punishment is not a requirement to being saved. Hebrews 6:2 states that one of the principal doctrines of the faith is "eternal judgment." This sounds like it disagrees with what I just said. However, some think that eternal judgment means being condemned to eternal sleeping or eternal annihilation. They are definitely mistaken. But does an error in their theology mean condemnation to hell? As long as that person is trusting in the shed blood of Jesus, the one and only Son of God and risen Savior, that He died on a cross for them and rose from the dead, that they receive Him as their Lord and Savior, and they have repented for their sins, then they have fulfilled the requirement for salvation. As I said, I cannot understand how a believer cannot understand that hell is eternal torment, but I have met some such believers. This is one of the reasons we all need to read the Bible daily in order to renew our minds and correct our misconceptions.

Some have actually become angry because I have pointed out that the Bible does teach eternal sufferings for the unrepentant. Many listeners have called in to the radio shows I have been a guest on to say to me, "God would never allow anyone to suffer in hell. People are annihilated at hell's entrance." This is what I have been confronted with many times. This is also why God allowed me to see and experience all I did in my vision: so that I could present to them my testimony and the scriptures that are so very clear on the subject. Unfortunately, many still persist in their misconceptions.

The Bible gives clear answers to the truth about the eternal torment of hell: Matthew 13:40, 49–50; 22:13–14; 25:30, 41, 46; Mark 3:29; Luke 12:46–48; 16:22–31; John 3:36; 5:29; 15:6; 2 Thessalonians 1:9; Revelation 14:10–11. I will spell these and other verses out in chapter 31, "Do People in Hell 'Cease to Exist'?—Annihilationism" Almost every reputable Bible teacher, pastor, scholar, and commentary supports the biblical view of eternal torment, and I have included many quotes from them ahead.

OTHER CHRISTIANS WHO HAVE SEEN HELL (SHEOL)

There have been many other witnesses to such experiences besides myself—both in the Bible and in more recent times.

Lester Sumrall had a vision of hell. We shared his experience in our first book on pages 95–96. In his vision, he saw a long and wide highway filled with people walking. He was carried far down the road to the end. At the end he saw an abrupt cliff, and the procession of people moving ever forward could not stop. The ever-surging river of humanity was sweeping the people forward. They were being pushed off the cliff, falling into an abyss, a fiery pit, all clawing in the air, horrified, as they fell into the flames of that pit. Lester Sumrall states in his book *Run With the Vision*, "One thing that continued to drive me was that tormenting vision of a world going to hell. Every day, it was the one predominating thought of my mind. When I was asleep I often dreamed about it. The vision would not let me go."[9]

At seventeen years of age Kenneth Hagin was dying of a disease and received a vision from the Lord. He left his body three times and went to the gates of hell, where he saw the flames and a demon. After this experience, he became a Christian and a well-known Bible teacher.

John Bunyan, who wrote *The Pilgrims Progress*, also had a vision and wrote a book called *Visions of Heaven and Hell*.

The prophet Jonah is one man in the Bible who quite possibly had seen hell (Sheol). He tried to run from God when he was instructed to deliver a warning of coming judgment to the people in the city of Nineveh if they did not repent of their evil ways. While he was on the run, God caused him to be tossed over the side of a boat into the sea. Jonah was swallowed by a large fish and spent three days inside his belly. Perhaps it is there that he had a vision of hell, or actually died and went to hell (Sheol). In Jonah 2:2 he said, "Out of the belly of Sheol [hell] I cried." And in verse 6 he said that "the earth with its bars closed behind me forever; yet You have brought up my life from the pit."

Two highly respected commentaries state that he was either just inside the gates of hell or just outside the gates:

Although Jonah is on the verge of entering Sheol, the Lord hears his cry and delivers him....Like a Palestinian city, Jonah views the underworld as having a gate which was locked secure by bolts and bars: there could be no escaping from it. Once in Sheol, Jonah would be imprisoned there forever.[10]

He had been in Sheol's belly. Sheol, the world of the dead, is depicted as a monster in whose maw Jonah was trapped. He was as good as dead before Yahweh graciously answered his appeal....He found himself at death's door. The gates of hell prevailed against him, clanging shut with a terrible finality—or so it seemed.[11]

The New American Commentary states, "The expression [in Jonah chapter 2] also may refer to the gates of Sheol, the underworld, conceived to be a fortified city (cf. Ps. 9:13; Is. 38:10). If these bars were closed behind a human being, they remained finally shut. Jonah had a sense of despair, his utter hopelessness."[12] "A third possibility is that Jonah actually suffocated and died in the great fish and then later God brought him back from the dead....This is implied also by Jonah's prayer, when he said, '...out of the belly of hell (i.e., "sheol," 'the place of the departed spirits) cried I, and thou heardest my voice' (Jonah 2:2)."[13]

Some say that Jonah's situation was not a vision, but that he may have actually died and actually gone to hell. Whatever the situation, he most likely saw Sheol, and God rescued him out of it.

HIDDEN

There is another significant part of my experience that I would like to point out: the Lord had blocked from my mind, or hid from me, that I was a Christian. In *23 Minutes in Hell,* I explained that He had done that because He wanted me to experience the hopelessness real unbelievers will feel in hell. If I would have had the understanding that I was a Christian, I would not have experienced the utter hopelessness. God needed me to be a "firsthand" witness of what it is to actually be an unsaved person in hell in order to relay the gravity of this message.

I would like to give some additional scriptural support and some commentaries' opinions on how God can block certain knowledge from our minds. We know God can do anything, but scriptural support is needed here.

When Jesus appeared after His resurrection to two disciples as they walked along the way to Emmaus, Luke 24:16 states, "Their eyes were holden that they should not know him" (KJV). These disciples were kept from knowing Jesus's identity. *The MacArthur Bible Commentary* says, "They were kept by God from recognizing Him."[14] *Matthew Henry's Commentary on the Whole Bible* states, "For here it is said that their eyes were held by a divine power."[15] "Partly He was in another form (Mark 16:12), and partly there seems to be an operation on their own vision."[16]

In his book *Systematic Theology*, Wayne Grudem writes, "It is true that two of Jesus' disciples did not recognize him when they walked with him on the road to Emmaus (Luke 24:13–32), but Luke specifically tells us that this was because 'their eyes were kept from recognizing him' (Luke 24:16), and later, 'their eyes were opened and they recognized him' (Luke 24:31)."[17] God apparently hid the fact, just for that time, that He was Jesus. Then, as we just saw, Luke 24:31 states, "Their eyes were opened" when Jesus "took bread, and blessed it, and brake, and gave to them" (v. 30, KJV).

"This suggests that God had prevented them from recognizing Jesus earlier, which they otherwise would have," says Randy Alcorn, in his book *Heaven*.[18]

Of the woman who went to the tomb to care for the body of Jesus, John 20:14 says, "She turned herself back, and saw Jesus standing, and knew not that it was Jesus" (KJV). *The MacArthur Bible Commentary* says, "Perhaps, however, like the disciples on the road to Emmaus, she was supernaturally prevented from recognizing him until He chose for her to do so (see Luke 24:16)."[19]

According to Daniel 4:34, our understanding can return to us the same way in which it was taken—by God's doing. *Matthew Henry's Commentary on the Whole Bible* supports this by saying, "His understanding and memory were gone.... God justly makes him less than a man.... He has the use of his reason so far restored to him.... He [God] has the power to humble the haughtiest... those that walk in pride he is able to abase (v. 37)."[20]

In the story of the Shunammite woman in 2 Kings 4, the prophet Elisha said, "Let her alone, for her soul is vexed within her: and the Lord hath *hid it from me*, and hath not told me" (v. 27, KJV). The woman had come to the man of God because her son had died, and God had not made Elisha aware of her circumstances before time. These are just a few examples. Another sure proof that God can hide something from our mind is my marriage. I shared that my wife and I have been married since 1997. Well, she still thinks I'm wonderful! Praise the Lord! That is abso- *Cute* lute, definite, concrete proof that God keeps certain things hidden!

HOW I KNOW IT WASN'T JUST A BAD DREAM

In the vision, my spiritual body was separated from my physical body. I know this because on the return from the trip into hell, I could see my body lying on the floor of my room as I hovered above the roof of our home. This shocked me, and I thought, "How could that be me?" As I have said previously, you can have a spiritual body in a vision (1 Cor. 15:44). The spirit body is separate from your physical body. The spiritual life seems much more real than the physical life. One reason might be because the spirit, or soul, is eternal.

Once the shock of seeing my own body lying there registered, God allowed my spirit body to rejoin with my physical body, and I immediately went into a traumatized state. The horrors of hell entered back into my mind. You see, on the way back, I was with the Lord, and the horrors in my mind had gone. First John 4:18 says, "Perfect love casts out fear." Since I was with God and because God *is* love, there was absolutely no fear. When the Lord's presence left, the horrors returned. My wife had to pray for me for a while before I came to myself and was aware that I was back. I was then able to ask her to pray to the Lord and ask Him to remove the horrors from my mind. He graciously did so and allowed me to only retain the memories. He separated the memories from the terror. You may ask, "How could He do that?" He is a supernatural God, that's how. The Bible says that the Word of God is able to divide both soul and spirit, and joints and marrow (Heb. 4:12).

It still was an entire year before I would be settled down from this experience. The reality of the vision made me want to warn everyone I saw about that place. I didn't want to necessarily share my experience with anyone, but I was compelled to talk to everyone regarding his or her eternity. I wanted to warn them how to avoid hell at all costs! I could hardly go to sleep each night without at least talking to one person who didn't know the Lord. I was almost obsessed with this desire to warn others. I will always have the desire to warn everyone I can, but my "settling down" resides in the fact that all I can do is to tell others; God does the rest.

Concerning the psychological trauma that could have haunted me after such a horrifying experience, God has been most gracious toward me. I will forever have the picture burned into my mind of people burning and the deafening screams of the lost. But I am blessed that my "settling down" has not been a recovery from fear, lack of sleep, bad dreams, or any of the like. I have had no problems whatsoever in that regard. God took all of that away immediately during the moments right after my return while my wife prayed for me.

WHY SHOULD YOU BELIEVE ME?

It is not my experience I want you to believe. My experience just points the way to what the Bible has to say. I have been reminded by some readers, radio listeners, and audience members about the story in Luke 16 where the rich man in hell asked Abraham if Lazarus could return from the dead and go and warn his brothers, for he had five brothers. The rich man thought, "If one went unto them from the dead, they will repent." Abraham said, "If they hear not Moses and the prophets, neither will they be persuaded, though one rose from the dead" (vv. 30–31, KJV).

Based on this story, the question is then asked, "Why would God send you with this message about hell, if Abraham told the rich man that people wouldn't be persuaded, though one rose from the dead?" There are two reasons why I don't fit that scenario. One reason is that I didn't die. I'm not coming back from the dead. This was a vision, as I explained previously. Secondly, I am not telling anyone to believe me and be persuaded. I am just a signpost to point people to the Scriptures. I do not feel responsible for making people believe my experience, but it is so very important that you take me seriously enough to check out the Bible for yourself. I don't want you to take my word for it. The Bible has so many scriptures in it for you to read for yourself. I want you to have the confidence to say for yourself, "God said it; I read it!"

So I ask you, please don't write this off as being from some extremist, because that is not at all in my nature. I am only sharing with you what I saw and what the Scriptures say. If at the end of this book you decide to throw it in the trash, it is your decision. Proverbs 18:13 says, "He who answers a matter before he hears it [the facts], it is folly and shame to him."

I do not have any reason to subject myself to anyone's criticism or skepticism. You may be thinking, "Oh, yes, you do. You're selling books!" Let me share with you that my wife and I traveled for seven years around the country before the book was published. We went wherever we were asked to come and didn't get paid a dime. We paid our own way and took time off of work just so people couldn't use that as an excuse not to believe. My wife had a high-paying job, and we arranged our trips on her two days off each week and also used up her three weeks of vacation every year to be able to go.

We didn't know that seven years later I would be asked to write a book. Yes, the book is selling, but we now travel full-time and have left our real estate careers. We have never self-promoted this in any way. We have prayed and asked the Lord to direct us. We told Him that if He wanted a book, then He would have someone approach us. We were amazed and honored when our publisher came to us, as they are a very reputable and respected publisher. But at the same time, we were very reluctant to share this with the world. It is something I didn't even want to share with my parents. However, since we were being asked to speak at churches, we figured that putting all of the verses that relate to my experience in a book would be beneficial for others to read. We also knew the Lord was telling us to write it.

My wife and I have been very comfortable and successful in our real estate careers. I didn't need this change, but the Lord had other plans. The life that He has chosen for us at this time is so very different from how we lived before. As a matter of fact, I used to get sick to my stomach the night before I would speak. I would cringe when the phone rang with another invitation. I have always disdained public speaking. All through my school years, I never once gave a speech. I always declined. I finally had to change my attitude, and I am now able to look at this with a different perspective. The Lord spoke to me one day and said, "Bill, it is not about you being comfortable but about you being obedient." That was sobering!

Sometimes God pulls us out of our comfort zones. As Christians we all have been given a job to do for Him. And just like me, many of us have been given dreams or visions to let us in on what that job is. We must get over our desire to be comfortable, and do as He asks. In his book *Out of Your Comfort Zone*, R. T. Kendall shares, "If you want an increase in your anointing, and if you go where the anointing is to be found, you will almost certainly be required to move outside your comfort zone." He goes on to quote John Steinbeck, saying, "It is the nature of man as he grows older…to protest against change, particularly change for the better."[21] There is no better employer than God. He has great benefits, and we are so very honored to do whatever He asks.

My goal is not to justify myself but to get the truth to everyone. This is a "heads up" message. I don't want to see even one person go to that place, and I will do all I can to use my experience as a means to point people to the truth. The wonderful thing about all of this is that there have been thousands come to the Lord through this testimony, and an equal number of Christians have become much more motivated to witness. I have actually been very surprised at how many thousands believe me and how few oppose the message. At the end of my experience, when I was alone with the Lord, I told Him that I didn't want to share this with anyone. "They will think I'm crazy or had a bad dream," I said. The Lord said, "It is not your job to convict their hearts; that responsibility belongs to the Holy Spirit [1 John 5:6]. It is your part to go and tell them."

Some have said to me, "God doesn't need you, Bill, and He doesn't need to add to the Bible with your story." Well, they are right. God doesn't need me at all, and I am not adding anything to His Word, only pointing others *to* His Word. Because many are not pointing out the consequences that will be suffered for rejection of the provision (Jesus Christ) for our sins, God is drawing attention to this area in His Word. Even churches are avoiding the subject of hell, or downplaying it severely. God is trying to send a warning message to those who don't know Him and a wake-up call to some of those who do, by any means necessary—even giving Christians visions of the horrors of hell's fire.

CHAPTER 14

EXPOUNDING ON
23 MINUTES IN HELL

ANY HAVE SAID TO ME, "I WOULDN'T WANT TO GO THROUGH what you experienced. That must have been so horrible." Yes, it was something I never would want to go through again, not even for one minute. However, I would not trade that experience for the world. I have a despicable hatred for hell, yet I value the minutes spent there. It is a place of unexplainable fear, yet I highly treasure what God has allowed me to see. I say this because it has given me a much greater appreciation for what I have been spared from. I have gained a much greater compassion for the people who don't know God, a strong desire to warn them of what lies ahead and how they can avoid it, an increased burden to share the good news of the gospel, and a deeper and more intimate love for our Lord and Savior.

There are no words to adequately describe hell's horror. In John MacArthur's teaching on hell called "Hell—the Furnace of Fire," he quoted another writer, saying:

> There is no way to describe hell. Nothing on earth can compare with it. No living person has any real idea of it. No madman in wildest flights of insanity ever beheld its horror. No man in delirium ever pictured a place so utterly terrible as this. No nightmare racing across a fevered mind ever produces a

terror to match that of the mildest hell. No murder scene with splashed blood and oozing wound ever suggested a revulsion that could touch the border lands of hell. Let the most gifted writer exhaust his skill in describing this roaring cavern of unending flame, and he would not even brush in fancy the nearest edge of hell.[1]

HELL IS NOT JUST "SEPARATION FROM GOD"

Some pastors and scholars state that hell is merely separation from God, but not actual torment, as if "separation" would not be so severe. Indeed, hell is separation from God. But to many, that implies no real pain experienced. What they don't understand is that separation from God is much worse than anyone can ever imagine. Most of the great leaders of the past, along with the early church fathers, believed that there was great torment in being separated from God. Many also believe that the fiery torments are part of the suffering as well. To quote just a few who commented about the fire, Pope Benedict XVI told a parish gathering in a northern suburb of Rome, "Hell is a place where sinners really do burn in an everlasting fire..."[2] Dr. Albert Mohler, president of the Southern Baptist Theological Seminary, said in the book, *Hell? Yes!* by Robert Jeffress, "Scripture clearly speaks of hell as a physical place of fiery torment and warns us we should fear."[3]

Charles Spurgeon said:

> Do not begin telling me that there is metaphorical fire: who cares for that? If a man were to threaten to give me a metaphorical blow on the head, I should care very little about it: he would be welcome to give me as many as he pleased. And what say the wicked? "We do not care about metaphorical fires." But they are real sir—yes, as real as yourself. There is a real fire in hell, as truly as you now have a real body—a fire exactly like that which we have on the earth in everything except this—that it will not consume, though it will torture you.[4]

John Calvin said, "Everlasting destruction and the torment of the flesh await all those whom He will drive from His presence."[5] John Piper said, "I know of no one who has overstated the terror of hell. We are meant to tremble and feel dread. We are meant to recoil from the reality."[6] Psalm 116:3 says, "The pains of Sheol laid hold upon me; I found trouble and sorrow." In the Gospel of Luke Jesus quotes a rich man who is in hell. The rich man says, "I am tormented in this flame" (Luke 16:24). David describes hell as a "horrible pit" (Ps. 40:2). Amos 5:18–19 says that hell "will be darkness, and not light. It will be as though a man fled from a lion, and a bear met him!"

There are many other verses we will look at ahead. To think that by saying "separation from God" somehow reduces the torments one suffers in hell is a great misnomer. Everything good we experience is from God (James 1:17). To be separated from Him would be the same as being separated from all good. You can't have the good without God. Some people tend to think that the good things we experience, such as sunshine, fresh air, food and water, sleep, and beautiful scenery are from "mother nature." But they do not come from "mother nature"; they come from Father God. John Calvin said, "How wretched it is to be cut off from all fellowship with God."[7]

NO STRENGTH

As I mentioned in my first book, in regard to having no strength in hell, the Bible says, "The way of the LORD is strength for the upright" (Prov. 10:29). You are not His upright in hell. Isaiah 14:9–10 states, "Hell from beneath is moved for thee to meet thee at thy coming....All they shall speak and say unto thee, Art thou become weak as we?" The word *weak* is the same word used in Judges 16:7, where Samson became physically weak when his hair was cut off. According to *Strong's Exhaustive Concordance*, it means "weak, sick, afflicted."[8] Also, Psalm 88:4 says, "I am counted with those who go down to the pit; I am as a man who has no strength." Most people in life enjoy strength, and in sports they train for their entire lives to get strength. We eat properly and sleep sufficiently to achieve the most strength and health possible. But the Bible says that the joy of the Lord is our strength (Neh. 8:10). God told Joshua, "Be strong" (Josh. 1:6). Caleb said he was strong, like he was at forty, now being eighty-five (Josh. 14:11). David said, "The king shall have joy in Your strength, O LORD" (Ps. 21:1). It is God's strength we enjoy. Strength is a blessing from God. In hell, it is the antithesis.

CAN'T BREATHE

In hell, it is so very difficult to even capture one breath. It is far worse than a mountain climber being at too high of an altitude where he cannot get adequate oxygen, or a person who has an asthma attack and can't breathe. This goes on forever. Isaiah 42:5 says that God gives breath to people who dwell *upon* the earth. It is not to those *under* the earth. In the Bible, the words *upon*, *beneath*, *below*, and *above* all are very specific, as is every word of the Bible. If you are in hell, then you are beneath the earth and, therefore, would not derive that benefit of the breath of God.

ODOR!

Have you ever wondered about a volcano? It spews out burning rock, brimstone, and sulfur. Where does that sound like it comes from? I believe God lets us have a glimpse of hell. The spewing lava flow should be enough to scare anyone to at least think, "Hey, that might be what hell is like." I believe the lava flow and burning sulfur are a visual warning from God as to a glimpse of the hell below. Also, the odor from the sulfur in hell is similar to the toxic odor coming from the volcano. In Hawaii, there are signs posted near the volcano where you cannot pass, as the fumes it produces are considered toxic. I once received a call from a man who had a near-death experience where he went to hell. He said he will never forget the sulfur odor in hell, so putrid and foul. Then, after his experience, he was in Pearl Harbor, and he smelled that same odor. He wondered where it was coming from. A man told him that sometimes the trade winds carry the smell from the big island, from the volcano. They smell it every so often. He said that was the same foul smell he remembered when he was in hell, and he would never forget it. Neither will I!

NO MERCY

There is no mercy in hell. Psalm 36:5 says, "Thy mercy, O LORD, is in the heavens" (KJV). Mercy is not under the earth; it is from heaven and upon those who fear Him. (Ps. 103:17). Those in hell do not fear Him. You will never receive any mercy in hell, there will never be an angel—or anyone—to come and rescue you, and the cavalry will never come over the hill. The demons hate God (John 15:18), and therefore they also hate His creation. Hatred comes from the demonic realm. They will torment those in hell, mainly because they hate God; by tormenting His creation, in one sense they would be striking back at Him. Lester Sumrall said in his book *101 Question and Answers on Demon Powers*, "They possess humans in order to strike back at God. God is too great and powerful for them to attack directly, so in their hatred they turn to His greatest creation, mankind, and oppress and destroy them."[9] This is talking about demons possessing people on the earth, not in hell. However, the demons have the same opportunity and abilities to attack the humans in hell as well. If they can possess and harm people on the earth, would hell be any less? This is at least until Judgment Day, when the devil and his demons will then be cast into the lake of fire and receive their full torment (Matt. 8:29; Rev. 20:10).

NO REST, NO SLEEP

You can never go to sleep in hell. Revelation 14:11 says that "the smoke of their torment ascends forever and ever; and they have no rest day or night." In hell there is no rest from the torments—and no actual rest of any kind, or sleep. Isaiah 57:20 says, "But the wicked are like the troubled sea, when it cannot *rest*." But Psalm 127:2 says that God "gives His beloved sleep." In hell, you are not His beloved. Therefore you do not get the blessing of sleep ever again. Psalm 4:8 says, "I will both lie down in peace, and sleep; for You alone, O Lord, make me dwell in safety." The promise of this verse will never be fulfilled in hell.

NO WATER, NO LIFE, NO BLOOD

There is no water, ever, not even one drop. Deuteronomy 11:11 says that water is the rain of heaven. It represents life (Rev. 21:6). There is no life in hell (Rev. 6:8; 20:13–14) and therefore no water (Zech. 9:11; Luke 16:24) and no blood (Lev. 17:11), because the life of the flesh is in the blood. There is only death in hell.

Some have said, "Why would you need water, or even food, if you are a spirit body or just simply a soul?" Remember, in Luke 16, the rich man thirsted and wanted just one drop of water to cool his tongue. He was thirsty, and he had a tongue. He had eyes, a mouth to talk, and thereby must have had a body. Lazarus was "comforted" in Abraham's bosom.

Since the rich man thirsted in Hades, he possessed the ability to drink and most likely to eat. He was a soul, and yet a soul thirsted. In the wilderness, the Israelites ate the manna from heaven. The Bible says it was "angels' food" (Ps. 78:24–25). Angels are spirit beings, and yet they eat manna, which could be consumed by humans. Did God convert the food over for human consumption? Who knows! The point is, angels do eat, and they are spirit beings. There is a heavenly banquet being prepared for all the saints. In Matthew 22:3–4, Jesus states that, "The kingdom of heaven is like unto a certain king, which made a marriage for his son....Again, he sent forth other servants, saying, Tell them which are bidden, Behold, I have prepared my *dinner*: my oxen and my fattlings are killed, and all things are ready: come unto the marriage" (kjv). Luke 12:37 says that when the Lord comes, He shall "have them to sit down to *eat*, and will come and serve them." In Luke 22:30, Jesus said, "...that you may *eat* and *drink* at My table in My kingdom." Randy Alcorn, in his book *Heaven*, said, "The resurrected Jesus invited His disciples, 'come and have breakfast.' He prepared them a meal and then ate bread and fish with them (John 21:4–14). He proved that resurrection bodies are capable of eating food, real food."[10] Wayne Grudem said, "With regard to the nature of Jesus' resurrection body…had a physical body with 'flesh and bones' (Luke 24:39), which could eat and drink…"[11]

Some other verses that substantiate this are found in Isaiah 25:6; Matthew 8:11; 26:29; Luke 14:15; 22:16, 18; Revelation 7:17; 19:9). In hell, you will forever thirst (Zech. 9:11). Revelation 6:8 associates death and hell with hunger. Proverbs 19:15 says, "An idle soul shall suffer hunger" (KJV). In heaven we will never hunger or thirst, as on the earth (Rev. 7:16). Hell would, of course, be worse than what we may experience during the hardest days on Earth.

NAKED

Job 26:6 records one being "naked" in hell. The word *naked* is the same Hebrew word used in Genesis 2:25, *arom*, where Adam and Eve were naked in the garden.[12] It is also the same word used in Job 1:21, where he said, "Naked I came from my mother's womb…"

Job 26:6 means primarily that God does oversee hell and looks upon it. It is not hidden from Him. I believe, secondarily, it means actually physically naked, because of the definition and usage of the word *naked*. There are other verses that imply nakedness and shame together, as I mentioned in *23 Minutes in Hell*. It is another form of vulnerability. We have seen how people were stripped naked in the concentration camps, which added shame, increased their vulnerability, and exposed them to the extreme climate. That kind of evil and merciless act originates from the demonic realm and should be expected in hell.

SCREAMS

The screams of those in hell are so very loud that they absolutely pierce right through your very soul. It never ceases. "There is no peace, saith my God, to the wicked" (Isa. 57:21, KJV). Peace is from God (Phil. 1:2; 4:7, 9; Col. 3:15; 1 Thess. 5:23, Titus 1:4; Heb. 13:20).

John Wesley said, "…but one unvaried scene of horror upon horror!

There is <u>no music</u> but that of groans and shrieks; of weeping, wailing, and gnashing of teeth, of curses and blasphemies against God..."[13]

No Purpose

There is no purpose of any kind in hell. All is over, lost, and gone. Ecclesiastes 9:10 says, "...no work, nor device, nor knowledge, nor wisdom in the grave [Sheol]..." (KJV).

In hell, you are a nobody. There is no reward for your accomplishments. No fame, fortune, or status is recognized. Ecclesiastes 6:4 says, "His name shall be covered with darkness" (KJV). Psalm 88:12 states, "...the land of forgetfulness." You are forgotten to all (Isa. 26:14).

Maggots

While I was in hell, I saw maggots by the millions crawling along the walls. I couldn't see well enough through the flames to see if there were maggots on any of the people. But the Bible states over and over, "Where their worm dies not, and the fire is not quenched" (Mark 9:44, 46, 48). Notice it says *"their* worm," not *"the* worm." Each has their own worms. Isaiah 14:11 states, "The maggot is spread under you, and worms cover you."

John MacArthur says, in his teaching "Hell—the Furnace of Fire," "When a body is put into a grave, worms begin to consume it. Once the body is consumed, the worms die. But in hell, the worms that consume the bodies will never die because the bodies will never be totally consumed. In other words, the Lord was saying that the unrelieved torment of the body will go on forever in hell."[14] Job 24:20 says that "the worm shall feed sweetly on him" (KJV). (See also Job 21:26; Isaiah 66:24.) According to the *Holman Illustrated Bible Dictionary*, "Maggots are spread out as your bed beneath you and worms for your covering."[15] Just imagine, maggots eating your flesh for eternity. That is a very horrifying thought, indeed!

No Thoughts of God in Hell

Some asked, "Did you think of God, and do people in hell pray to God?"

I can tell you that I did not think of God. Remember, it was hidden from my mind that I was a Christian, so God didn't come to my mind. I know I heard the demons blaspheming God, but I only heard their words and didn't think of Him myself. There were no sounds of anyone praying to God that I recall. The scriptures that address this somewhat are as follows:

- Psalm 6:5—"For in death there is no remembrance of thee: in the grave [Sheol] who shall give thee thanks?" (KJV). *Thee* in this verse is God, according to many of the commentaries.

- Isaiah 38:18—"For the grave [Sheol] cannot praise thee, death can not celebrate thee" (KJV). *Vine's Expository Dictionary on Old Testament Words* tells us that the King James sometimes uses the word *grave* when it should say "Sheol," as Sheol never represents nor is it synonymous with the grave.[16]

- Psalm 88:10–12—"Shall the dead arise and praise thee? Shall thy lovingkindness be declared in the grave? or thy faithfulness in destruction? Shall thy wonders be known in the dark? and thy righteousness in the land of forgetfulness?" (KJV). From the satirical tone of these verses, we can assume these questions are rhetorical; therefore, the answer to all of them would be no.

Based on what we have just read, I would say that no one will be praising the Lord or praying.

Senses Are Keener

Many people have asked questions about one's senses in hell, such as: "How could you have known that you were deep in the earth? How could you have known the pit you saw was a mile across? How could you have known it was ten miles away from you when first viewed?" Well, I can't explain exactly, but your senses are sharper and keener in the spiritual realm. There are only two verses that would possibly indicate that you are capable of a greater awareness. In Zechariah 5:2, Zechariah tells of a vision he had: "And he said unto me, What seest thou? And I answered, I see a flying roll; the length thereof is twenty cubits, and the breadth thereof ten cubits" (KJV). Zechariah wasn't told the measurement, yet he knew it! How did he know, and why is it recorded for us? This is only a hint of proof about knowing more in the spiritual realm. In Luke 16, the rich man recognized Abraham and Lazarus. How did he know what Abraham looked like, especially from a great distance? There may be some explanation for that, as Abraham may have had some kind of distinguishing feature, and it could have been obvious. Who knows? But also Lazarus, being a great distance off, would be very difficult to recognize, especially since hell is filled with smoke (Rev. 14:11). These are only some indications of sharper senses. If you study Ezekiel 32:18–31 and Isaiah 14:9–18, you will discover more of this "awareness."

Dr. Erwin Lutzer, a conservative and well-known scholar, said that those in Sheol exist "with heightened perception and a better understanding."[17] Some scholars point out that the rich man in Luke 16 showed signs of a greater awareness, in that he understood why he was there. The rich man said, "But if one went unto them from the dead, they will *repent*" (v. 30, KJV). This is something he most likely didn't fully comprehend in life, since he didn't do it. Yet, in hell, he knew repentance was the key. He knew what was necessary in order to receive salvation. You see, when Abraham began telling him that he had received the "good things" in life and Lazarus the "evil things," many would misunderstand that to mean that being rich will cause one to be cast into hell and being poor will get you to heaven. But he understood that was not the case! This was not what Abraham meant. It was only by repentance, as he said in verse 30. This is what some of the commentaries point out in regard to him having a greater awareness.

Dead, but Alive

It is difficult to explain how it is that you are dead but still exist and feel pain in hell. Death is separation from God, and God is the source of all life. Your soul lives on forever, yet it is disconnected from the source of all life. There is, perhaps, one simplistic analogy that may grasp one aspect of this reality. It is, in a sense, like living in a negative, like a piece of 35 mm film you receive. It is not the true photo, with color and life. It is the reverse of the image, negative and lifeless. It is like being a shadow and not the real person. It's like Daniel Block reported on the Israelite burial practices; they are like "living corpses" or "shadowy images."[18] As far as living in a separated state from God and all life, there is no way I can describe the horrendous feeling of being separated from God. It is the most empty, lonely, abandoned, and completely destitute feeling one could ever imagine. According to *Harper's Bible Dictionary*, "The dead are referred to as 'shades,' pale reflections of the men and women they had once been (Isa. 14:10; Eccles. 9:10)."[19]

Matthew Henry's Commentary on the Whole Bible says, "Their punishment will be no less than destruction...both as to body and soul. This destruction will be everlasting. They shall be *always dying, and yet never die.* Their misery will run parallel with the line of eternity."[20]

On the Edge

The only moment I had to reflect back about my life here on the earth was a few seconds in two instances. Other than that, the terror fills your mind completely, leaving no calm moments to ever escape in thought. My point is, your mental escapes are ever so limited as you are too occupied with fear and horror to ever have even a minute, only seconds, to reflect on your past. You feel as if you will go completely insane, but the reality is, you never do. You stay right on the edge. If you did actually go insane, it would be a form of escape, and there is no escape of any kind, so insanity never quite occurs. Remember the rich man in hell? He asked questions, seemed rational in his thinking, and understood why he was there. He didn't argue that he should be let out. He knew God was just and that it took repentance on his part before he died.

Two passages from the Book of Isaiah and Ezekiel give additional support for those in hell being rational and in their right mind. Isaiah 14:9–10 says, "Hell from beneath is moved for thee to meet thee at thy coming....All they shall speak and say unto thee, Art thou also become weak as we?" (KJV). And Ezekiel 32:21, 24 says, "The strong among the mighty shall speak to him out of the midst of hell....Yet have they borne their shame with them that go down to the pit" (KJV). My point is, these are able to speak rationally knowing they bear shame. This would not be the case with someone who is insane. There is no rest for the wicked—not even mentally.

FEAR

The fear level is so far beyond anything you can imagine. Psalm 73:18–19 says, "Thou castedst them down into destruction....They are utterly consumed with terrors" (KJV). This was so very true of my own experience. I can't begin to express the terror and fear that consumed me. I mention in another chapter how everything good comes from God, including His love, which casts out all fear. There is no hint of God or His love in hell. The fear and torment were unrelenting and clung to me anxiously like a thick cloud. It is hard for me to relate to anyone this level of fear. That is why I mentioned in *23 Minutes in Hell* my being attacked by a shark when I was younger. It was a terrifying experience, and I hoped that people could relate that experience to the degree of fear experienced in hell. But truly hellish fear is completely incomparable.

HOPELESSNESS

When you are in hell, you are separated from God, and that is hopeless indeed. There is absolutely not even one tiny ray of hope for all who enter hell's gates. Isaiah 38:18 states, "Those who go down to the pit cannot hope for Your truth." (See also Ecclesiastes 9:4.) On Earth, we could at least die and escape whatever we were facing, but in hell, you exist forever and can never escape or stop the pain. Your desire is to die, but you are now what is called "the living dead." Daniel I. Block said it this way:

> That which survives of the deceased is not simply the spiritual component of the Human being, but a shadowy image of the whole person, complete with head and skeleton…Israelite burial practices, which suggest that the tomb was not considered the permanent resting place of the deceased. While the physical flesh decomposed, the person was thought to descend to the vast subterranean mausoleum in which the dead continued to live in a remarkably real sense as "living corpses."[21]

There is a verse that says, "For in Him we live and move and have our being" (Acts 17:28). Without Him, only death and horror exist. Job 7:9 says, "He that goeth down to the grave [Sheol] shall come up no more" (KJV).

FEELING WHAT GOD FEELS

Some have asked me to describe in more detail what Jesus looked like and what His voice sounded like. First of all, I cannot tell you what He looked like, as I did not see Him, only an outline of a man. The light that surrounded Him was so very bright that I was unable to see any of His features. The light was like nothing I had ever seen. It was so pure, and a white that I had never encountered. It was bright, but it didn't hurt my eyes. His presence was not even describable. I can see why Paul said that in heaven he saw and heard things that were not lawful for him to utter (2 Cor. 12:4). There are truly no words. The feelings I had were completely overwhelming. I felt infinite power, eternal majesty, absolute authority, inexpressible love, and unsurpassed peace. There was a comfort beyond my ability to even comprehend. His voice was full of strength and yet so very compassionate. It was totally authoritative and also tender. This is actually a futile attempt, and a gross understatement of who He is and how it was to be in His presence. My ability to express the greatness and awesomeness of God is extremely limited. No one could ever pen words adequate enough to express His majesty.

He did allow me to experience two of His attributes: first, His awesome and infinite power. To see all the billions of stars, the expansive universe, and how much He is in control of everything was completely overwhelming. Just think of how many stars and galaxies there are. Psalm 147:4 says, "He telleth the number of the stars; he calleth them all by their names" (KJV). They all have a name! Can you imagine! That alone is inconceivable. I was in awe of His majesty and power.

I looked at our planet, the vast oceans and how they do not even move (Prov. 8:29). If I tried to walk across a room with a bowl filled with water, it would be very difficult not to spill it, yet God has the earth spinning at a thousand miles per hour and the vast oceans not even moving an inch. Everything on the earth is in perfect balance and harmony. I thought about all the people who exist and that He knows how many hairs we each have on our heads (Matt. 10:30). He also knows every thought and intent of man's heart (Heb. 4:12). Not a sparrow falls to the ground that He doesn't know about (Matt. 10:29). I could go on for hours telling of all the things I felt. My point is, we do serve a BIG God, and He is not only in total control of everything, but He is also well able to answer our prayers.

He also allowed me to experience a portion of the amount of love He has for each one of us. We have all heard about His love before, but I can tell you, I never knew just how very much He loves us all. I have mentioned how much I love my wife, more than I could ever express or tell you. If I told you a dozen reasons why I love my wife, you would be convinced that I do indeed love her. If I went on for another five or six hours about how much I love her, you'd think I was a bit fanatical. If every thought I had toward my wife represented a grain of sand, how many grains of sand would I exhaust? Maybe a handful?

God's thoughts for us are more than all the sand granules on the entire earth! How many thoughts would that be if each granule represented a thought? Psalm 139:17–18 says, "How precious also are Your thoughts to me, O God! How great is the sum of them! If I should count them, they are more in number than the sand." This is literal. He loves us that much! It is amazing to feel that kind of love, that much love, generating from Him! It so far surpasses our ability to love that we cannot even grasp or understand it. Ephesians 3:19 says that His love "passes knowledge."

Because of this great love, God feels such sadness when He sees even one person going to hell. We looked back, and I saw the tunnel we just came up out of, and I saw people falling back down that tunnel, one after the other, after the other, after the other. It was so very sad. I couldn't stand feeling the pain of what God feels. He allowed me to feel just a fraction of what He feels, and I had to ask Him to stop. Ezekiel 33:11 says, "I have no pleasure in the death of the wicked." I believe He revealed to me just a small amount of His great power and a small amount (in comparison to the amount He has) of His great love for mankind. Numbers 12:6 says, "I the LORD will make myself known unto him in a vision, and will speak unto him in a dream" (KJV). Not that I am anyone to have been allowed this—I am the least—but He made known to me a small piece of Himself, and the impact it had on me surpasses any words I could declare. Some would say that God is not sad at all for those going to hell. God has absolutely no pleasure in the death of the wicked, as we saw above in Ezekiel 33:11. God, of course, must have His justice fulfilled, just as a righteous judge in our courts must see that the law is upheld and that the criminal is rightly sentenced. Remember, however, that Jesus wept over Jerusalem (Luke 19:41), and His desire is to see all men repent and be rescued from going to hell (Acts 2:21; Rom. 10:13; 1 Tim. 2:4). For as John 3:16 says, "For God so loved the world..."

WHY HE ALLOWED ME TO FEEL PAIN

There is another point I would like to make clear. God allowed me to feel a small amount of the pain one will feel in hell. I only felt a fraction of its torment. Some have said, "God would not allow someone to experience that pain, especially a Christian! So why would He allow that?" I can tell you this much: in order for me to be able to share with others that there is actual pain felt, that it is not simply allegorical or metaphorical, He allowed me to experience some pain. I understood that I was only experiencing a small part of the pain, that it was being blocked or softened by God.

You might still ask, "Why would God allow you to feel any pain at all, when He paid the price?" First of all, I didn't "pay the price" for anyone's salvation by suffering pain. That would be like saying, "Since Jesus suffered on the cross for us, then no Christian should ever bear any pain, at any time, for any reason." In addition, I can answer your question with a question: Why did He allow the apostles to suffer the way they did? They were sawed in half, hung upside down on a cross, stoned, shipwrecked, thrown in dungeons, beaten, chained, and so forth. If God would allow even His best to suffer for the sake of the gospel, then how much more I, who am not to be compared with any of these great men? Besides, even though twenty-three minutes seemed like twenty-three weeks, it was still only twenty-three minutes. What I experienced was minor in comparison to what the great men in the Bible had to go through.

Please understand, though, as I mentioned in *23 Minutes in Hell*, God is not the one who steals and causes pain in our lives. In John 10:10, Jesus told us who was behind it. Jesus said, "The thief does not come except to steal, and to kill, and to destroy. I have come that they may have life, and that they may have it more abundantly." God's desire is not to cause pain to anyone, but to bless and help people. In addition, man exercises free will and makes unwise decisions which result in pain, suffering, loss, and destruction. Besides, I had told the Lord a long time ago that I was willing to do whatever He would want me to do at any time. My life belongs to Him totally and completely.

CHAPTER 15

WHY DOES A CHRISTIAN NEED TO KNOW ABOUT HELL?

S OME OF THE CHRISTIANS WHO HAVE HEARD MY TESTIMONY SAY things like, "I'm not going there, so there is no need to hear about it. It doesn't bring peace or joy. It doesn't focus on God's love, and it doesn't encourage my faith. I do not believe it is a subject that I need to think about for any reason."

There are three reasons I would like to show you as to why we all need to know about it:

1. To have a greater appreciation for our own salvation and from how much we have been spared

2. To help us walk in holiness by fearing the Lord

3. To cause us to have a greater desire to witness

GREATER APPRECIATION FOR SALVATION

Knowing just how severe hell really is will cause us to appreciate our own salvation much more than we do. We will realize just how horrendous a place we were saved from. Edward Donnelly said, "The doctrine of hell should lead us to appreciate more than we do the love and merits of the Lord Jesus Christ...from how much we have been spared....But it is not until we gaze into hell that we really appreciate the love of our Savior."[1] Grant Jeffrey said in his book *Journey Into Eternity*, "William Booth declared that he wished his Christian workers could observe the terrors of hell for a few minutes to properly motivate them to preach salvation to a world of sinners."[2]

When the people who went down with the *Titanic* were rescued from the frozen, icy waters of the North Atlantic, they were rescued with tears. Being grateful of what they were saved from brought tears to their eyes. There were both tears of joy and tears of sadness. That is somewhat of the attitude the Lord would expect from all those He rescues from hell—to be grateful with a godly sorrow. Second Corinthians 7:9–10 says, "Now I rejoice, not that ye were made sorry, but that ye sorrowed to repentance; for ye were made sorry after a godly manner....For godly sorrow worketh repentance to salvation" (KJV).

Billy Graham said, "Repentance also involves a genuine sorrow for sin....Repentance without sorrow is hollow....With repentance comes a change of purpose, a willing turnaround from sin."[3]

When we realize that there is a wrath to come (Rom. 1:18; Eph. 5:6) because of our sins, we should be all the more grateful for what He has done for us. Edward Donnelly said, "Hell brings us to our knees....Hell inspires us with a new adoration for Him who loved us and gave Himself for us."[4]

Randy Alcorn said, "The high stakes involved in the choice between heaven and hell will cause us to appreciate heaven in deeper ways, never taking it for granted, and always praising God for His grace that delivers us from what we deserve and grants us forever what we don't."[5]

INCREASED FEAR OF THE LORD

The second reason for knowing about hell is this: understanding how severe the punishment is in hell should cause us to be more desirous to walk in God's ways. Due to a lack of the fear of the Lord, many in the body of Christ live compromised lifestyles. They feel little conviction of their sin. This is partly because our society today is so very tolerant of sin, and we think that God is the same way. A lack of the fear of the Lord brings with it a slackness in our walk, and we become more susceptible to a life-style of sin. Proverbs 16:6 says, "By the fear of the LORD one departs from evil." John Calvin said, "For as promises are necessary for us, to excite and encourage us to holiness of life, so threatenings are likewise necessary to restrain us by anxiety and fear."[6]

A 2006 Barna poll said that, "Although large majorities of the public claim to be 'deeply spiritual' and say that their religious faith is 'very important' in their life, only 15% of those who regularly attend a Christian church ranked their relationship with God as the top priority in their life."[7] George Barna goes on to say in this poll, "American Christians are not as devoted to their faith as they like to believe. They have positive feelings about the importance of faith, but their faith is rarely the focal point of their life or a critical factor in their decision making."[8]

As Christians, we are called to holiness. Romans 6:22 says, "But now being made free from sin, and become servants to God, ye have your fruit unto holiness, and the end everlasting life" (KJV). (See Ephesians 1:4; 1 Thessalonians 3:13; 4:7; 2 Timothy 1:9; 1 Peter 1:15–16.) In his book *The Fear of Hell*, Solomon Stoddard says, "From hence we may learn that the consideration of the pains of hell is singularly useful for promoting holiness; and it would be greatly beneficial to carnal men if they had more of the fear of hell. It would make them more solemn, more prayerful, more loose from worldly enjoyments, and more cautious how they behaved themselves. And it would be a great benefit to godly men if they had more of the fear of hell; for it would help them against a lukewarm and slumbering spirit."[9]

I don't believe this means we walk around sad and looking religious. God wants us to enjoy life and live in His joy which is our strength! (See Nehemiah 8:10; Proverbs 17:22.) Living holy and enjoying life are not contrary to one another. God even gives us the grace or ability to live holy (1 Thess. 3:13). However, we have a responsibility to receive and cooperate with His grace by faith. Some Christians make excuses for their sloppy, sinful lives by saying, "Oh, I'm under grace. The Lord understands my heart." Grace wasn't given as an excuse to sin, but as an empowerment to live holy.

The Bible says in Hebrews 12:14, "Follow peace with all men, and holiness, without which no man shall see the Lord" (KJV). Jesus said, "If thine eye offend thee, pluck it out: it is better for thee to enter into the kingdom of God with one eye, than having two eyes to be cast into hell fire" (Mark 9:47, KJV). The word *offend* means "to cause one to sin or fall." That is very severe language: dig out your eye rather than sin, because you would be in danger of hell fire. Of course, it is not the actual digging out of the eye; it is comparing the action of taking such severe measures as that to get rid of the thing that is causing us to sin.

In this same regard, Robert Peterson responds to Jesus's warning in his book *Hell on Trial*: "Jesus warns his hearers to restrict themselves, to perform radical spiritual 'surgery,' rather than yield to their sinful desires. The reason? Because the Savior loves sinners and wants them to avoid the terrible reality of hell."[10]

Sinning habitually places one in a dangerous position. If we practice such sin, the Bible says we will not enter heaven (1 Cor. 6:9–10; Eph. 5:5; Rev. 21:8). One of the problems created from a lack of the fear of the Lord is that the truth about hell is not being taught. It is not even discussed in many churches. R. T. Kendall said, "We are to maintain a healthy respect and fear of God's justice and forgiveness: 'But with you there is forgiveness, therefore you are feared' (Ps. 130:4)."[11] Jeremiah 32:40 says, "I will put My fear in their hearts so that they will not depart from Me." In their book *The Way of the Master*, Ray Comfort and Kirk Cameron said, "Scripture makes it very clear what it is that causes me to flee from sin. It is the 'fear of the Lord' (Proverbs 16:6)."[12]

A few years ago there was a lengthy article in the *Los Angeles Times* on the front page of the religious section. It was called "Hold the Fire and Brimstone." I pulled out some of the quotes that give us a sense of the position held by many churches today. Here are some of the highlights:[13]

- "Mention of hell from pulpits is an all-time low. The down-playing of damnation shows the influence of secularism on Christian theology."

- "The violence and torture that Dante described…no longer resonates with churchgoers."

- "Where once hell was viewed as a literal, geographic location, it is more often seen now as a state of the soul."

- "Hell's chief punishment is the separation from God."

J. I. Packer said, "The subject of divine wrath has become taboo in modern society, and Christians by and large have accepted the taboo and conditioned themselves never to raise the matter."[14]

There have been many other articles in newspapers as well, stating more of the same. There was a report on CBN News called "Most Don't Believe in Hell." In the article, president of the Southwestern Baptist Theological Seminary, Paige Patterson said, "You can traverse the entire United States on any given Sunday morning, and you very probably will not hear a sermon on the judgment of God or eternal punishment. Evangelicals have voted by the silence in their voices that they either do not believe in [the doctrine of hell] or else no longer have the courage and conviction to stand and say anything about it." One pastor said, "Preaching a sermon like, 'Sinners in the hands of an angry God' wouldn't work today, when most Americans seemingly have it all."[15]

Another article dated March 27, 2007, in the *Times Online* quoted Pope Benedict XVI as saying, "[Hell] really exists and is eternal, even if nobody talks about it much anymore."[16]

Grant Jeffrey said, "In our generation the preaching and teaching about the reality of hell has virtually disappeared from seminaries, Bible colleges, and from many of the pulpits throughout the land. Today, the average person in the western world feels almost no real threat from the teaching about hell."[17]

Robert W. Yarbrough reports that "a recent official statement of the Evangelical Alliance Commission on Unity and Truth Among Evangelicals (ACUTE) in Great Britain states, 'The interpretation of hell as eternal conscious punishment is the one most widely attested by the Church...'"[18]

The Bible says in Psalm 89:7, "God is greatly to be feared in the assembly of the saints" (KJV). The word *feared* in the Hebrew is *aras* and means to "shake in terror."[19] Hebrews 12:21 quotes Moses as saying, "I exceedingly fear and quake" at the Lord's presence (KJV). Moses was called the "friend of God," yet he shook at God's presence. How much more for you and I?

The attitude and reaction to God in many churches in America does not demonstrate this kind of holy fear. Deuteronomy 10:12 says, "And now, Israel, what doth the LORD thy God require of thee, but to fear the LORD thy God, to walk in his ways, and to love him..." (KJV). In this verse you can see that the fear comes first, and then you are able to walk in His ways and love Him. If you don't hear about hell and the judgment to come, your fear of the Lord can easily slip away.

I do not want anyone to misunderstand in regard to having a godly fear. There is a level of comfort that we can have when we come to Him. He is our Father. As Christians, we are to be able cry out to God, *"Abba,* Father," which means "daddy" (Mark 14:36; Rom. 8:15; Gal. 4:6). Because of this, we can have a feeling of complete comfort and love as you would feel toward a good earthly father. (Sadly, many haven't experienced a loving, good earthly father and so have a warped view of the heavenly Father.) You would come in full assurance of His love for you in peace and trust.

While this seems quite the contrary to a "shake in terror," how does one blend the two? How do the two coincide? I believe it is when we have first established in our hearts a true fear and reverence for God. When we understand His hatred of our sin and that He is a holy God, we begin to grasp why we all should fear Him. God's hatred for our sin is also because of His great love for us. He knows that sin will destroy our lives. When we truly love God, we feel such remorse when we sin because we don't want to hurt or offend Him in any way. We can feel bad enough if we hurt our spouse. How much more, God! David said, "Against thee, thee only, have I sinned" (Ps. 51:4, KJV). His sorrow was because he sinned against the one who loved him the most, and that was his Creator. Once we have this fear and awesome respect for Him, we now can come to Him as our Abba Father.

The Bible says in 1 John 4:8, "God is love." It also says in Hebrews 12:29 that "God is a consuming fire." Hebrews 12:28 says, "We may serve God acceptably with reverence and godly fear." Philippians 2:12 says to "work out your own salvation with fear and trembling." So as you can see, what we need is to have both in our lives.

In his book *The Fear of the Lord*, John Bevere explains it well:

> Apart from His love we cannot even know the Father's heart. Earlier in this very epistle, Peter comments on the love which is to burn in our hearts for the Lord, "whom having not seen you love" (1 Pet. 1:8). We are called to have a personal love relationship with our Father, but Peter is quick to add the balance of the fear of God. Our love for God is limited by a lack of holy fear. Our hearts are to bear the light and warmth of both flames.
>
> You may wonder how this love could be limited. You can only love someone to the extent that you know them.... True love is founded in the truth of who God really is. Do you think He reveals His heart to those who take Him lightly? Would you? In fact, God has chosen to hide Himself (Isa. 45:15). The psalmist refers to His place of hiding as the secret place (Ps. 91:1).
>
> It is here in secret that we discover His holiness and His greatness. But only those who fear Him will find this secret refuge. For we are told: "The secret of the Lord is with those who fear Him, and He will show them His covenant" (Ps. 25:14)....
>
> Those who have been born again know God as Abba Father. But that does not negate His position as Judge of all flesh, (Gal. 4:6–7; Heb. 12:23). God makes it clear: "The Lord will judge His people" (Heb. 10:30).[20]

I believe Bevere summed it up for us to see both sides.

INSPIRED TO WITNESS

The third reason to know about hell is that it will help inspire us to witness. Some have cooled from the excitement they had when first saved to share so readily and enthusiastically with others the good news. But we must not let that die, because it is what we are commanded to do (Mark 16:15).

In 2 Corinthians 5:10–11, Paul speaks of the judgment seat. Even though this is the reward seat for Christians, most commentaries state Paul was also incorporating references to the judgment in general and about hell. He said, "Knowing, therefore, the terror of the Lord, we persuade men" (v. 11). When we understand judgment and hell, we will have a greater desire to convince man of a wrath to come and how to escape it. We will be more persuasive and place more effort toward that goal. Here is what some of the commentaries have to say about that verse:

According to the *Believer's Bible Commentary*, "This verse is commonly taken to mean that since Paul was aware of God's terrible judgment on sin, and the horrors of hell, he went everywhere seeking to persuade men to accept the gospel."[21]

The *New Testament Survey* by Robert Gromacki says, "They needed to know about the severity of hell in order to preach out of a sense of urgency....The terror of the Lord, not of men, motivated Paul to preach with a proper heart, not in mere outward appearance."[22]

"The coming judgment," *Jamieson, Fausset, and Brown's Commentary on the Whole Bible* says, "[is] so full of terrors to unbelievers....Ministers should use the terror of the Lord to persuade men."[23]

In the *Parallel Commentary*, Matthew Henry says, "Let all consider the Judgment to come, which is called, The Terror of the Lord. Knowing what terrible vengeance the Lord would execute upon the workers of iniquity, the apostle and his brethren used every argument and persuasion to lead men to believe in the Lord Jesus, to act as His disciples."[24]

Most Christians really don't bother to witness. Bill Bright has been quoted as saying that only 2 percent of Christians witness.[25]

Some don't because they feel they don't know enough about the Bible. Others don't because they feel it is just not their gift. Their other services in the church cause them to feel less of an obligation to witness. And still others are just plain fearful to talk to people.

Some churches emphasize worship and do not encourage the people to open their mouths and share with the unbeliever. They feel that worship is the only thing of importance, so witnessing is something not really mentioned. We all should definitely *worship God as our first priority* every day, as it is so very important and foremost, but we cannot leave the other undone. True worship is also obedience to God's Word (Matt. 4:10).

Ray Comfort gives a great analogy in *The Way of the Master*:

> There was once a respectable captain of a ship whose crew spoke highly of him. They esteemed him to a point where everyone knew of the crew's professed love for him. One day, however, the captain saw, to his horror, that an ocean liner had struck an iceberg and people were drowning in the freezing water ahead of his ship. He quickly directed his vessel to the area, stood on the bridge, and made an impassioned plea to his crew to throw out the life preservers. But instead of obeying his charge, the crew lifted their hands and said, "Praise the captain...praise you...we love you! You are worthy of our praise." Can you see that their adoration *should have been displayed by their obedience to his command*? Their "admiration" was nothing but empty words.[26]

Ray went on to say:

> Evangelist Bill Fay has spoken at more than fifteen hundred conferences and churches. At each meeting, he asks how many have shared their faith in the previous year. Never once has he found a church where more than ten percent raised their hands.[27]

That is a sad commendation for the church. Jesus told us all to go into all the world and preach the gospel (Mark 16:15). We all can do it. All we need is to learn a few verses and go share those verses along with our own testimony. Robert Murray M'Cheyne said, "As I was walking in the fields, the thought came over me with almost overwhelming power, that every one of my flock must soon be in heaven or hell. Oh, how I wished that I had a tongue like thunder, that I might make all hear; or that I had a frame like iron, that I might visit everyone, and say, 'Escape for thy life!'"[28]

In *Hell Under Fire*, Sinclair Ferguson says, "Behind everyone we know and meet stands the shadow of judgment. They themselves do not see it; we know they may have spent all their lives denying it or hiding from it. But one day the account will be presented, the verdict will be past, the judgment given. Knowing this, how can we remain silent?"[29]

"If you ever get to the point," Norvel Hayes says in his book *Rescuing Souls From Hell*, "where you don't care about winning souls, where you don't want to testify for Jesus or help those who are beaten down, then you had better get down on your knees right then and pray—one hour, two hours, three hours, however long it takes—until that compassion comes back to you. If you don't, I'm warning you, you'll end up living in a world of spiritual darkness."[30] This is so true. Unfortunately many Christians do not have a passion to warn people of hell's fire.

I believe Ray Comfort's ministry has some of the best teaching and training materials on evangelism to equip the saints. All of us can listen to teaching CDs, read our Bibles, and prepare ourselves. The Bible says in 2 Timothy 2:15, "Study to shew thyself approved unto God" (KJV). Jesus said to me, "Many make excuses why they don't witness. They say, 'I didn't feel led.'" It's true we are all to be led by the Spirit of God, and not to be rude, forceful, or condemning, but always respectful. However, many times we fear man instead of fearing God and don't open our mouths.

> Many Christians will not witness unless they sense the Spirit of God prompting them to speak to a particular person. I'm not that spiritual. I share my faith whenever and wherever possible. As far as I'm concerned, the starting gun went off 2,000 years ago with a loud, "Go into all the world and preach the Gospel to every creature" (Mark 16:15). My conscience continually prompts me to speak.[31]
>
> —Ray Comfort

I think Ray Comfort has the right attitude. My wife and I had an experience in September of 2007 that put to action this very attitude that he expressed above. We were asked to speak at a church in South Africa. We knew the pastors very well, so we boarded a plane and were off to South

Africa. It was a long way to go, but it was the most rewarding experience in traveling that we have ever had. The church was beyond excellent. The people were very dedicated to their commitment to witness and serve the Lord. All the leadership had fasted, prayed, and handed out flyers prior to our coming. The members of the congregation also were fasting and praying for souls, and most of them had brought someone they knew who didn't know the Lord to the meeting. They had passed out over fifty thousand flyers and were all so excited about what God was going to do. The level of expectancy was through the roof. Their hearts were committed, and they believed God would save their loved ones and co-workers. Well, their work paid off, as there were approximately twelve hundred people who came forward to accept Jesus as their Lord and Savior. My point is that it was a team effort that caused this great move of God. May we all have that kind of enthusiasm and commitment to serve Him.

If any of us have a fear of talking to others about the things of God, all we need do is to pray and ask God to help us overcome it, and He will. Some don't realize this, but He holds us accountable to open our mouths and testify for Jesus. Ezekiel 33:8 states, "If thou dost not speak to warn the wicked from his way, that wicked man shall die in his iniquity; but his blood will I require at thine hand" (KJV). (See also Acts 18:6; 20:26.) That sounds like we will share in some of the guilt of the lost souls we could have spoken to. That's why Paul said, "Woe is me if I do not preach the gospel" (1 Cor. 9:16).

In speaking about hell, Charles Spurgeon said, "If we hold back from declaring 'all the council of God' (Acts 20:27) at least part of the responsibility of their ruin will lie at our door."[32] Edward Donnelly said, "If we fail to tell our friends about Christ we will be held partly accountable for their damnation, but the final responsibility rests with the individual concerned."[33] In *Run With the Vision*, Dr. Lester Sumrall said, "'Oh, God,...do you mean I can be responsible for Africa's going to hell even though I have never been to Africa?'...God left no doubt in my mind. I was impressed that every Christian is responsible for taking the message of God's grace and salvation to those who have never heard."[34]

I don't know about you, but I don't want to stand before God and have

Him say to me, "Why didn't you speak to this one or that one about Me?" I want to please Him. It's time we all stop making excuses and be a doer of the Word. Colossians 1:27–28 says, "Christ in you, the hope of glory: Him we preach, *warning* every man."

Charles Spurgeon said, "Soul winning is the chief business of the Christian. It should be the main pursuit of every true believer."[35]

Edward Donnelly said, "The doctrine of hell should motivate us to speak out."[36] Jesus called His disciples to teach them how to "catch" men and women (Matt. 4:17–20). Norvel Hayes again said, "The greatest thing that can happen for you and for others is for you to open your mouth and share the Gospel of Jesus Christ."[37]

JESUS IS OUR EXAMPLE

Some have said that this message is not loving enough, that Jesus would not talk of hell and punishment, but only of love and forgiveness. Jesus did speak of love, but He spoke more of hell and judgment than anyone else in the Bible. Robert Jeffress said, "Thirteen percent of the 1850 verses in the New Testament that record the words of Jesus deal with the subject of eternal judgment and hell. In fact, Jesus had more to say about hell than He did about heaven."[38] There are forty-six separate verses that Jesus Himself spoke about hell and destruction. (See Appendix A.) He warned us over and over of the consequences of sin.

John Wesley said, "Before I can preach love, mercy, and grace, I must preach sin, Law, and Judgment."[39] Ray Comfort said, "Only when he [the sinner] sees his depravity before his holy Creator and the severity of God's judgment will the cross make sense! Only then will he cry out in despair, 'Woe is me, I'm undone! Or smite his breast with "God be merciful to me, a sinner!' The more he sees his guilt, the better."[40]

James 4:6 says, "God resists the proud, but gives grace to the humble." Jesus would give the Law to the proud. Since there are many who are prideful and arrogant, and who think they are "good enough" for heaven's citizenship, this type of person usually cannot be won through telling them of God's great love. Using the Law is necessary to show them their sin and how far we all fall short from His standard. Romans 3:19 says, "…that every mouth may be stopped, and all the world may become guilty before God." Jesus used the Law when He could see that they were trying to justify themselves. Ray Comfort states, "He [Jesus] always preached Law to the proud and arrogant, and grace to the meek and the humble (see Luke 10:25–26; 18:18–20; John 3:1–17). Never once did the Son of God give the good news (the message of the cross, grace, and mercy) to the proud, the arrogant, or the self-righteous."[41] The reason for this is, as Ray continues, "With the Law, we should break hardened hearts, and with the gospel, we should heal broken hearts."[42] A. W. Pink said, "The unsaved are in no condition today for the gospel till the Law be applied to their hearts, for 'by the Law is the knowledge of sin.' It is a waste of time to sow seed on ground which has never been ploughed or spaded! To present the vicarious sacrifice of Christ to those whose dominant passion is to take fill of sin is to give that which is holy to the dogs."[43]

Charles Spurgeon said:

> One other reason why this soil was so uncongenial was that it was totally unprepared for the seed. There has been no plowing before the seed was sown, and no harrowing afterwards. He that sows without a plow may reap without a sickle. He who preaches the gospel without preaching the Law may hold all the results of it in his hand, and there will be little for him to hold. Robbie Flockhart, when he preached in the streets of Edinburgh, used to say, "You must preach the Law, for the gospel is a silken thread, and you cannot get it into the hearts of men unless you have made a way for it with a sharp needle; the sharp needle of the Law will pull the silken thread of the gospel after it."[44]

Romans 7:7 says, "I would not have known sin except through the Law." In the book *What the Bible Is All About*, Henrietta C. Mears states:

> As long as a person is not a murderer or thief, he would swear that he is righteous. How does God show such a man what he

really is? By the hammer of the law. As long as a person thinks he is right, he is proud and despises God's grace. This monster of self-righteousness needs a big axe, and the law is just that. When anyone sees by the law that he is under God's wrath, he begins to rebel and complain against God. The law inspires hatred of God. What does this beating by the hand of the law accomplish? It helps us to find the way of grace. When the conscience has been thoroughly frightened by the law, it welcomes the gospel.[45]

People need to see their need for a Savior. They must be shown first the Law; then grace can be given.

In saying that, we must also have our preaching delivered in an attitude of concern, love, and care for the individual. If that person sees that we genuinely care for him, he will receive what we are saying, even though it is strong and direct. Charles Spurgeon said, "I hate to hear the terror of the Lord proclaimed by men whose hard countenances, harsh tones, and unfeeling spirits betray a sort of doctrinal dehydration: all the milk of human kindness is dried out of them....If we are to be used by God as soul winners, we must have in our hearts a great deal of tenderness."[46] If that individual to whom you are speaking senses or sees that your uncompromised message of salvation is delivered with a sincere concern for their souls, it will be received much more readily.

LIVING WITNESS

Our most important way of witnessing to others is by living out the faith we have in our everyday lives. Without saying a word, our actions speak volumes. As a matter of fact, most of our lives should be a continual witness by the way we live, by the friends we keep, and by what we participate in and do not participate in. We should always strive for being the best worker in our workplace. Our work should be done with excellence, and we should make every effort to keep our word. Criticizing another is one of the worst things we can do. To preach to someone and then be a poor example does much more damage than good.

When we understand the severity of hell, we will want to go and warn others. I am not talking about condemning people or pounding them with scripture. We can simply share with them about God's goodness and also explain to them that there are eternal consequences if we die in our sin. It is not a message of condemnation but rather a message of warning. If you love others, you will warn them. The severity of hell is a very strong motivator.

I would like to share some comments from some of the great men of the past and present who have stated what I am attempting to express:

> The doctrine of judgment to come is the power by which men are to be aroused. There is another life; the Lord will come a second time; judgment will arrive; the wrath of God will be revealed....It is absolutely necessary to the preaching of the gospel of Christ that men be warned as to what will happen if they continue in their sins.[47]
>
> —Charles Spurgeon

> I have come to realize the need for greater discussion of hell. To be silent on the eternal destination of souls is to be like a sentry failing to warn his fellow soldiers of impending attack.[48]
>
> —Bill Bright

> We shouldn't be afraid to make sinners tremble; which is worse: a little trembling because of guilt, or eternity in the lake of fire.[49]
>
> —Ray Comfort and Kirk Cameron

> One of the most obvious results of a consideration of hell should be a renewed zeal for evangelism.[50]
>
> —Edward Donnelly

> The fear of hell is the only thing most likely to get worldly people thinking about the Kingdom of God.[51]
>
> —John Gerstner

To omit hell from a discussion with a non-Christian is to miss the greatest incentive a person has for becoming a Christian.[52]

—Robert Jeffress

As you can see, understanding the severity of God's judgment on sin should motivate Christians to do what the Lord has given us orders to do (Mark 16:15). As we pointed out earlier, many churches are not preaching about hell, and others have downplayed it to the point where many think it will not be all that bad. Some have rated being in hell the same as staying at a two-star hotel, even air-conditioned.

Hell is far worse than your mind can ever conceive. It is important for Christians to know this. Time is short, and what we do here counts for our eternity. Hopefully, we all will have a better overall eternal perspective on life and our assignment from our Lord. Lester Sumrall writes "that the Lord said to him, 'If you plow like the Israelite farmer, with a tractor piercing deeply into the soil and many furrows wide, you can bring a million souls to heaven!' God showed me that plowing deep is my personal relationship with Him. Plowing wide is my working with others of the same spirit. I must recruit others to help me in the harvest."[53] I think he summed it up nicely for us. We as Christians are all ambassadors for Christ, so let us represent Him in the best possible way. May we all be "about my Father's business."

CHAPTER 16

"ARE YOU IN, OR ARE YOU OUT?"—A TRUE STORY

ONE NIGHT MY WIFE AND I WERE IN TEXAS HAVING DINNER WITH a dear pastor and his wife when we received a message from my brother-in-law, Greg. His tone was extremely anxious for us to return his call.

I called him immediately, and he proceeded to explain to me that a very close friend and business associate of his, Bill, was dying of pancreatic cancer and would not live through the night. The doctor said he would die in a matter of hours. Bill and his wife, Ruthie, had known for months that he had little time to live. In fact, in a conversation with Greg about a month earlier, Bill commented that he had been faced with a lot of difficult tasks and dilemmas in his life, but that he was not going to be able to come up with a solution to get out of this one. His words were "I'm not getting out of this one, Greg." Bill was normally a controlling person and always prepared. But on this night, he was very anxious. However, Bill had something very special going for him that few people were fully aware of at the time. Bill's wife Ruthie is a strong believer in Christ and she had been praying for Bill's soul on a daily basis.

Greg told me that they had been friends for many years, and that they had done many business transactions together. Bill had made a lot of money in his life for himself and for his partners, raised a great family, contributed substantial sums to charity, and to the best of Greg's knowledge honored every financial and friendship commitment he had ever made. Bill did not publicize it but he had an invalid sister whom he fully supported financially and medically until the day she died. Greg had been Bill's accountant and friend for over twenty-five years and had personally witnessed Bill's integrity in all of his business, friendships, and family dealings.

On occasion, Greg would try to share with Bill something about God, but he would never have any of that. Bill said that God was fine for Greg, but not for him. Now that he was about to die, Greg asked him once more if he would talk to his brother-in-law, which is me, about eternal things, and at least hear what I had to say. At this point, he was so weak that he could barely talk, but he could utter out a yes-or-no answer. He responded yes that he would listen. Greg was surprised and thrilled, to say the least! So Greg called me, told me the story, and asked if I would call right away, as Bill didn't have much time.

I picked up the phone and called him in California, and Bill's wife, Ruthie joined the call. At first, we talked a bit about our mutual love for Janice and Greg, as they are two of the finest people we each know. I then got right to the point. I acknowledged that I understood he had acquired a great deal of knowledge in business and other areas, but that I wanted to share something with him that perhaps he had not had the opportunity, or maybe interest, to learn. "We all learn different things on our journey through life that we can share with each other, if we are willing to listen," I said. I then proceeded to share with them God's overall plan and the bottom line on what it takes to gain entrance into heaven. I explained that it was not based on whether he and his wife were "good" or "bad," that it was based on an entirely different premise. It had to do with what God did for us, not what we can do for Him. I told them that without forgiveness of their sins and acceptance of Jesus as their Savior, they would never see heaven but only torment and hell. I explained that Jesus gave His life for ours so that we wouldn't have to remain dead spiritually. I explained that to be dead spiritually didn't mean "to cease to exist." What it does mean is to be separated from God. And to be separated from God means to be separated from all good, as everything we experience that is good comes from God. I went on to say that all that is necessary for each of us to do is repent and ask Jesus to come into our life to be our Lord and Savior. To repent takes humility, to be able to admit we are not good enough, and we need a Savior. Most do not possess the humility to admit that truth. He listened and gave an occasional yes, as he was following along with his wife. They shared with me that they loved each other very much and couldn't imagine being apart. I told them that there was only one way that they would be able to see each other after he died, and that would be if he accepted the Lord as his Savior. After answering some questions, I asked Bill if he wanted to accept Jesus as his Lord and Savior. He said, "Yes, positively yes." Bill mumbled that he was also scared of dying. I told him that once you ask forgiveness and accept Jesus, you will no longer need to fear death.

I asked Bill to repeat this prayer in his heart after me. I said to him, "Say this after me: God in heaven, I know that I am a sinner and I cannot save myself. It is not by my good works, but by Your Son's shed blood on the cross that I can be saved. I believe You sent Your only Son, Jesus, to be crucified on a cross and that He died and rose again from the grave and lives forevermore. I ask You to forgive me of my sins. I repent. I'm sorry for my sins. I ask You to come into my heart. I accept You now as my Lord and Savior. Thank You for forgiving me and saving me. In Jesus's name I pray, amen." Well, they were so very happy. He immediately started saying, "I love You, Jesus. Thank You for saving me. I love You, Jesus. I love You, Jesus." He kept saying it over and over, where earlier, he could not even mumble more than one word. He was so excited. We hung up, and then they called Greg and his wife, Janice, right away. They told them how happy they were that they were both going to heaven. When Greg and Bill would do a business deal together, they would always say to each other, "Are you in, or are you out? If you're in, it's 100 percent, not 50 or 60 percent. You're in all the way, or nothing." So after Bill prayed with me, Greg said to him, "Bill, this covenant, this prayer, this request for forgiveness deal is 100 percent, so you understand that right? So either you are in all the way, or you are out all the way." Bill replied, "I'm in 100 percent."

With what was probably one of Bill and Greg's last conversations, they concluded that the main beauty and satisfaction of their twenty-five-year personal and business association was obviously not merely about the money, but rather the preparation for the phone call that set the stage for

Jesus to secure Bill's place in heaven for eternity. God is so good that He arranged all of that for this man's salvation. He cares for each one of us in that same manner. This man never cared for the things of God; yet God, in His mercy, saved him in his last moments.

As you can see, God is always ready to extend mercy to anyone who asks. I would like to ask you, the reader, a question: Would you step up to the plate for your friend, as Greg did for Bill, and tell them the truth? Or would you be afraid you might offend them and their beliefs? Thankfully, Greg was able to see the big picture. By the way, Bill ended up living another three weeks, as his wife said he suddenly had this renewed energy and zeal for life! They had three more wonderful weeks together and then looked forward to seeing each other in heaven. They will be together for eternity now.

Three weeks later, my wife and I were in North Carolina when we received a call from Greg. We were driving on the freeway, heading for the airport. Greg told us that Bill died three days before, and he was on the way to his funeral. He wanted to know what would be a good scripture to share, as he was asked to speak about Bill. We quickly thought of a verse and told Greg. He thanked us and shared how good it was that Bill and his wife had another three weeks together and had that time to reflect on things. At the same time, he was extremely sad to lose his friend. Greg and Janice went to the funeral. Greg was so choked up he couldn't stand up to say anything, but he really wanted to share that verse we had given him. He just couldn't. Then the pastor got up to take over and the first thing out of his mouth was that exact verse of scripture! Greg was shocked. Greg knew God did that.

Now let me ask you one more question: If you are someone out there like Bill, who doesn't know the Lord Jesus—and, of course, you know that you are going to die one day—are you in, or are you out? It is your choice. Deuteronomy 30:19 says, "I set before you life and death, blessing and cursing, therefore choose life." It is up to you!

CHAPTER 17

TRUE STORIES AND TESTIMONIES

MY WIFE AND I HAVE BEEN SO BLESSED TO SEE MANY WHO HAVE accepted Jesus as a result of *23 Minutes in Hell*. We believe that many more will be drawn in by the grace of God. Here are some true stories that we have experienced ourselves or heard from others. Later in the chapter we share testimonies that people have shared with us about how God impacted them through my testimony.

One day, a man, while sitting in rush hour traffic, felt impressed to get out of his car, tap on the window of the car ahead of him, and give the driver one of the CDs with me sharing my testimony on hell. The man's first thought was, "No way, I'm not going to do that. The driver may think I'm some kind of crazed person knocking on his window."

However, the man kept sensing he should do this, so he finally got out of his car. He knocked on the window and handed the man a CD. The driver said he was just praying that he would be able to get a CD to give to his family and have them listen. He shared that he had read our first book, *23 Minutes in Hell*, and really wanted a CD but didn't know where to get one. What are the odds of that happening?

Another time, we received an e-mail that there was a husband and wife and son who had not seen each other for fifteen years. The parents were divorced, and they wouldn't speak to one another. None of them were Christians. One day, the son had come across my book and received the

Lord after reading it. He then wanted to find his parents and share it with them. When he found each one separately, both parents had just read the book and had accepted the Lord into their lives! All three read the book at just about the same time, separate of each other knowing.

Another time, the same thing happened to a husband and wife, who had been separated, and each read the book and were saved. They then got back together.

There was a woman who wrote us and said that she would carpool to work every day. One day she had my book in her car. One of the ladies asked what it was about. She read the beginning of the book aloud, and then everyone wanted her to read more. Each day that they met to carpool, the ladies would ask her to continue reading. They couldn't wait to carpool to read the book! One woman accepted the Lord.

Another special occurrence happened when my parents were taking a trip to Maryland from Florida. On the way, their car broke down. They needed to be towed in. Well, the tow truck came and took them to the nearest auto repair. It turned out that the auto repair place couldn't fix the car. There were other garages in the area, but they felt led to go back approximately sixty miles to where a dealer was located. It was far out of the way, but the man towed them back.

When they arrived, the service writer was so very nice and helpful. In the course of the conversation, my parents shared my book with him. He said that his wife had read the book and really wanted to meet me. She had also given out many books. His wife mentioned that she would love it if we ever came to their church. They both had recently started a church and had a couple hundred people already coming. Many young people were already being drawn there, and his wife thought it would affect them so much for us to come and share the reality and severity of hell. They believed it would encourage them to be more effective witnesses.

Well, we ended up going, and we really took to them and all the youth. God moved on hearts and ignited those youths for Him. Many were saved, and we know it was a divine connection. We will see them again, as a friendship has developed.

The book has found its way into many of the prisons around the country, and many prisoners have written to us sharing how the book has changed their lives. Many have received the Lord, ceased from sinning, and desired a fresh start with God. The fact that the book is in so many prisons is amazing in itself. Many prisoners identify with the prison cells in hell. They indicate that now they don't feel as bad spending their sentence in a cell, when they would have had to spend an eternity behind bars in hell. They thanked me over and over for the book. One prisoner wrote to the prison chaplain after reading my book and said on his request form, "Urgent! I must talk with you immediately about salvation."

MEETING IN DAYTONA

In 2008, I was asked to speak at a church in Daytona Beach, Florida. After the service, a lady approached my wife and me. She explained that she had brought her son, an atheist, to the service. He listened to my experience but he still didn't believe in God, heaven, or hell. I was in the back of the church at this time talking with the people, so I asked her if she could bring him back to meet me.

He came back to meet me, and I shook his hand. When I saw him, I felt impressed by the Lord to really take a few minutes and be especially attentive to him. I looked him in the eye and sincerely thanked him for taking the time to come and listen. (It was miracle that he actually came to listen!) I told him that I respected the fact that he stayed right through to the end and did not leave early. I said to him, "I know you don't know me, and who am I that you should listen to me, but all of us learn something in life that the other doesn't know. I said, "Even Mark Twain said, 'We're all ignorant. It's just about different things.'" I asked him to please consider and at least investigate what the Bible has to say regarding our eternity. I continued, "The decision you make is a permanent one. Please don't dismiss this lightly." He said, "OK," and looked me in the eye intently. Then he and his mother left.

The next day he was crossing the road and in the middle of the street his legs froze. He couldn't move. He collapsed on the ground and started having heart palpitations. He was scared. He looked up and saw a cross planted along the side of the road. Perhaps it was a memorial for someone who had died near that location. But what are the chances that a cross would be there? He said that conviction came all over him, and all he could think of was that man, Bill Wiese, and how sincere I was as he looked me in the eyes. He said to himself, "I believe what he told me was true." He called out to the Lord to save him! Someone found him on the ground and took him to a hospital. The medical personnel couldn't find anything wrong with his heart or legs. By this time, he felt fine and went home.

He came back to that same church the next morning, which happened to be Easter Sunday. This young man shared that he was radically saved and will be coming to church from now on. This happened because his mother prayed for her son all the time. If you have a praying mother or grandmother and you don't know the Lord, just give up—God will win.

GOD'S TIMING

My wife and I traveled to a meeting in a very small town out in the middle of nowhere. We had been invited to a wonderful church and corresponded with the church secretary for over two years. Thankfully, she sent us a few reminders by e-mail that they still wanted us to visit. We kept the e-mails, prayed about when to go, and then put something on the calendar. We flew into the state and then drove and drove, praying we would find the church. We were two city kids driving for miles along these back country roads late at night navigating via the Holy Spirit! Later we found out that the computerized map didn't give us the most direct route. However we got checked in, slept, and then got ready for the service.

After the service, an elderly man came up to me and said, "I was given your book about a year ago, and I looked at it and threw it in the trash." This man continued to share with me that he had walked away from the Lord completely and didn't want anything to do with Him. He said, "One year later, last week, I was at a restaurant twenty miles from here, and I overheard the conversation at the next table. They mentioned Bill Wiese was speaking just twenty miles away at a church next weekend." He said that he thought to himself, "This couldn't just be a coincidence. What is the chance of Bill Wiese coming way out here to this small town and me overhearing this conversation? This is too obvious! I should go." With a big smile on his face, he said, "So here I am, and I have now come back to the Lord. I've given my life back to Him. Thank you for coming. I would have gone to hell if you didn't come. Thank you!" (Believe me, all the credit goes to the Lord. He's the one who did it all!)

After the service at this same church, a father came up to us and explained that his son did not believe in God. He said that he never would give his heart to the Lord, no matter who the speaker was at the service. The father shared, "He refused to accept Jesus, until today. My son is now saved! Thank you for coming." He thanked us over and over as his son was now a Christian. His son came forward without anyone nudging him. My wife and I saw this father, with tears in his eyes; join his son at the altar a few minutes following. He was so grateful to the Lord.

Another young man reached for my hand to thank me for coming. He looked so serious and sincere as he said, "You have no idea what I was going to do before you came. You have no idea. Thank you so much for coming." He wouldn't let go of my hand. He was so touched and so thankful. I felt that he was planning to commit suicide.

SMALL-TOWN PASTOR WITH A BIG HEART

We traveled to a very small town approximately an hour and a half from Tulsa, Oklahoma. The pastor, Phil, picked us up at the airport and took us to our hotel. By the time we reached the hotel, we were all beginning to think this really was a divine connection. Pastor Phil shared with us a vision the Lord had given him many years earlier. It was about getting the body of Christ to unite and really work together. He shared that there are so many separate denominations working independently and by working together we could get so much more done. God gave him a plan that he recently published in a book to share it with those pastors and ministers who are interested.[1]

Pastor Phil had been building relationships with several other pastors in his town for the past fifteen years. These four other pastors were from different denominations, and they all came together to have me speak at their local high school gymnasium. This was an outreach to the community, an evangelistic effort for souls, and surely everyone could agree on that. So my wife and I came, and the service was exceptional.

However, before the meeting ever took place, this is what Pastor Phil and the four operating pastors did: they purchased 1,040 copies of *23 Minutes in Hell* from the publisher and sent one to everyone in their city. The entire population is 1,300. They didn't want anyone in their city to go to hell because they didn't hear the truth from them.

At the meeting, over seven hundred people showed up. That is more than half the town! The pastors were all united, and the unity was so amazing. Souls were saved, and church leaders and members worked together to make it happen. This was a firstfruit of Pastor Phil's vision to unite Christian churches. After that meeting, all the pastors said that they wished they could all meet on a regular basis with their congregations, as unity brings such strength.

Testimonies

... because your book is so well written and compelling, it may be the most timely, relevant book I've read, besides the Bible. Could not help but believe that the Holy Spirit was assisting you in getting down every word I've read, and I'm just on page 105!

Your humility, excellent research, persuasiveness, and comprehensive command of Scriptures denoted in your book make it a massively important book. Thank you for this special gift!

—G.W.

Thank you for sharing your life-changing testimony. I recently bought a copy of *23 Minutes in Hell* and it has really caused the fire of evangelism to burn deeper in my heart.

—A.H.

As a born-again Christian for the last twenty-seven years, I was moved far beyond tears after reading about your ordeal. Your testimony has changed me in ways I cannot explain or understand. Thank you for writing the book, but I praise Jesus Christ for using you to tell the message....I just wanted to tell you what the book did for me, and I'm sure it will inspire me to speak with others lovingly about heaven and the importance of accepting Jesus as Savior.

—M.L.

I just read your book last night. It only took me four hours straight. I couldn't put it down. I am twenty-seven years old and your typical youth Christian. This book gave me the shock that I needed and an amazing insight to questions that I have always had for the Lord.

Honestly, when logging on-line anymore, sexual sin has almost no power over me anymore thanks to your experience. I can effectively eliminate any temptation of porn or similar temptations. Now I just need work on driving at rush hour home!

In summary, THANK YOU! You helped me tremendously. I have decided I am simply done with "my way."

—B.S.

I am currently reading the book *23 Minutes in Hell* by Bill Wiese, and this book has made me realize the importance of accepting Jesus Christ as my Savior and Lord over every aspect of my life. Also, this book has given me a desire to preach to others of the importance and the opportunity to receive Jesus as Lord.

—Charles

I read your book and I have to share with you what is going on. It touched me and made me realize what I should be doing as a Christian, and that hell is a place I don't even want to think about going to. Your book really opened my eyes again, and I know what I have to do now. I haven't been going to my youth group for a while now, but I think it is time I go back.

I thank you so much for this book. It's already changed my life and I'm so grateful for that. Thank you for opening my eyes, I was blind and had fallen off the path but now I can see!

—M.B.

I wanted to start out by saying thank you for sharing your experience with me. I haven't really been making Jesus number one in my life the past five or six years, but thanks to your testimony, He is today! My eyes were opened when I heard you preaching about hell. I have realized that I have been selfish and not taking my Christian walk seriously. I know that we are all here for a purpose now, and that is to make sure that nobody misses out on the great opportunity of meeting our Lord Jesus Christ. I have shared your story with my family and people I don't even know.

I just want to thank you, again, for helping me to renew my walk with Jesus. God has given me a boldness to tell others what I know, and now I think I have found my purpose on this earth. Thanks again!

—A.R.

Just wanted to say thanks for your book. It really woke me up! I have asked Jesus into my life!

—J.I.

I gave your book to my husband on Father's Day. We both read *23 Minutes in Hell*, and it has been the hottest topic in our family. It has changed the way I look at life and I have such compassion to tell everyone about Jesus Christ. My unsaved mother-in-law is interested in the topic and she has begun to ask questions. One of our sons is reading it for a book report. Your story has given me such joy and ideas to minister to others. I thank God for your journey and your story. THANK YOU!

—C.P.

I'm twenty-one years old. I just wanted to let you know that I read your book *23 Minutes in Hell* and I was so fascinated by the story. At first, when I picked up the book I did not know what to expect. I thought it would be interesting to read about someone being in hell, but I never knew that it would change my aspects about God. I never thought that I would believe in God so deeply and I never knew that I had sinned so much, thinking that small things didn't count. Your book made me realize that small things do count and it started to make sense to me. I just want to remind you that all this is coming from a person that has never picked up a Bible. I went to church but never really listened. I was forced to go to church by my parents. Your book helped change all of that in just two days. I feel like a new person.

I just wanted to say thank you. Thank you for opening my eyes to reality. I believed every word you said about hell and how there is a God that wants the best for us. And I believe it is up to us to follow Him or turn our backs. I prayed to God to forgive me for all my sins. I felt something so powerful inside of me when I said those prayers that even words cannot describe how I felt. So now I'm here and I wanted to share with you how much the big impact your book has caused in me.

Your book has changed my life and I wanted to help other people save their lives too, so I told many of my friends about your book. One of them bought the book and some of them are taking turns reading it. I am hoping that they too feel the same way after they read it, and I hope to be a good help to save them from the "pit."

—W.F.

I am an ex-satanist, occultist, Wiccan, you name it and I've done it. Your book and video helped me turn back and asked to be saved by the REAL JESUS CHRIST!

—B.W.

I'm a twenty-three-year-old college student. You've saved my life, and I just want to thank you. [She heard and read my account of hell.] I cried. I cried through almost the whole thing. I felt so bad at all of the sins I had committed and the blasphemies. I was so ashamed and so sorry. I apologized to the Lord for the rest of the night and asked for forgiveness. I immediately believed your story. I just knew it was truth beyond a shadow of a doubt. I know God exists and that Jesus Christ is my Savior.

I called my mom the next day and she was so overjoyed for me, that I've fully accepted the Lord. It may not have happened if it weren't for your incredible journey. I thank God every day for blessing me with the opportunity to change, for opening my eyes to the only truth. I hope your book and words continue to reach and heal people. I don't want anyone to go to hell.

—S.M.

Just got through reading Bill Wiese's book *23 Minutes in Hell*. Excellent testimony! I'm a Seventh-Day Adventist believer. I've been brought up believing there is no hell, only "soul sleep." Family and friends are either Jehovah's Witness or Seventh-Day Adventist. But after reading the book, I'm convinced there is a hell. The Holy Spirit used the book to open my eyes to the truth! Thank you so much. I am ever grateful for coming across this book.

—M.U.

We were shown a video of a talk Bill Wiese gave about his experiences in hell. (I had previously read the book.) I brought a friend with me, and because of your testimony my friend that I had prayed for and witnessed to for twenty years finally got saved. I am so grateful. Thank you so much!

—Sherleen

About a year ago I began to backslide into idolatry toward a singer. I actually said, "He is my idol." I did not know how far I had gotten. I've also been asking the Lord to give me, the fear of God....A Christian friend lent your book to me.

My ignorance of the holiness of God became surreal. I had to wonder, if God chose me from the beginning and saved me by His Son's blood, then He knew I would backslide. But if I had died without repenting of my idolatry, amongst many sins, like lying, what would have happened to my eternal soul?

Today I am seeking God and I've repented. Again, thank you very much.

—Monica

I write these lines only to express my deepest respect and thankfulness for the boldness and straightforwardness of your testimony and your book. I do believe that this will make a difference in this once so God-fearing nation, which now has become so sadly backslidden in almost every way!

I also would like to tell you that your testimony so TOTALLY changed my way of thinking, praying, living, and ministering that I can say without a doubt that nothing EVER impacted me like this. (And I've been through a lot...)

—Daniel

I am a believer in Christ as my Savior, and have been for many years. However, I have always found it difficult to witness to others. I have been praying for the Lord to help me spread His good news to as many as possible. He answered that prayer with your book. I have never been more motivated and determined to witness in my life than I am now. I just wanted to thank you for sharing your story.

—Michelle

I had been struggling. I was dabbling with drugs again and was miserable. I hate to read. I spotted *23 Minutes in Hell* and something inside of me told me, "You have got to read that book." I know now that it was the Holy Spirit.

I believed in hell prior to reading this book. I acknowledged that it was a literal place, but I never realized how severely Scripture described it and how awful of a place it really is. God obviously wants us to talk about it and inform the saved and unsaved about it. Why else would He mention it over 150 times in His Word?

Other than the Bible itself, this is the most influential book I have ever read. God changed my life through you because you had a willing heart. Thank you.

—Dan

I'm fifteen years old. I just got done reading your book and it opened my eyes.

I thank God I got this book. If I wouldn't have read this I would probably be going to hell cause I do not know God that good. So thank you much...I have a whole different look about things now...And I promise you I will be praying more and thanking God more and more.

—Amanda

I am ten years old, and I am absolutely shocked! When I looked at the cover of the book, *23 Minutes in Hell*, I got a little nervous. But I just kept reading it until I was at the tenth page of "The cell." It is an amazing book, and I am so happy you wrote the book. I believe in God, and I think that this book has really changed the way I live. It makes me think when I do something wrong. I stop doing the wrong thing, and go the right way. I must admit though, I did get a bit scared, but then I just talked to my mom about it, and she made me feel A LOT better.

—Emily

In the store (where I work), they have a section where they have a rack of Christian books. I have always been "Christian," but your book caught my eye and I bought it immediately. I haven't been able to put it down. I also found myself driving to the bank in tears. I couldn't stop and all I could say is, "I don't want to go there, Lord. Please forgive me for my sins. I want to go home with You." Even when I was in the bank, I couldn't stop crying. A very nice gentleman asked me if I was all right, and I said, "Yes, thank you." A lady gave me a tissue and the gentleman asked me again if I was all right. That is when I told him about reading your book and how frightened I was. He invited me to his church and I went because I need to make sure that I am right with God and Christ. Anyone can say they are Christian but it doesn't mean they are. I want and need to do everything the best I can to be right with the Lord! I need Him and I love Him with everything I am. I am writing to you and yours to say thank you very much. I needed the kick to refocus on what I need to actually be doing and for whom I am doing it for. Thank you again.

—Claudia

Yesterday, my father came into my office and asked if he could talk with me. I told him to sit down and he began to explain his first true experience with God. He told me that he picked up the book *23 Minutes in Hell* from his wife's collection of Christian books and sat down to read it. He stated that he has always been envious of my mother's, mine, and his wife's relationship with the Lord.

My dad gave his life to the Lord about ten years ago. However, it seems more like he has been going through the motions. He has stated numerous times that he believes Jesus died for him but that he has never felt like he has been able to communicate with the Lord. He said that he sat down and read this whole book. He said he sobbed through it and that he felt the Lord talking to him. For this I thank you!

When he was telling me his story I instantly felt like I had to read this book. I went straight to the bookstore and bought it. I sat down last night and experienced the most amazing four hours of my life. I have been a believer for a while now. I gave my life to the Lord when I was twenty-one (Dec. 7, 1999). I feel like I have a good relationship with God and I try every day to be the best disciple possible. However, I have never truly felt like I have been able to grasp what it is that He wants me to do with my life. I have always felt like I was suppose to spread the Word of the Lord, but I have never known exactly how to do this! During this whole book I felt like He was telling me something. I know in my heart that I am supposed to help spread the Word through this book. I feel like I am suppose to budget buying a few of these books every month and send them to people who I know need to read this.

First thing this morning I ran into my dad's office and told him that I too had a life-changing experience reading this book. I told him that I felt that I was suppose to send this book to more people. He said that he felt the same calling. So, we have made a plan to buy as many books each month that we can afford. We are going to send them to people who we know need God in their lives. We are going to make laminated cards asking each person to read this book with an open heart and mind. Also we are going to ask that each person pass it on to someone else when they are done. If they want to keep it that would be great, but we are going to ask they would buy a new one and pass it on with the same note. We are going to sign it "your loving friend."

Thank you so much for writing a book about your experience!

—Jeff

The following e-mail was passed on to us from our friend who delivered the CDs to the young people.

> Just wanted to say thank you for the CDs. Thank you for listening to God's voice on this. We were able to give 200 out during Halloween day at two schools. I met the principal and vice principal. They asked who I was and what was I doing. You see, a few days earlier there was a shooting and two teens died so they were on high alert. I told them what we were doing and said we meet every week on campus. The V.P. asked for a CD and I told the principal my church was praying for the school. She was grateful. Students received the CDs as we handed them out and stated that this could be 23 minutes that could change your life.
>
> —Eric

Here is another e-mail passed on to us from our friend. Names have been changed in this e-mail.

> Earl has a friend named Bob. Bob's son was recently murdered. The father, Bob, went into a tailspin emotionally and spiritually.
>
> Earl contacted him and began ministering. Part of Earl's ministry was the presentation of your hell testimony. Bob listened while driving home. To quote Bob, "I could not stop listening. I began to pray to the Lord for the first time in a long while. As I did so, the Lord spoke to me. He said, 'I have taken your son because he was caught in a snare. He is in heaven.'" Needless to say, he repented and was greatly comforted by God.
>
> But the story continues. Bob then gave the CD to one of his friends. He listened and came to faith in Christ.
>
> Another one of Bob's friends had become suicidal until he was warned that he would go to hell if he committed suicide. Bob gave his friend your CD testimony and they listened

together. Then, this suicidal friend broke, wept, and gave his life to Christ!

Your book terrified me and gave me a deeper love (not sure how that was even possible) for God and His Word. I have started to read the Bible...I do plan on taking a serious trip through it and doing the best I can, even if it's just a little bit a day. I also plan on attending church tomorrow, and believe it or not I'm really excited about going. I do plan on joining a church and continue to go every Sunday. And I seriously could not ever THANK YOU enough for writing this book and sharing your story.

—Casey

I would just like to thank you for sharing your story with me. I have not yet finished reading the book. I just felt that I have never been moved by any other book like I have this one. Upon reading the book, I was skeptical if you were actually a visitor in hell. When reading the book, something made me believe that what you have to tell is true. If your hopes when writing this book were to save at least one soul, your hopes have been fulfilled.

—Brent

I have always sensed that God called me into ministry for a specific and significant purpose. That sense of purpose was on reaching people and helping believers walk in victory in their life. Yet, at the same time, though I certainly had a passion and certain sense of urgency, after your book, my sense of purpose has been highly focused and clarified, and the urgency dramatically heightened!

—Chris

Thank you so much. YOU BLEW MY SOCKS OFF with your book, *23 Minutes in Hell*. All this time I thought that I was a good Christian. Now I see that I was only kidding myself after I read your book. Now I am on the road to being a real Christian, praise God.

—John

I would like to purchase ten copies of *23 Minutes in Hell*. I feel this book is one of the most important books ever written other than the Bible and is essential reading by everyone.

—Eddie

I ordered your book, *23 Minutes in Hell*, and received it in the mail yesterday. I ordered your book because while I believed hell existed, I didn't know much about it.

I admit I was a bit skeptical as to how much truth would be in your book, but I knew at the least it would paint a better picture of what the horrors of hell *might* be like and your book painted a picture that was more than enough to keep me on my toes. After reading the book, I was no longer skeptical. I believe every word you said for many reasons. One being, if you were out to deceive people, the book would have at least implied some things against God and His will, but your book did nothing but glorify Him. Secondly, any questions I had as far as the validity of your experience were answered in the second half of the book. And third, the book has more than enough biblical references to back up your claims.

So I want to thank you, Bill, for spreading God's Word and sharing your experience with me through your book because I now have a better understanding of how horrible hell is and am compelled to become even closer to God.

I am currently in Baghdad, Iraq, on my second tour here. Less than two weeks ago, one of our teammates was killed, and it has taken its toll on me, very personally. Since then, I have realized that life is short and that I must live right for God, which is one of the things that inspired me to order your book.

—Jonathan

I loved the book you wrote about hell. I am a Christian and know Jesus died for my sins and to save me from hell, but I never thought exactly what hell would be like. Now I know! I don't want anyone to go there. This is gonna give me a new boldness to tell people about Jesus and what He has done for all of mankind. Understanding the torment has motivated me.

—Pam

I'm seventeen years old, and I just got done reading your book, *23 Minutes in Hell*. It only took me about a few hours to read it (and I NEVER read), but I couldn't put the book down for a second! When I got done reading it, I started praying a lot and taking in the fact that hell really does exist. During the whole book, you talk about spreading the message of the Lord to other people, and I just wanted to tell you and thank you myself for getting the message out to ME!! That's one more person that you saved from a horrendous eternity! Thank you SO much—I can't even explain the way that I feel now.

—Kayla

I am already a Christian and I attend church. My whole family read your book together and it changed all of us! I am turning thirteen and I am starting to slide off course a little bit. When I read your book, that night I was strictly back on course. I keep your book on the counter so every time I make a sin I will see that on the counter and pray immediately. THANK YOU SO MUCH!

—Ryan

Your book is a lifesaver. Even though I am halfway through your book, I am making some changes in my life as I write this. Thank you again.

—Dustin

I just finished reading *23 Minutes in Hell* about two weeks ago. While reading it I knew that I had to find out how to buy as many copies of your book as I could to give away to others.

Right after I finished your book, a woman in my real estate class asked if she could see the book. I handed it over thinking, well if I don't get this back at least I know I shared it with another. I ended up trying to tell the entire classroom what your book was about, and that is so not like me to have a room full of people looking and listening to me. Nonetheless she read the book and would like to buy as many copies as she can to hand out as well. Thank you for your obedience.

—Krystal

I am a pastor in training. I got your book from a friend of mine and after reading it, I am taken away. This is a very powerful testimony. This story made me immediately break down and start praying for family and friends. I plan on sharing this with many people that I may come in contact with the rest of my earthly life.

—Matt

I purchased your book *23 Minutes in Hell* this morning not really expecting to get much out of it. Wow! I was wrong in so many ways! I read your whole book within four hours. I just couldn't put it down worth anything! It had me crying in many parts, and I am amazed at what you have experienced. I am sixteen years old. And I just want you to know how much you have done for me and my life. Your story has changed my whole look on the world! I am so glad that I read this book now. I wasn't sure about if there was a hell or not, and you, my friend, have made it VERY clear to me, that it is real! So I would like to thank you. I am going to pass this book on and share your story with my friends that don't believe in hell!

—Tiffany

I haven't read a book so fast in years. I was just mesmerized! I've also never written to anyone about a book, but I just had to tell you how it really spurred the urgency in me to witness to others. After reading your incredible story I feel an urgency to witness to my neighbors and again to my family.

—Darlene

I wept reading your book. I was truly saddened by the thought of anyone going to hell to spend eternity. I feel by reading your book that you have given me a much greater understanding of God's love toward us and have brought me closer to Him.

—Maureen

I read your book in two days and was captivated. I am a born-again Christian of thirty-two years. I must say that this book drew me closer to the Lord and has given me a fire down inside to share the pangs of hell with my unbelieving loved ones so much more. Sometimes I get discouraged and just think, "Let them go to hell if that's what they want." But after this book, I know I have to start fighting again for their souls, in prayer and words.

—Pat

One thing I want to tell you is the fact that I am not a book reader. Once I began to read your book I could not put it down. I will have to say once I got past the experience in "hell" part of the book, I thought, oh here we go; this guy is going to get all religious on me. Your vivid description of hell compelled me, however, to continue on with reading about the explanations you described. As yourself, I too am a skeptic. I believe your story is real, I just don't think you could make something like that up. It scared me to a point that I slept with the lights on last night. I was in the army. I am not scared of the dark; however, after reading your book the lights were on!

I realized when I got to the part of your book where the sinners prayer is, that I had no choice but to except Christ back into my life. My mom was laying on the couch and I asked her to come and pray with me and she did. I had a warm feeling come over my body and I could not control the fact that I had to do what I did. I then realized that the reason I came to see my mom was not to do chores but rather to become saved.

I'm sure I will face opposition to my decision in the upcoming weeks and I look forward to that. I am going to take this book and give it to anyone who will be willing to read it. I suppose I will lose a few old friends and that is OK because my soul is not going to that horrible place you described. For all of the people who don't believe I would say this. Is it really a chance you want to take? Like you said, *eternity*. That was a scary word a couple of days ago. I like the sound of it now. I for one think a few years on this earth are nothing compared to a lifetime in hell. Thank you again and GLORY BE TO GOD.

—R.W.

I just want you to know I found your book and testimony powerful. I have been a Christian since I was nine years old. I have served the Lord and I have grown in a relationship with Him. You may find this strange, but being saved for so long (I'm fifty-two now), I thought many times I should be happier about going to heaven. I have taken so much for granted. I prayed and asked the Lord to renew my joy about being a Christian. Does that make sense? Sometimes we become stagnant, or I did. A good friend of mine gave me your book and CD. She too is a Christian and she was so excited about it. I took the CD on a little trip I had to make by myself and...well, it was an answer to prayer! I was crying and praising the Lord that He has SAVED ME FROM HELL! What a turning point! Praise came so easy and still does! I have such a passion about telling people about the Lord now! I don't want anyone to go there! AND you have scripture to back it all up, which is extremely important. Thank you for sharing your experience.

—Jyl

After reading your book, my wife and I lent it to a good friend. (Our friends) read your book while driving across town to work. They took turns reading through the book. Their grandson is about nineteen and your book changed his life! He went back to Wisconsin and told many of his HS friends about the book and they now have been gloriously saved!

—Tim

Thanks for writing this book! We as Christians need to hear this.... We always hear about God's love and mercy, which is all part of who God is, but we never hear of God's wrath and this part of what will happen to the unsaved. After reading your book, I looked at everyone that I knew that was unsaved in a different light. I feel I have a new purpose in exposing them to the love of Jesus and in showing them the way, the only way, which is Christ our Lord. I don't want even one soul to ever have to endure that punishment. We must get the Word out! Thanks for inspiring me and for scaring me and for giving me a godly fear that I have needed.

—Elaine

I just wanted to let Bill know that his book has really touched my life. It has really opened my eyes to the reality of hell. I was saved when I was really young, but during my teens I started living for myself. I have recently recommitted my life to Christ as a result of Bill's book. I've read it twice and want to buy his book for friends and family.

—David

I have enjoyed your book! I could not put it down. I gave it to my sister and my husband to read. They were also awed by the revelation God allowed you to experience. We have since told others about the book. I felt the Lord prompting me to give the book to others, and I am seeing God at work as He is opening doors to witness through discussions about your testimony. Thanks!

—Tracy

You are dear, dear people and your ministry flies in the face of the spirit of the age—even within the body of Christ. Thank God for His mercy in sending you with His message of warning and mercy.

—Cherry

Thank you for renewing my fervor to see souls saved. This book has stirred the "joy of my salvation" once again. I am so grateful to our Lord and Savior, Jesus Christ, for saving me from a horror I could not even fathom. Thank you for your courage to speak His Word with boldness to a generation that chooses to ingest a watered down version of the Truth that soothes our "itching ears." I encourage you to shout it and proclaim it from the rooftops. Our youth need to hear it. They must hear it. I pray God will open unexpected doors for you, doors that will bring many, many souls to Him.

—Marly

Over the past few years I have felt like I didn't really know what my purpose was in life as a Christian, and I caught myself praying that Jesus would just come back soon and I would just live happily ever after in heaven. After reading your book I broke down in tears! I realized why I am here and as a Christian what my purpose is. I have prayed more than ever that God would use me to witness to unbelievers, and your book has been a great tool for me to do so. I have given it to Christians and to unbelievers. I feel like your experience can not only bring people to Christ but renew faith in Christians and remind them what God's plan is for their life. Thank you for sharing your amazing story, and I believe God will continue to bless your life.

—Kelly

I wanted to write you and tell you that, first off, I believe your testimony of hell. I first heard about your experience on a CD in Australia. When I first heard your testimony, I was fired up to evangelize. A couple of weeks later, I got a group of friends together and we listened to your testimony. We then went out into the streets and evangelized with skits and testimonies. Seven people were saved that night. Your testimony pumped us up to see people accept the Lord!!!

I'm reading your book right now and it makes me want to stand up and preach about Jesus to everyone…but in our culture that might be viewed as insanity. I just wanted to let you know that your experience has encouraged me so much! Excited for heaven!!

—Luke

PART TWO

CHAPTER 18

AN OVERALL PERSPECTIVE

I WOULD LIKE TO GIVE YOU AN OVERALL PERSPECTIVE OF GOD'S eternal plan. How did this whole thing start? Why did God create man?

John G. Lake said, "What did God create man for anyway? Answer: The chief end of man is to glorify God and enjoy Him forever. God's purpose in the creation of mankind was to develop an association on His own plane."[1]

God made man because He desired fellowship and wanted someone to bless. He wanted a relationship. The Bible says that, "In the beginning God created the heavens and the earth" (Gen. 1:1). God made the earth for man first. Then He made the man and woman on the sixth day of creation. He gave them the entire planet to explore and rule. Everything was perfect, and man was designed to live forever.

The earth had an abundance of food, fruit, vegetables, nuts, and so forth. No animals were used for food, as there was no killing or death. "There was, therefore, nothing bad in that created world, no hunger, no struggle for existence, no suffering, and certainly no death of animal or human life anywhere in God's perfect creation."[2]

God's first instructions to the man and woman, who were named Adam and Eve, were that they could eat of every tree in the garden, "but of the tree of the knowledge of good and evil you shall not eat, for in the day that you eat of it you shall surely die" (Gen. 2:16–17). God didn't explain why; He simply gave them a command and a warning of what would happen to them if they were to disobey and eat of its fruit.

In addition to everything in the earth, God had also created millions of angels. One of the angels had been given more authority than the rest. He occupied the position of chief angel and had been endued with an abundance of beauty and wisdom (Ezek. 28:12–14). Billy Graham states, "[Lucifer] was the most brilliant and most beautiful of all created beings in heaven. He was probably the ruling prince of the universe under God, against whom he rebelled. The result was insurrection and war in heaven."[3]

On a certain day, Lucifer decided he wanted to be God. His desire was to rule all things, including God, even though he knew he was a created being (Ezek. 28:15). Pride had arisen in his heart (Isa. 14:13–14; Ezek. 28:15–17). "Satan desired to rule over heaven and creation in the place of God. He wanted supreme authority!...Lucifer was not satisfied with being subordinated to his creator. He wanted to usurp God's throne."[4] He convinced one-third of all the angels that he was the one who should rule in heaven (Rev. 12:4–9). There was a brief battle, and he and his comrades were thrown out, down to the earth and down to hell (Sheol), which was prepared for him (Isa. 14:12–15; Ezek. 28:17; Matt. 25:41; Rev. 12:7–9). This act of rebellion was after God had created the earth and formed man from the dust of the earth. This is confirmed by Dr. Henry Morris, who says, "Satan's fall did not occur until after the creation week of Genesis 1, for at that time God had pronounced the whole creation 'very good' (Gen. 1:31)."[5]

According to Billy Graham, "It is difficult to suppose that their fall occurred before God placed Adam and Eve in the Garden...at the end of all creation, and pronounced everything to be good. By implication, up to this time even the angelic creation was good."[6] Some time after Adam and Eve were placed in the garden, Satan entered it and tempted them.

Two questions you may be asking right now are: "Why did God put the tree there in the first place if man was not to eat of it? And why would obtaining that knowledge be harmful to man?"

To answer the first part of the question, God wanted man to have choice. He wanted man to choose to obey Him, just as we want our spouse to love us by choice, not by command. God gave man a command with a warning, but man had a choice. If a command wasn't given to not partake of that tree, man would not have had the "choice" to follow God's instruction. God doesn't want us following Him out of demand. I heard a minister once say, "Love lets you make your own choice, but love demanded man would know his choice."

Josh McDowell said, "But genuine love cannot exist unless freely given through free choice and will, and thus man was given the choice to accept God's love or to reject it. This choice made the possibility of evil become very real.... God is not evil nor did He create evil."[7] God is love, and by love's very nature man had to be allowed a choice. God did not merely give man the choice, but He gave the warning as well. Real love does that. As a loving parent, think about how you explain to your child the consequences that will result from his or her decisions. You warn your child. You don't just say, "Do whatever you want."

Pastor Chuck Smith writes in his book *What the World Is Coming To*:

> By yielding themselves to the suggestion of Satan (eating of the forbidden fruit), they acted doubly. It was a disobedience to God which took them out of fellowship with God, but it was also an obedience to Satan which brought them into submission to Satan. At that point man forfeited the right to the earth. The title deed of the earth was passed over to Satan, and the world became Satan's. Jesus came to redeem the world back to God— to buy the "field." "The kingdom of heaven is like unto treasure hid in a field; the which when a man hath found, he hideth, and for joy thereof goeth and selleth all that he hath, and buyeth that field" (Matthew 13:44).
>
> The "treasure" in the field is the church. Jesus died to purchase the earth. It was God's to begin with. God created it, but He gave it to man. Man, in turn, forfeited it to Satan, and Satan has been the ruler of the world ever since.[8]

Now for the second part of the question, "Why would obtaining that knowledge be harmful for man—the knowledge of good and evil?" At this point, man didn't even know what bad or evil was. It is hard for us to grasp what it means to have no knowledge of evil. Nowadays a world without evil would be difficult for us to imagine, but then to not even know what evil is, is not even possible for us to contemplate. Man in the garden didn't even have it in his mind what "evil" is. God knew that if man gained knowledge of evil, he would be tempted by it and would indulge in it, thereby separating himself from God. The nature of God cannot dwell with any evil. The two are incompatible. The main reason that man would become evil is because he disobeyed God in the first place by eating of the fruit of that tree. God told him clearly not to, yet he did it anyway.

Back to the garden—how did man end up disobeying God's command? Well, remember that head angel God threw out of heaven earlier? This same angel named Lucifer, or Satan, approached Adam and Eve one day and told them they could eat of the tree despite what God had told them. Satan said, "Ye shall not surely die....Ye shall be as gods" (Gen 3:4–5, KJV). He lied to them, but they had a choice to make: believe God, that they will die if they partake, or believe Satan, that they will be as a god. God had to allow them this choice.

> It is deadly to doubt God's Word! Satan's strategy is to persuade us to rationalize....How easily Satan covers with a light color ideas that are dark. His intrigue comes to us colored in the light of our own desires....God created us in His image, and He desires that the creature worship the Creator as a response of love. This can be accomplished when "free will" is exercised.[9]

John G. Lake tells us, "The result was that because of the suggestion of Satan there developed calls of the earth for the earthly. After a while he partook of things earthly and became earthly himself. Therefore the fall of man was his fall into himself. He fell into his own earthly self, out of his heavenly estate, and the separation was absolute and complete."[10] The passage that mentions the word *earthly* is 1 Corinthians 15:48–49 (NIV). This verse will give further validity to the state to which man had fallen.

Here is another point to understand. God has made us eternal beings. We do not simply cease to exist at death. Since God made us eternal, when we die we can only spend eternity with Him or spend eternity in hell.

Walter Martin said in his book *The Kingdom of the Cults*, "The teaching of the Word of God that the soul of man, whether regenerate or unregenerate, exists after the death of the body."[11] He made us to live with Him forever, and He made hell for the devil and his angels (Matt. 25:41). If we don't want anything to do with God, there is no other place for our soul to go.

JESUS—OUR SUBSTITUTE

Only Jesus, who is God, became a man and lived that perfect life without ever sinning even once. Only a perfect man could make the exchange for our lives. He was tempted in all points, as we are, and thereby can identify with our pain and our weaknesses. He was rejected, betrayed, lied about, beaten, hungered, thirsted, tortured, and finally nailed to a cross and killed for you and me.

You may ask, "Why did He have to suffer such a horrible death?" If a really evil criminal was captured, and he had mutilated, raped, and killed small children, we would want the judge to pronounce the severest punishment. Some would want him locked up forever. Others think the death penalty would be more appropriate. Still others would want to see him suffer the way he caused those innocent children to suffer. He probably deserves all of the above. Well, sin is so exceedingly sinful to God that the punishment for it should be the severest in God's eyes. Jesus took that punishment upon Himself for us. If He would have let Himself off easy, like a quick blow to the head, then death, He would not be applying an appropriate punishment for the sin. He would then not be considered a "just judge." The Bible states that God is truly just, fair, and righteous. He remained faithful to His Word, even to the death and punishment of His own Son. He loves us that much.

Chuck Missler states, in regard to the Lord's death on the cross, "His crucifixion was not a tragedy: it was an achievement targeted before the foundation of the earth."[12] God foretold the future in the Bible of what would happen to Jesus, where He would be born, where He would travel to, the punishment, the betrayal, the type of death, His burial, His resurrection, and so on. (See Psalm 22; 26:16, 18; 34:20; 41:9; Isaiah 7:14;

50:6; 53:1–5, 7, 12; Zechariah 9:9; 11:13; 12:10; and approximately three hundred other verses.) These scriptures were all written prior to any of it taking place. They were written at different times, by different people, in different cities and countries, and all were fulfilled exactly as God had spoken. Jesus was the fulfillment of them all.

CHAPTER 19

HELL, HADES, SHEOL, GEHENNA— WHAT IS THE DIFFERENCE?

MANY HAVE INQUIRED WHAT THE DIFFERENCE IS BETWEEN Sheol, Hades, the pit, hell, Gehenna, Topheth, Tartarus, and the Abyss. First, the use of the word *hell* should only be used when referencing the "lake of fire," which is the future location of the current "Sheol," or "Hades" (Rev. 20:13–15). However, most use the word in general to refer to Sheol, Hades, or hell. The technical quotes from the scholars will be just ahead, but a brief description is as follows:[1]

Abyss is a bottomless pit mentioned in Revelation 9:2 and other places. It is a special pit where certain demons are held in chains.

Gehenna is the Latin word for the Hebrew term "Valley of Hinnom," which came to mean "hell" along with *Topheth*.

Hades is the Greek word and equivalent of Sheol.

Pit sometimes is the equivalent of Sheol. There are thirteen different words for "pit," but only three or four are used as a synonym for Sheol. The book *Hell Under Fire* points out some of this. If you look up the word *pit*, you will see sixteen different words, thirteen in the Old Testament, and three in the New Testament.

Sheol is the Hebrew word to refer to hell and means "the realm of the dead."

Tartarus is used only once, in 2 Peter 2:4, and is a Greek word meaning "place of torture and torment lower than Hades."

The current place of torment is called Sheol in the Hebrew and Hades in the Greek. Many scholars believe that on the one side was the torment side, currently called Hades, and on the other side was Paradise. They were separated by a "gulf fixed" (Luke 16:26). Up until the time of the Ascension, Hades also encompassed both sides, according to the *Vine's Expository Dictionary*. After the Ascension it now only refers to the torment side. Paradise was believed to have been removed when Jesus descended for three days in the heart of the earth and then arose and took the saints with Him. This is not conclusive and is debated, but there seems to be enough evidence in Scripture, and many commentaries' views, to support this belief. After Judgment Day, death and hell will be delivered up and cast into the "lake of fire" (Rev. 20:13–14). It will be cast into "outer darkness" (Matt. 25:30). The lake of fire currently has no occupants.

The pit is usually referred to as Hades, or Sheol. There are thirteen different words in the Hebrew for the word *pit*. Only three or four are synonymous with hell. Those being "sheol" and "Bowr" and *"shachath"* and *"be'er,"* in a couple of incidences (Ps. 55:23; 69:15). *John MacArthur Study Bible* says, "The 'pit' was another word for Sheol, the realm of the dead."[2] Matthew Henry's commentary refers "to the pit of destruction, to the bottomless pit, which is called destruction."[3]

There are three other words for "pit" in the New Testament that refer to the abyss. They are the Greek words *phrear* and *abussos* and *bothynos* or *bothros*. This is a separate area reserved for certain demons that will be released during the tribulation period (Rev. 9:2, 11; 11:7; 17:8; 20:1). There is yet another separate area called "under darkness" that is reserved for some other demons who "left their first estate" (Jude 6, KJV; see also 2 Pet. 2:4). This place is called Tartarus.

I will simply list many of the commentaries and leaders' statements regarding these places. What I can tell you is that I was in Sheol, or Hades.

I felt it was deep in the earth. I descended to get there and ascended when leaving. In my opinion, Scripture describes its location as down deep in the earth. As for the location, scholars are not in agreement as to it being literally in the lower parts of the earth.

ABYSS

The bottomless pit (the abyss in the Greek). This is the dwelling place of demons. When he opened the entrance to the abyss, billows of smoke poured forth, as if from a huge furnace, veiling the landscape in darkness.[4]

—Believer's Bible Commentary

Transliteration of Greek word *abussos*, literally meaning "without bottom."[5]

—Holman Illustrated Bible Dictionary

The bottomless pit—Greek, "the pit of the abyss"; the orifice of the hell where Satan and his demons dwell.[6]

*—Jamieson, Fausset, and Brown's
Commentary on the Whole Bible*

Bottomless pit. Lit. "pit of the abyss." Mentioned seven times in Revelation, it always refers to the prison where some of the demonic hordes are incarcerated, the place of severest torment and isolation (vv. 1, 2, 11; 11:7; 17:8; 20:1, 3; see notes on 2 Pet. 2:4, Jude 6, 7).[7]

—The MacArthur Bible Commentary

The bottomless pit, or the chaotic deep . . . it describes the prison of disobedient spirits.[8]

—Nelson's New Illustrated Bible Dictionary

Abussos–Bottomless a noun denoting the abyss. KJV, "bottomless pit." It describes an immeasurable depth, the underworld, the lower regions. The abyss of sheol. The abode of the dead.[9]

—*Vine's Complete Expository Dictionary of Old and New Testament Words*

SHEOL AND HADES

Hades is the Greek for the O.T. word Sheol, the state of departed spirits. In the O.T. period, it was spoken of as the abode of both saved and unsaved.[10]

—*Believer's Bible Commentary*

In the ancient near Eastern world in which the Bible originated, death was called "the land of no return," and was viewed as an inescapable underworld prison. The OT pictures the realm of the death (or Sheol) as being under the earth, comparing its entrance to a deep pit (Ps. 88:4–6)....Amos makes the hyperbolic suggestion that by digging deep one might reach Sheol (Amos 9:2). The afterlife, like the pit that represents it, is pictured as dark and deep (Ps. 88:6), mucky (Ps. 40:2) and disgusting (Job 9:31).[11]

—*Dictionary of Biblical Imagery*

Sheol and Hades are identical, Psa. 16:10; Acts 2:27....It has gates, Isa. 38:10; Matt. 16:18; and bars, Jon. 2:2–6.[12]

—*The Great Doctrines of the Bible*

When the term Hades is used as the equivalent of the Hebrew Sheol, as it is in Acts 2:27–31, where Peter is quoting from Ps. 16:8–11, it refers simply to the grave.... [Sheol], Place of the dead...In a number of texts persons are spoken of as descending to Sheol or of going into a pit (Ps. 88:6, 10; Amos 9:2). This likely indicates that the Hebrews saw Sheol as something beneath their feet.... The KJV often translated it as "hell" (sheol)... but this is surely a bad translation, since hell as the "lake of fire" is no one's dwelling place until final judgment (Rev. 20:14).... Sheol itself is a broad term that, depending on the context, may signify the abode of both the righteous dead and the ungodly dead.[13]

—*Holman Illustrated Bible Dictionary*

"Paradise" and "Abraham's bosom," the abode of good spirits in Old Testament times, are separated by a wide gulf from Hell or Hades.... There has been placed a vast impassable abyss between the two states.[14]

—*Jamieson, Fausset, and Brown's
Commentary on the Whole Bible*

The Old Testament uses '*sheol*' to describe the abode of the dead and divides it into parts (Deut. 32:22) as the righteous go there (Gen. 37:35) and the unrighteous (Ps. 9:17)...[15]

—*The Life of Christ*

We've learned that the Hebrew word *sheol* is used for the realm of the dead in the Old Testament. The New Testament, however, was written in Greek, and there we find *sheol* translated by the Greek word *hades*...sheol is always translated "hades"; they are one and the same...the word *hades* is never used of the grave, but always refers to world of departed spirits.[16]

—Erwin W. Lutzer

Hades...the New Testament equivalent of the Old Testament grave or Sheol. Though sometimes it identifies hell (Matt. 11:23), here it refers to the general place of the dead.[17]

—*The MacArthur Bible Commentary*

...Sheol, which referred to the realm of the dead in general, without necessarily distinguishing between righteous or unrighteous souls. The imagery Jesus used paralleled the erroneous rabbinical idea that Sheol had two parts, one for the souls of the righteous and the other for the souls of the wicked—separated by an impassable gulf.... Later, Paradise was described as the place of the righteous dead in Sheol (Luke 16:19–31).[18]

—*The MacArthur Bible Commentary*

The New Testament term used to describe the afterlife is *hades* and is equivalent to the Hebrew term *sheol*.[19]

—*The Moody Handbook of Theology*

In Old Testament thought, the abode of the dead, Sheol is the Hebrew equivalent of the Greek *Hades*, which means "the unseen world." Sheol was regarded as an underground region Num. 16:30; Amos 9:2, shadowy and gloomy, where disembodied souls had a conscious but dull and inactive existence (2 Sam. 22:6; Ec. 9:10). The Hebrew people regarded Sheol as a place to which both the righteous and unrighteous go at death (Gen. 37:35; Ps. 9:17; Is. 38:10; death, NIV: Deut 32:22; the realm of death, NIV), a place where punishment is received and rewards are enjoyed.... As a deep underground place, the pit became synonymous with Sheol: the abode of the dead, the netherworld of departed spirits.[20]

—*Nelson's New Illustrated Bible Dictionary*

Sheol was below the surface of the earth (Ezk. 31:15, 17; Ps. 86:13). Hades... is therefore the N.T. equivalent of Sheol.[21]

—*New Bible Dictionary*

The pit (shahat) is synonymous for Sheol...[22]

—*Unger's Commentary on the Old Testament*

For the rendering "hell" as a translation of hades, corresponding to Sheol, wrongly rendered "the grave" and "hell."

Hades—the region of departed spirits of the lost (but including the blessed dead in periods preceding the ascension of Christ).

Sheol—It never denotes the grave, nor is it the permanent region of the lost; in point of time it is, for such, intermediate between decease and the doom of Gehenna....It is used with reference to the soul of Christ, Acts 2:27–31;...A more probable derivation is from *hado,* signifying "all receiving."[23]

—*Vine's Complete Expository Dictionary*
of Old and New Testament Words

When a person who is not a Christian dies now, he is in a waiting place called Hades, translated "hell" in your King James Bible. This place called Hades is actually in the center of the earth, and those unrighteous dead are in it....It was the abiding place of everyone who died, but it was divided into two sections.[24]

—Chuck Smith

Jesus firmly believed that hell is just as real as heaven. In John 14:2, Jesus promised His disciples, "I go to prepare a place for you." The Greek word for "place" is *topos,* which means, "a geographical location." Heaven is not a state of mind, but is the eternal destination for those who trust in Christ. In the same way, Jesus taught that hell was an actual destination rather than a state of mind. Read carefully how Jesus described the fate of the unrighteous: "These will go away into eternal punishment, but the righteous into eternal life" (Matthew 25:46). My point is simply this: You can't have one group of people going to an actual location (heaven) and the other group of people going to a state of mind. Just as Jesus described heaven as a real place, He taught that hell is a real place.[25]

—Robert Jeffress

On one side of Hades was Abraham's Bosom, which held the souls of all those saints who had died with faith in God during the Old Testament period until the time of the resurrection of Christ (Luke 16:23). Those souls in Abraham's Bosom were conscious in a pleasant place of waiting until Jesus Christ descended into Hades after His death on the cross.[26]

—Grant Jeffrey

GEHENNA

The best known biblical image for hell derives from a deep, narrow gorge southeast of Jerusalem called "The Valley of Ben Hinnom."...The Greek word Gehenna, "hell," commonly used in the N.T. for the place of final punishment, is derived from the Hebrew name for this valley....The sight of mutilated corpses, human bones, maggots, flies, animals, and birds ripping strips of flesh off dead bodies as well as the smell of rotting and burning flesh convey a sense of horror and revulsion to which those who have viewed the aftermath of modern atrocities and warfare can fully attest.[27]

—*Dictionary of Biblical Imagery*

English equivalent of the Greek word (*geena*) derived from the Hebrew place-name (*gehinnom*) meaning "valley of Hinnom" and came to be used in NT times as a word for hell....In the period between the OT and NT, Jewish writing used the term to describe the hell of fire in the final judgment.[28]

—*Holman Illustrated Bible Dictionary*

Tophet, Lit. a place of abomination. Idolatrous Israel had burned to death human victims in the valley just south of Jerusalem, an area sometimes called The Valley of Hinnom (2 Kings 23:10, see note on Jer. 19:6). Later it became known as Gehenna, the place of refuse for the city, with constantly

burning fires, symbolizing hell. The defeat was so complete that
the fires burn continually.[29]

—*MacArthur Study Bible*

Here is Tophet ordained and prepared for them, v. 33. The
valley of the son of Hinnom, adjoining to Jerusalem, was called
Tophet...and there is fuel enough ready to burn them all; and
they shall be consumed as suddenly and effectually as if the
fire were kept burning by a continual stream of brimstone, for
such the breath of the Lord, his word and his wrath, will be to
it....Our Savior calls the future misery of the damned Gehenna,
in allusion to the Valley of Hinnom....It is deep and large,
sufficient to receive the world of the ungodly; the pile thereof is
fire and much wood. God's wrath is the fire, and sinners make
themselves fuel to it; and the breath of the Lord (the power of
His anger) kindles it, and will keep it ever burning.[30]

—*Matthew Henry's Commentary on the Whole Bible*

Hell, the place of eternal punishment for the unrighteous...Hell
also translates Gehenna, the Greek form of the Hebrew phrase
that means "The Valley of Hinnom."...In the time of Jesus the
Valley of Hinnom was used as the garbage dump of Jerusalem.
Into it were thrown all the filth and garbage of the city including
the dead bodies of animals and executed criminals. To consume
all this, fires burned constantly. Maggots worked in filth. When
the wind blew from that direction over the city, its awfulness
was quite evident. At night wild dogs howled as they fought over
the garbage. Jesus used this awful scene as a symbol of hell. In
effect He said, "Do you want to know what hell is like? Look at
"Gehenna."...The word *Gehenna* occurs 12 times in the New
Testament. Each time it is translated as "hell"....

Apparently, the Valley of Hinnom was used as the garbage
dump for the city of Jerusalem. Refuse, waste materials, and
dead animals were burned here. Fires continually smoldered,

and smoke from the burning debris rose day and night. Hinnom thus became a graphic symbol of woe and judgment and the place of eternal punishment called Hell. Translated into Greek, the Hebrew "Valley of Hinnom" becomes Gehenna, which is used 12 times in the New Testament (11 times by Jesus and once by James), each time translated as "hell" (Matt 5:22; Mark 9:43, 45, 47; Luke 12:5; James 3:6).[31]

—*Nelson's New Illustrated Bible Dictionary*

It was a place in the Valley of Hinnom where human sacrifices were offered to Moloch (2 Kings 23:10; Jer. 7:31), and it became the city dump, where fires were kept burning continually. Hence, it came to denote Gehenna (eternal hell)....Fire of Gehenna (Rev. 20:11–15) is literal, but it is also supernatural, symbolizing the destiny and punishment of the unsaved, Satan, and demons.[32]

—*Unger's Commentary on the Old Testament*

Geenna represents the Hebrew *Ge-Hinnom* (the valley of Tophet) and a corresponding Aramaic word; it is found twelve times in the N.T.[33]

—*Vine's Complete Expository Dictionary*
of Old and New Testament Words

The Greek word *Gehenna*, used frequently for hell in the New Testament, is derived from the Hebrew *ge hinnom*....It is developed into a prophetic symbol of judgment. The transferred use of this place name for the final state of the lost employs it as a symbol of judgment. It is the wasteland of humanity, inhabited by all those who reject Christ and his revelation. Those who do not belong to the Kingdom of God are there.[34]

—Sinclair B. Ferguson

It is interesting to note that Tophet and Hinnom became symbolic of hell. Jeremiah 19:6–7 describes quite graphically the horrors of this place. If it can be this awful on Earth, how much more the eternal domain of hell.

> Therefore, behold, the days come, saith the LORD, that this place shall no more be called Tophet, nor The valley of the son of Hinnom, but The valley of slaughter....And their carcasses will I give to be meat for the fowls of the heaven, and for the beasts of the earth. And I will make this city desolate, and an hissing; every one that passeth thereby shall be astonished and hiss because of all the plagues thereof. And I will cause them to eat the flesh of their sons and the flesh of their daughters, and they shall eat every one the flesh of his friend...
>
> —Jeremiah 19:6–9

Because of their worshiping of false gods, God allowed this (v. 13).

HELL

> The abode of the dead; the underworld where departed souls were believed to dwell; Specifically, in the Hebrew Scriptures, Sheol, and in the Greco-Roman tradition, Hades.[35]
> —*The American Heritage Dictionary of the English Language*

> The best known biblical image for hell derives from a deep, narrow gorge southeast of Jerusalem called *ge hen hinnom*, "the Valley of Ben Hinnom," in which idolatrous Israelites offered up child sacrifices to the gods Molech and Bael (2 Chron. 28:3; 33:6; Jer. 7:31–32; 19:2–6, NIV).[36]
> —*Dictionary of Biblical Imagery*

> The popular notion of heaven and hell as the abode of the souls of the dead is more or less correct.[37]
> —*Encyclopedia of Biblical Words*

The place of eternal punishment for the unrighteous. The NKJV and KJV use this word to translate Sheol and Hades, the Old and New Testament words, respectively, for the abode of the dead. Hell also translates *Gehenna*, the Greek form of the Hebrew phrase that means "the vale of Hinnom"—a valley west and south of Jerusalem.[38]

—*Nelson's New Illustrated Bible Dictionary*

Geenna represents the Hebrew *Ge-Hinnom* (the valley of Tophet) and a corresponding Aramaic word; it is found twelve times in the N.T. The abode of condemned souls and devils. The underworld place or state of torture and punishment for the wicked after death, presided over by Satan.[39]

—*Vine's Complete Expository Dictionary*
of Old and New Testament Words

TARTARUS

There is another word to describe a special place in hell called "Tartarus." It is a Greek word translated as hell. It only appears one place in Scripture, in 2 Peter 2:4.

Tartarus was regarded by the ancient Greek as the abiding place where rebellious gods and other wicked ones were punished. Its only N.T. use is in 2 Pet.2:4.[40]

—*Holman Illustrated Bible Dictionary*

This passage indicates that there is a special part of hell in which God imprisoned those fallen angels who chose to defile mankind in the ancient past before the Flood by having illicit sexual relations with the women of earth (Genesis 6:1–5).[41]

—Grant Jeffrey

The abode of evil angels who sinned during the times of Noah.[42]

—Erwin Lutzer

The Greeks taught that Tartarus was a place lower than Hades reserved for the most wicked of human beings, gods, and demons. The Jews eventually came to use this term to describe the place where fallen angels were sent. It defined for them the lowest hell, the deepest pit, and the most terrible place of torture and eternal suffering.[43]

—The MacArthur Bible Commentary

In 2 Peter 2:4, signifies to consign to Tartarus, which is neither Sheol nor Hades nor Hell, but the place where those angels whose special sin is referred to in that passage are confined "to be reserved unto judgment;" the region is described as "pits of darkness."[44]

—Vine's Complete Expository Dictionary
of Old and New Testament Words

TOPHET

Isaiah 30:33 says, "For Tophet is ordained of old; yea, for the king it is prepared; he hath made it deep and large: the pile thereof is fire and much wood; the breath of the LORD, like a stream of brimstone, doth kindle it" (KJV).

> ... the destruction of the wicked in the Valley of Topheth, south of Jerusalem (v. 33). Here, Yahweh will set up piles of wood on which the bodies of the enemies of his people will be placed, and with the breath of his mouth he will set these stacks of wood aflame.[45]
>
> *—Baker Commentary on the Bible*

The burning fires of Topheth (hell) are ready to welcome the wicked king.[46]

—Believer's Bible Commentary

Tophet—lit., "A place of abomination"; "the valley of the sons of Hinnom," southeast of Jerusalem, where Israel offered human sacrifices to Moloch by fire; hence a place of burning....Hence it came to express hell....Tophet is the receptacle "prepared for the devil (antitype to the king, ch. 14:12–15) and his angels," and unbelieving men (Matt. 5:22; 25:41; Mark 9:43, 44).[47]

—Jamieson, Fausset, and Brown's
Commentary on the Whole Bible

A place of abomination....an area sometimes called the Valley of Hinnom...Later it became known as Gehenna, the place of refuse for the city, with constantly burning fires, symbolizing hell. The defeat was to be so complete that the fire burned continually.[48]

—The MacArthur Bible Commentary

Here is Tophet ordained and prepared for them (v. 33). The valley of the son of Hinnom, adjoining to Jerusalem, was called Tophet....and there is fuel enough ready to burn them all....Our Savior calls the future misery of the damned Gehenna, in allusion to the valley of Hinnom....It is deep and large, sufficient to receive the world of the ungodly; the pile thereof is fire and much wood. God's wrath is the fire, and sinners make themselves fuel to it.[49]

—Matthew Henry's Commentary on the Whole Bible

Tophet—a place southeast of Jerusalem, in the Valley of Hinnom, where child sacrifices were offered and the dead bodies were burned or consumed. (Is. 30:33; Jer. 7:31–32; 19:6, 11–14; Topheth, 2 Kings 23:10).[50]

—Nelson's New Illustrated Bible Dictionary

WHERE IS HELL'S (SHEOL) LOCATION?

I believe that the current location for Sheol is down deep in the earth. The Scriptures bear this out, but commentaries do not all agree. Some say no one knows. Yet others say it is not in the earth, but perhaps another dimension. If one takes the Scriptures literally, then it becomes obvious. In reading the forty-nine verses that give the clues as to its location, I don't know how so many verses could be misunderstood. You decide for yourself. Here are a few comments from others:

> In the ancient near Eastern world in which the Bible originated, death was called "the land of no return," and was viewed as an inescapable underworld prison. The OT pictures the realm of the death (or Sheol) as being under the earth, comparing its entrance to a deep pit, (Ps. 88:4–6)....Amos makes the hyperbolic suggestion that by digging deep one might reach Sheol (Amos 9:2). The afterlife, like the pit that represents it, is pictured as dark and deep (Ps. 88:6), mucky (Ps. 40:2) and disgusting (Job 9:31).[51]
>
> *—Dictionary of Biblical Imagery*

> When the term Hades is used as the equivalent of the Hebrew Sheol, as it is in Acts 2:27–31, where Peter is quoting from Ps. 16:8–11, it refers simply to the grave...(Sheol), Place of the dead....In a number of texts persons are spoken of as descending to Sheol or of going into a pit (Ps. 88:6, 10; Amos 9:2). This likely indicates that the Hebrews saw Sheol as something beneath their feet.[52]
>
> *—Holman Illustrated Bible Dictionary*

> In Old Testament thought, the abode of the dead. Sheol is the Hebrew equivalent of the Greek *Hades*, which means "the unseen world." Sheol was regarded as an underground region, Num. 16:30; Amos 9:2, shadowy and gloomy, where disembodied souls had a conscious but dull and inactive existence

(2 Sam. 22:6; Ec. 9:10). The Hebrew people regarded Sheol as a place to which both the righteous and unrighteous go at death (Gen. 37:35; Ps. 9:17; Is. 38:10; death, NIV: Deut 32:22; the realm of death, NIV), a place where punishment is received and rewards are enjoyed....

As a deep underground place, the pit became synonymous with Sheol: the abode of the dead, the netherworld of departed spirits.[53]

—*Nelson's New Illustrated Bible Dictionary*

Sheol was below the surface of the earth (Ezek. 31:15, 17; Ps. 86:13). Hades...It is therefore the N.T. equivalent of Sheol.[54]

—*New Bible Dictionary*

Hell is in the center of the earth, "at least idiomatically."[55]

—Chuck Missler

So far as we can tell from Scripture, the present hell, Hades, is somewhere in the heart of the earth itself. It is also called "the pit" (Isa. 14:9, 15; Ezek. 32:18–21) and "The Abyss" (Rev. 9:2)....The writers certainly themselves believed hell to be real and geographically "beneath" the earth's surface.[56]

—Henry Morris

Patients who described hell said, "The place seems to be underground or within the earth in some way."[57]

—Maurice Rawlings

Another point: in regard to the rich man in Hades, in Luke 16:26, he was separated by a "great gulf fixed" from Abraham's bosom. This was not a state-of-mind condition, but it was an actual physical and geographical location. I believe that the many scriptures we listed in *23 Minutes in Hell* described the location as in the center of the earth. Some good scholars do not agree or say it is not conclusive from Scripture. I simply believe what the verses state. These are just some of those verses that mention hell's

(Sheol) location: Numbers 16:32–33; 1 Samuel 28:14–16; Job 11:8; Psalm 55:15; 63:9; 88:6; Proverbs 15:24; Isaiah 5:14; 14:9; Ezekiel 26:20; 31:14–16; 32:18–30; Amos 9:2; Matthew 12:40.

Since it mentions that Jesus spent three days and three nights in the heart of the earth (Matt. 12:40) where Abraham's bosom was most likely located, and then in 1 Sam. 28:14–16 it mentions Samuel ascending up out of the earth (Abraham's bosom, which was across from the torment side in Sheol), it is a strong possibility that scripturally, Sheol is down in the lower parts of the earth. It is not an important issue one way or the other. You can decide for yourself.

CHAPTER 20

IS THE FIRE REAL OR METAPHORICAL?

ONE OF THE MOST COMMON QUESTIONS I GET IS, IS THE FIRE IN hell real fire or allegorical? I covered that on pages 104–106 in *23 Minutes in Hell*; however, I do want to point out that I think many people make the mistake of not taking the Bible literally. In the Bible, there are many metaphors and allegories, idioms and colorful poetic language. However, where that occurs it is obvious. Other places state clearly its meaning.

I have found in my studies, that there are scholars on both sides in regard to literal fire in hell. This is not a crucial point and need not be argued. I am simply supplying some evidence that supports my opinion of literal fire. I'm sure that the fires mentioned in Scripture could also be as some of the commentaries state—fires of unfulfilled desires and lusts, mental anguish, and the burning memory of the foolish decision made in rejecting almighty God while the individual had the chance. I'm certain it will include that type of burning. But I also believe it is literal fire as well, as I've seen it with my own eyes. But the only thing of importance is what the Bible states. In John's vision and Ezekiel's vision, they saw some things that were difficult to try to explain. I'm more convinced because of Scripture, not because of my experience. I did see the flames, I felt the heat, and I saw people burning in fire. There was smoke, and that would take a literal fire to produce it.

Revelation 9:2 states that there arose a great smoke out of the pit, and "the sun and the air were darkened by reason of the smoke of the pit" (KJV). With a verse like this, it is impossible to argue the point that the fires down below are only allegorical. How could a metaphorical fire or flames of mental anguish produce real smoke? It would take a literal, burning fire to produce smoke that darkened our sky, not an allegorical or metaphorical fire. The commentaries below mention the smoke as well.

> The bottomless pit (the abyss in the Greek). This is the dwelling place of demons. When he opened the entrance to the abyss, billows of smoke poured forth, as if from a huge furnace, veiling the landscape in darkness.[1]
>
> —*Believer's Bible Commentary*

> Upon the opening of the bottomless pit there arouse a great smoke, which darkened the sun and the air....Out of this dark smoke there came a swarm of locusts.[2]
>
> —*Matthew Henry's Commentary on the Whole Bible*

Matthew 13 is another passage that indicates actual fire in hell. The *Holman Illustrated Bible Dictionary* gives a good interpretation of the passage:

> However, there is strong evidence to indicate that literal language is used and that the Bible does in fact teach literal fire and other sufferings. The parable of the tares in Matt. 13, which discusses eternal judgment, is helpful here. The Son of man, the world, children of the kingdom, the children of the wicked one, the devil, the end of the world, the angels, the gathering—all are literal figures in the parable. It is then natural to conclude that the burning of the tares should also be taken literally.[3]

The following scriptures are very clear and make it very possible to arrive at an interpretation of literal fire. They should not be easily dismissed.

Brimstone shall be scattered upon their habitation.... Surely such are the dwellings of the wicked, and this is the place of him that knoweth not God.

—Job 18:15–21, KJV

Upon the wicked he shall rain snares, fire and brimstone, and an horrible tempest.

—Psalm 11:6, KJV

You shall make them as a fiery oven in the time of Your anger; the Lord shall swallow them up in His wrath, and the fire shall devour them.

—Psalm 21:9

Let burning coals fall upon them; let them be cast into the fire, into deep pits, that they rise not up again.

—Psalm 140:10

And the streams thereof shall be turned into pitch, and the dust thereof into brimstone, and the land thereof shall become burning pitch. It shall not be quenched night nor day; the smoke thereof shall go up for ever.

—Isaiah 34:9–10, KJV

For, behold, the day cometh, that shall burn as an oven...and the day that cometh shall burn them up, saith the Lord of hosts...

—Malachi 4:1, KJV

The angels shall come forth, and sever the wicked from among the just, and shall cast them into the furnace of fire: there shall be wailing and gnashing of teeth.

—Matthew 13:49–50, KJV

And in hell he lift up his eyes, being in torments...And he cried and said, Father Abraham...send Lazarus, that he may dip the tip of his finger in water, and cool my tongue; for I am tormented in this flame. [He wanted just one drop of water to cool his tongue. Why would water suffice if it were mental anguish only?]

—Luke 16:23–24, KJV

The chaff He will burn with unquenchable fire.

—Luke 3:17

If a man abide not in me, he is cast forth as a branch, and is withered; and men gather them, and cast them into the fire, and they are burned.

—John 15:6, KJV

And he shall be tormented with fire and brimstone....And the smoke of their torment ascendeth up for ever and ever: and they have no rest day nor night.

—Revelation 14:10–11, KJV

These both [beast and false prophet] were cast alive into a lake of fire burning with brimstone.

—Revelation 19:20, KJV

And the devil that deceived them was cast into the lake of fire and brimstone, where the beast and the false prophet are, and shall be tormented day and night for ever and ever.

—Revelation 20:10, KJV

If you simply take what God said at face value and don't try and read anything into it, then literal fire seems apparent. To suggest, or even insist as some do, that all those verses are metaphorical or allegorical would require some solid evidence to validate that claim!

So many scholars state that the fire is not literal in hell. I haven't seen any scripture to support this belief. As you can see from the *Holman Illus-*

trated Bible Dictionary above, and the many verses, there is no reason to doubt the probability of real fire. The Bible mentions heaven having gates of pearl, streets of gold, and walls of precious stones; would we say that it is only metaphorical language and not to be taken literally? I think not! Most would agree that the pearly gates are literal. I believe that just as heaven is literal, so are the features of hell. What I have listed here should be enough information to be considered more than conjecture.

> Fire serves as an instrument of divine judgment. The destruction of Sodom and Gomorrah is the first example…(Gen. 19:24). Sodom and Gomorrah became a type indicating the severity of future judgment (Deut. 29:22–23; Isa. 13:19; Lam. 4:6; Luke 17:29; 2 Pet. 2:6; Jude 7). A special fire called "The fire of the Lord" consumed the outer edge of Israel's camp in the wilderness…supernatural fire fell from heaven and consumed the soldiers whom Ahaziah had sent to seize Elijah the prophet (2 Kings 1:12).[4]
>
> —*Holman Illustrated Bible Dictionary*

> Whenever the Bible writers used allegories or parables or other symbolic stories, they always either said so or else made it evident in the context.[5]
>
> —Henry Morris

> We are not under constraint to resolve how utter darkness can also have perpetually burning flames. These, I take it, are metaphors. But having said this—and here is a vital point—metaphors are used precisely in order to describe realities greater than themselves. Hell itself is not metaphorical but real; these vivid metaphors point to a reality more awful than themselves, indeed, terrible beyond mere words (hence metaphor rather than prosaic language is required).[6]
>
> —Sinclair B. Ferguson

Fire is a portrait of divine judgment, an image that features prominently in the preaching of John the Baptist (Matt. 3:10–12; 7:19; Luke 3:9,17).[7]

— *Encyclopedia of Biblical Words*

Below are a few who believe in literal fire.

Hell is a place where sinners really do burn in an everlasting fire, and not just a religious symbol designed to galvanize the faithful.[8]

—Pope Benedict XVI

Nothing is more painful and terrible to the body than to be tormented with fire; by this therefore the miseries and agonies of damned souls are represented.... They are burning forever in a fire, which not only cannot be quenched, but will never spend itself.[9]

— *Matthew Henry's Commentary on the Whole Bible*

Scripture clearly speaks of hell as a physical place of fiery torment and warns us we should fear.[10]

—Albert Mohler

There is a real fire in hell, as truly as you now have a real body; a fire exactly like that which we have on the earth.[11]

—Charles Spurgeon

Luke 3:17 also mentions fire: "But the chaff He will burn with unquenchable fire." Here's what some scholars have to say about this verse:

John refers here to Mal. 3:18; 4:1–2, "Then shall ye return, and discern between the righteous and the wicked...For behold, the day cometh that shall burn as an oven; and all the proud, yea, and all that do wickedly, shall be stubble; and the day that cometh shall burn them up, saith the Lord of hosts, that it shall leave them neither root nor branch."[12]

—*Matthew Henry's Commentary on the Whole Bible*

Think of the pain of even the smallest burn....We are not told how much of the suffering will be physical....It will be a hideous counterpart of the bush that burned with fire but was not consumed (Exod. 3:2). The wicked will burn with fire but they will not be consumed.[13]

—Edward Donnelly

Some have asked, "How could it be real fire but never consume?" Remember the burning bush? Moses saw it literally burning, but the bush wasn't consumed.

How Could I See If It Is Blackness or Darkness Forever?

Some have pointed out that in my book *23 Minutes in Hell*, I made a statement that in hell I could see through the flames and saw people burning. Some questioned that, as the Bible says hell is covered in complete darkness. In response, I do not know whether God illuminated it for me to see, when otherwise it would have been total blackness, or whether what I saw was accurate and actual in the amount of light seen from the flames. The light I did see didn't travel far beyond the sides of the big pit. The light did not spread as it would here.

A pit a mile across with that much fire would have produced a lot of light here on the earth's surface. The darkness seemed to overpower the light and consume it, as if it swallowed it up, so to speak. The darkness was so very heavy and thick that one could feel it (Exod. 10:21).

There is a verse in Job 10 that just possibly might have an explanation for this strange phenomenon. In verse 21 he mentions a land of darkness that man will go to. Verse 22 says, "A land of darkness, as darkness itself...and where the light is as darkness" (KJV). Many of the commentaries do not associate that verse with hell, but most are vague on its meaning and state that it has to do with the grave. The grave, many indicate, is called a land of darkness. Could that land of darkness include Sheol?

According to *Jamieson, Fausset, and Brown's Commentary on the Whole Bible*, "Job in a better frame has brighter thoughts of the unseen world."[14] This commentary mentions the unseen world. It may only be a possibility that the little light in Sheol is so dark it is "as darkness."

Jesus tells us in Luke 16 that the rich man could see Abraham in his bosom, across a "great gulf fixed" (v. 26). The Bible says, "...blackness of darkness forever"; "...in darkness, in the deeps"; and "mist of darkness...reserved forever" (Jude 13; Ps. 88:6, KJV; 2 Pet. 2:17, KJV). So how could he see if it was always darkness? The Bible says it was forever dark, and yet the rich man could see. Some said he could see from the light coming from Abraham's bosom. But if that was the case, why didn't the Bible say, "...blackness, except for the light produced from Abraham's bosom before the resurrection"?

Certain things cannot be explained. That is why I pointed out the properties of a black hole in our first book. A black hole does not let light escape, so it appears black. The gravitational pull is so great that even light cannot escape. Hell could be similar in the sense, or perhaps the gravity is so strong at the center of the earth that even light cannot shine forth. Or it could have been, as I said, the Lord illuminated it for me so that I could describe it, as He did in the cell. These are all possibilities to consider that make for interesting discussion. The most important thing to know, however, is that hell is real and an actual place of torment for those who do not choose to accept God.

IS GOD RESPONSIBLE FOR THE FIRES OF HELL?

Yes, He is. Some do not agree, but I believe that the following scriptures will spell that out for us clearly:

> For a fire is kindled in mine anger, and shall burn unto the lowest hell.
>
> —Deuteronomy 32:22, KJV

Upon the wicked he shall rain snares, fire and brimstone, and an horrible tempest.

—Psalm 11:6, KJV

According to *Matthew Henry's Commentary on the Whole Bible*, "The fire of God's wrath...will burn certainly and furiously to the lowest hell."[15]

Let burning coals fall upon them; let them be cast into the fire, into deep pits, that they rise not up again.

—Psalm 140:10

The pile thereof is fire and much wood: the breath of the LORD...doth kindle it.

—Isaiah 30:33, KJV

"God's wrath is the fire and the breath of the Lord (the powers of His anger) kindles it, and will keep it ever burning."[16]

Lest my fury come forth like fire, and burn that none can quench it.

—Jeremiah 4:4, KJV

Seek the LORD and live, lest He break out like a fire in the house of Joseph and devour it.

—Amos 5:6

...into everlasting fire prepared for the devil and his angels.

—Matthew 25:41

In this last verse, who did the preparing? The Lord did!

Matthew Henry's Commentary on the Whole Bible says, "The fire is the wrath of the eternal God fastening upon the guilty souls and consciences of sinners that have made themselves fuel for it...and being kindled and kept burning by the wrath of an immortal God."[17]

But the chaff He will burn with unquenchable fire.

—Luke 3:17

Other verses that talk of the wrath of God, His fury, and His fierce anger are as follows: Exodus 15:7; Deuteronomy 32:22–24; Psalm 73:27; 90:7–11; Proverbs 11:23; Job 21:30; 31:23; Isaiah 34:1–4; 66:15; Jeremiah 4:4; 25:37; Romans 1:18; 2 Thessalonians 1:9–10; Hebrews 10:27–29; 2 Peter 2:9.

The fires of hell are most likely even hotter than fire on the earth's surface. The temperature of a match is said to be 1,400 degrees, and the temperature of the lava from a volcano is said to be 2,000 degrees. Scientists say the temperature at the earth's core is approximately 12,000 degrees. It is possible that the fury of God's wrath that "shall burn unto the lowest hell" (Deut. 32:22, KJV) is far greater in intensity than any heat achieved on the earth. Revelation 14:10 says, "The same shall drink of the wine of the wrath of God, which is poured out without mixture into the cup of his indignation; and he shall be tormented with fire and brimstone in the presence of the holy angels, and in the presence of the Lamb." What is God's wrath "without mixture" or "in full strength," like some versions mention? I don't think we want to know!

The feeling that came over me when I was standing next to the large, open pit of fire was an overwhelming sense of total, catastrophic disaster and absolute devastation. I watched the news and talked to some who saw the disaster from Hurricane Katrina firsthand and the tsunami devastation. These were scenes of complete disaster. It was almost surreal, like watching the planes fly into the World Trade Center. How could anything ever be this bad? Yet, in hell, it was far, far worse than all of that.

I now have such an appreciation for just about everything, and I take nothing for granted. I truly appreciate life and all it has to offer, especially my wife. We are all truly blessed to have life and to be able to enjoy our family, friends, sleep, food, drink, and, above all, the Lord's presence. No one can really imagine what a world would be like without Him.

CHAPTER 21

WHO WERE THE "SPIRITS IN PRISON"?

WHO WERE THE "SPIRITS IN PRISON" JESUS PREACHED TO? MANY have asked the question, but I must say that there is no way to know for certain. This is not an issue of eternal importance, and the information I will give is only speculative. First Peter 3:19–20 reads, "By which also he went and preached unto the spirits in prison; which sometime were disobedient, when once the longsuffering of God waited in the days of Noah, while the ark was a preparing, wherein few, that is, eight souls were saved by water" (KJV).

I have read many of the scholars' opinions, and they do vary. There is no way to ascertain who the spirits were, as there is only this one verse in 1 Peter to go on. There seems to be three perspectives many of the commentaries take on this. They are as follows:

1. The spirits in prison were fallen angels before the Flood.

2. The spirits in prison were people who lived up to the Flood.

3. The spirits in prison were all those saved before Christ's death and resurrection.

The majority consensus is that they were the fallen angels before the Flood.

197

The fallen angels, who corrupted the generation who lived before the flood.... The spirits in prison are not the souls of dead human beings but fallen angels. According to Jewish tradition (1 Enoch 6:20), they deceived and corrupted the generation who lived before the flood, teaching them the acts of sin (Gen. 6:1–2). As a result, they were locked up in prison at the time of the flood, to be held for judgment (2 Pet. 2:4). Jesus preaching to these spirits was not an offer of salvation, but a proclamation of His final victory.[1]

—*Baker Commentary on the Bible*

Among evangelical Christians, there are two commonly accepted interpretations. According to the first, Christ went to Hades in spirit between His death and resurrection, and proclaimed the triumph of His mighty work on the cross. There is a disagreement among proponents of this view as to whether the spirits in prison were believers, unbelievers, or both. But there is fairly general agreement, that the Lord Jesus did not preach the gospel to them. That would involve doctrine of a second chance which is nowhere taught in the Bible. Those who hold this view often link this passage with Eph. 4:9 where the Lord is described as descending "into the lower parts of the earth." They cite this as added proof that He went to Hades in the disembodied state and heralded His victory at Calvary. They also cite the words of the Apostle's Creed—"descended into hell." The second interpretation is that Peter is describing what happened in the days of Noah. It was the spirit of Christ who preached through Noah to the unbelieving generation before the flood. They were not disembodied spirits at that time, but living men and women who rejected the warnings of Noah and were destroyed by the flood. So now they are spirits in the prison of Hades. This second view best fits the context and has the least difficulties connected with it.[2]

—*Believer's Bible Commentary*

The most satisfactory explanation of 1 Peter 3:19–20 seems rather to be one proposed...by Augustine: the passage refers not to something Christ did between his death and resurrection, but to what he did "in the spiritual realm of existence" (or "through the Spirit") at the time of Noah. When Noah was building the ark, Christ "in spirit" was preaching through Noah to the hostile unbelievers around him.... The people to whom Christ preached through Noah were unbelievers on the earth at the time of Noah, but Peter calls them "spirits in prison" because they are now in the prison of hell.[3]

—Wayne Grudem

Between Christ's Death and Resurrection His living spirit went to the demon spirits bound in the abyss and proclaimed that, in spite of His Death, He had triumphed over them (see notes on Col. 2:14,15). Spirits in Prison: this refers to fallen angels (demons) who were permanently bound because of heinous wickedness. The demons who are not so bound resist such a sentence (cf. Luke 8:31). In the end, they will be sent to the eternal lake of fire (Matt. 25:41; Rev. 20:10). Peter further explains that the abyss is inhabited by bound demons who have been there since the time of Noah and who were sent there because they overstepped the bounds of God's tolerance with their wickedness. See 1 Peter 3:20 where is says that they were "disobedient...in the days of Noah."[4]

—*The MacArthur Bible Commentary*

While Jesus' body was dead, His living divine spirit actually went to the abode of demons and announced His triumph over sin, Satan, death and hell.[5]

—*The MacArthur Bible Commentary*

The sin of these people, they were disobedient and rebellious. Their bodies were drowned (flood) and their spirits cast into hell, which is called a prison.[6]

—*Matthew Henry's Commentary on the Whole Bible*

Spirits in Prison—those to whom Jesus preached in connection with His death and resurrection (1 Pet. 3:19). Several interpretations have been suggested for this puzzling passage. Some believe the reference is to departed human spirits, especially those of Noah's day who heard preaching by the Spirit or by the pre-incarnate Christ through Noah. These spirits, who are disembodied, now await final judgment. Others believe the phrase refers to the spirits of the departed saints of the Old Testament to whom Christ, at His death proclaimed liberty from the bonds of death. However, the Greek word for spirits used in this verse is never applied to human spirits. It is always used to refer to supernatural beings, both good and evil (Luke 10:20; Heb. 1:14).

The most logical explanation of this passage is that Jesus made a proclamation of His victory over death to the rebellious angels who had been placed in prison. His proclamation was also a form of judgment on them because of their sin and rebellion. This idea also seems to be supported by 2 Peter 2:4 and Jude 6.[7]

—*Nelson's New Illustrated Bible Dictionary*

Nor is the phrase here "preached the gospel" (*evangelizo*), but "heralded" (*ekeruxe?*) or "preached"; but simply *made the announcement* of His finished work.[8]

—*Jamieson, Fausset, and Brown's Commentary on the Whole Bible*

What the above commentary is stating is that Jesus didn't "preach" as we think of the traditional preaching of the gospel, but rather He announced that He was victorious.

As you can see, there are differing opinions. You can draw your own conclusions.

CHAPTER 22

WHAT IS THE SIGNIFICANCE OF THE NUMBER 23?

GOING BACK TO NOVEMBER 23, 1998, IT WAS 3:00 A.M. WHEN I found myself falling and landing in a prison cell. I somehow was keenly aware of time, and I know it was three o'clock in the morning when I left our home. I then entered a different type of time than we are familiar with here. It became eternity, a time without end, a clear understanding of never ending. As to the significance of the number 23, first of all it was on the 23rd that this occurred. We didn't realize that date until later, several months later. Whenever I thought of the date, I would say the 22nd, because it was the evening of the 22nd when we came home and went to bed. When I returned from this vision, I was screaming and woke up my wife. Before leaving the bed, she looked at our digital clock, which read "3:23." I was in vision for 23 minutes, and it happened on the 23rd day of the month. It was not all that significant, and we never even thought about it. Later on, we learned these things.

In biblical numerology, the number 23 means "death." There are a couple of other things we have discovered regarding the number. Six years later, when writing the book, we went back and forth with the publisher on all the changes before the final draft was complete. We had a deadline, which we passed, and then finally finished the last manuscript. After we overnighted the manuscript with our changes to the publisher, we noticed the stamp on the receipt from the post office. It was dated the 23rd. We did not realize the date at all until afterward.

During the first year after the experience, we were asked to speak at different Bible studies and churches. After that first year, we made a list of where we had spoken, and the list had 23 places we had been that year. We thought it was interesting, but not a big deal. A couple of other small points we noticed: the first book that I started to read in the Bible when I was saved was the Book of Matthew. I really studied it for years and loved it. I noticed one day just recently, because of November 23rd, that Matthew 11:23 reads, "And thou Capernaum which are exalted unto heaven, shall be brought down to hell" (KJV).

That may just be a coincidence. And then again, my favorite book in the Bible has been Proverbs for thirty years now. I have studied it also almost every day. I then checked out Proverbs 11:23, which reads: "The expectation of the wicked is wrath." Maybe also just a coincidence! Some people have written us and pointed out that it is interesting how Psalm 23 is frequently read at funerals; again, this is connected with death. There are other reasons in the Bible why 23 refers to death. According to *Matthew Henry's Commentary on the Whole Bible*, "The courts of judgment sat in the gate of their principal cities; the judges, ordinarily, were in number twenty three; these tried, condemned, and executed murderers; so that whoever killed, was in danger of their judgment."[1] It is interesting that there were 23 involved with death.

There is another possibility with the number 23 that some have mentioned. Before the Flood in Noah's day, some scholars believed that the earth's axis was perpendicular to the sun, and not tilted. This is why there were no seasons and why all was at an even temperature around the earth. The tilt is what gives us the seasons. Some say that at the time of the Flood, the earth was then tilted on its axis to 23.45 degrees. That time is when much death occurred. It is interesting that the tilt is 23 degrees! Pastor Chuck Smith of Calvary Chapel says, "According to many physicists a polar axes shift takes place about every five thousand years....Our present polar axes is set at a twenty-three degree pitch in its relationship to the sun. This slant gives the earth its seasons....Physicists tell us that a polar axes shift creates great convulsions throughout the earth, causing mountains to disappear....It is very possible that the flood in Noah's time could have been created by the polar axes shift. It would closely correspond to the time some physicists say the last shift took place."[2] This, again, is just a possibility, but one fact is certain: that the tilt is, indeed, at 23 degrees.

You might think these are all contrived, but I didn't notice any of them until long after. This may have marginal significance, but it still spoke to us, as God throughout His Word consistently has a specific significance to numbers.

Please understand that my wife and I do not look at everyday occurrences as "signs," nor do we encourage others to do so. People can get way off by reading a hidden message into their situation through numbers or the like. We do not live that way. We are simply sharing what occurred and sharing how this spoke to us as one of God's subtle signatures. I was reluctant to put this in the book, as many may try and now look at numbers in their life and make something of them, and that is not something you need to do. And yet others will think that this is all contrived. However, so many have asked, "Why 23?" When we wrote the title, we only called it *23 Minutes in Hell* because it was just that—23 minutes of time that had passed, and that is all!

CHAPTER 23

WHO WERE THE "CAPTIVITY CAPTIVE"?

ANOTHER SCRIPTURE MANY HAVE ASKED ABOUT IS EPHESIANS 4:8–9, which states, "He led captivity captive." Who were the "captivity captive"? The bottom line is, no one knows for certain. There are basically two possible views. One view says that they were Satan, sin, and death; the other, that they were the Old Testament saints who were in Abraham's bosom. Below are some of the commentaries' explanations for each

> Christ conquered Satan and death, and in triumph returned to God those who were once sinners and prisoners of Satan.... Christ's descent... into the very pit of the demons, "the spirits in prison."[1]
>
> —*The MacArthur Bible Commentary*

> Captivity—i.e., a band of captives. In the Psalms, the captive foes of David. In the antitypical meaning, the foes of Christ the Son of David, the devil, death, the curse, and sin (Col. 2:15; 2 Pet. 2:4), led as it were in triumphal procession as a sign of the destruction of the foe.[2]
>
> —*Jamieson, Fausset, and Brown's Commentary on the Whole Bible*

Also the leading "captive" of the "captive band" ("captivity") of satanic powers, may imply that the warfare reached to *their habitation itself* (Ps. 63:9). Christ, as Lord of all, took possession first of the earth the unseen world beneath it (some conjecture that the region of the lost is in the central parts of our globe), then of heaven (Acts 2:27, 28).[3]

—*Jamieson, Fausset, and Brown's*
Commentary on the Whole Bible

"And the graves were opened: and many bodies of the saints which slept arose"—These sleeping saints (see on 1 Thes 4:14) were Old Testament believers, who, according to the usual punctuation in our version—were quickened into resurrection—life at the moment of their Lord's death, but lay in their graves till His resurrection, when they came forth....They went to glory with their Lord, as bright trophies of His victory over death.[4]

—*Jamieson, Fausset, and Brown's*
Commentary on the Whole Bible

When Christ came and fulfilled all things even as at His burial, many rose from the dead, who doubtless ascended to heaven with Him.[5]

—*Jamieson, Fausset, and Brown's*
Commentary on the Whole Bible

...a conquest over enemies, especially over such as formerly had led others captive. He conquered those who conquered us; such as sin, the devil, and death. *Into the lower parts of the earth*; this may refer either to his incarnation, according to David, Ps. 139:15, My substance was not hid from thee, when I was made in secret, and curiously wrought in the lowest parts of the earth; or, to his burial, according to that of Ps. 63:9, Those that seek my soul to destroy it shall go into the lower parts of the earth. He calls his death his descent into the lower parts of the earth... He descended into the earth in his burial. As Jonas was 3 days and 3 nights in the whale's belly, so was the Son of Man in the heart of the earth.[6]

—*Matthew Henry's Commentary on the Whole Bible*

...And the graves were opened: and many bodies of the saints which slept arose. But it is more agreeable, both to Christ's honor and theirs, to suppose, though we cannot prove, that they arose as Christ did, to die no more, and therefore ascended with Him to glory.[7]

—*Matthew Henry's Commentary on the Whole Bible*

The word is used of the Messiah in Psalm 68:18: "You have led captivity captive," speaking of the freedom Jesus would bring (Eph.4:8).[8]

—*Nelson's New Illustrated Bible Dictionary*

"He led captivity captive" (marg., "a multitude of captives") seems to be an allusion to the triumphant procession by which a victory was celebrated, the "captives" taken forming part of the procession. See Jud. 5:12. The quotation is from Ps. 68:18, and probably is in a forceful expression for Christ's victory, through His death, over the hostile powers of darkness. An alternative suggestion is that at His ascension Christ transferred the redeemed Old Testament saints from Sheol to His own presence in glory.[9]

—*Vine's Complete Expository Dictionary of Old and New Testament Words*

When anyone from the Old Testament died, they went to Hades. That is why in the Old Testament Hades is referred to as the "grave" and "hell." It was the abiding place of everyone who died, but it was divided into two sections.... When Jesus died

He descended into Hades and preached, according to Peter, to those souls in prison (1 Pet. 3:19). According to Paul, when Jesus ascended He led these captives from their captivity (Ephesians 4:8). He emptied that portion of Hades where the faithful with Abraham had waited for God to fulfill His promises.[10]

—Chuck Smith

CHAPTER 24

DEMONS AND FALLEN ANGELS—IS THERE A DIFFERENCE?

SOME HAVE ASKED, "WHAT IS THE DIFFERENCE BETWEEN DEMONS and fallen angels?" Up front I will say that from what I have studied, and from numerous commentaries, there seems to be no difference. There are no conclusive scriptures that would say one way or the other. However, after saying that, I will list some verses, commentaries' opinions, and some other biblical reference books that will indicate that there is no difference, that they are one and the same. I know some have indicated that there are differences, but the only difference some have mentioned is that demons seek to inhabit a body, and fallen angels do not because they already have a body. I am not aware of any verses that would indicate that belief and have not found any commentaries that would support the theory. Also, Satan is a fallen angel, and he can possess someone, as he did Judas. In the instances that angels appear, they usually appear and look like men. Remember the angels who came to Abraham when they were going to destroy Sodom? We know that they looked like men because of how the evil men of Sodom desired them. Scripture provides fairly conclusive evidence that they are one and the same. The verses are listed ahead. There are also many similarities in demons and fallen angels, which you will see below. You decide for yourself. I have no insight into this as a result of my experience.

The language and imagery of angels and demons exhibit many parallels. Angels come in "legions" (Matt. 26:53) and so do demons (Mark 5:9). Angels have "rulers" or "princes" (Dan. 12:1) as do demons (Eph. 2:2). The "host of heaven" may be angels (Luke 2:13) or demonic idols of the zodiac (Acts 7:42). Angels or other heavenly beings were pictured with wings (Is. 6:2), so were demons (An [evil, idolatrous] spirit oppresses you with its wings, Hos. 4:19).[1]

—Dictionary of Biblical Imagery

So the Gospels do picture demons as living beings with malignant powers. Demons are personal beings, not impersonal influences (Matt. 8:31).[2]

—Encyclopedia of Biblical Words

It seems most likely that the demons and evil spirits of the N.T. are the angels that fell with Satan.[3]

—Encyclopedia of Biblical Words

Some scholars estimate that as many as one-third of the angels cast their lot with Satan when he mysteriously rebelled against his Creator...ones who are now desperate demons....Lucifer and his angels, who turned into demons.[4]

—Billy Graham

Satan's original rebellion resulted in one-third of the angelic host joining his insurrection and becoming demons.[5]

—The MacArthur Bible Commentary

The devils, once angels in the best sense, are reserved.[6]

—Matthew Henry's Commentary on the Whole Bible

"Demons—another name for fallen angels." A symbolic view of this initial fall appears in Rev. 12:3–4 where the dragon (a symbol for Satan) "drew a third part of the stars of heaven" (a symbol for angels) and "threw them to the earth." Thus, Satan has his own angels, presumably these demons. (Matt. 25:41; Rev. 12:9).[7]

—*Nelson's New Illustrated Bible Dictionary*

The devil is prince of demons (Matt. 12:24). Demons, as described in the Bible, are the angelic host who decided to follow Lucifer, the archangel, in his insurrection against God, Luke 10:18.[8]

—Lester Sumrall

The next two scriptures give more insight into this question.

1. Luke 10:17–18 says, "Even the devils are subject unto us..." The seventy disciples said that the devils were subject unto them, and immediately Jesus said, "I beheld Satan as lightning fall from heaven" (KJV). He identified the devils with Satan. Satan is a fallen angel and the devils are associated with him. Could that mean they are one and the same?

2. Matthew 12:24–26: The Pharisees accused Jesus of casting out the devil by Beelzebub. According to the Strong's, the word *devils* is the word *daimonion*, a noun, and means "demon, (pagan) – devils."[9] Jesus said, "If Satan casts out Satan, he is divided against himself. How then will his kingdom stand?" (v. 26). Jesus drew the parallel again of "devils," or demon, with "Satan."

Another point to consider is that some say that the difference between fallen angels and demons is that demons are always looking for a body to possess. Well, in Luke 22 we find that Satan possesses Judas, and we have just identified Satan as a fallen angel. Could this also indicate that demons and fallen angels are the same?

The Bible says in Luke 22:3, "Then Satan entered Judas..." The

MacArthur Study Bible says, "Judas was possessed by Satan himself."[10] Then in John 6:70–71, Jesus said, "Have not I chosen you twelve, and one of you is a devil? He spoke of Judas Iscariot..." (KJV). Notice that it was Satan who entered Judas, and Satan is also called a devil. (See also Luke 4:6.) Revelation 12:9 also says, "...that old serpent, called the Devil, and Satan..." (KJV). We know that Satan is also a fallen angel (Luke 10:18; 2 Cor. 11:14; Rev. 12:4–8). So Satan is a fallen angel, called a devil, and can possess someone. For those who say that fallen angels do not desire to inhabit a body, then how do you explain that?

In Mark 1:13, it says that Jesus was tempted of Satan in the wilderness. Then in Luke 4:2 it says, of those same forty days in the wilderness, that Jesus was tempted of the "devil." Satan is called the devil. Luke 4:5 states, "And the devil, taking him [Jesus] up into a high mountain..." This verse uses the word *diabolos* for devil. Strong's gives this definition of that word: "a noun, the devil, Satan..." Vine's says, "Devil...is one of the names of Satan."[11]

So, it appears that demons, devils, and fallen angels are one and the same. The definition of *demon* in the *American Heritage Dictionary* is "a Devil or evil being, an unclean spirit that possesses and afflicts a person."[12] So by definition, devils and demons are the same, and a devil possessed Judas, and that devil was Satan, a fallen angel.

Vine's Complete Expository Dictionary of Old and New Testament Words states, "In the N.T. it (demon) denotes 'an evil spirit.' It is used in Matt. 8:31, mistranslated, 'devils.' Christ cast them out of human beings by His own power. His disciples did so in His name, and by exercising faith, e.g., Matt. 17:20."[13]

Matthew 8:28, 31 says, "There met him two possessed with devils....So the devils besought him, saying, If thou cast us out, suffer us to go away into the herd of swine" (KJV). These were the demons that were in the demoniac man running through the tombs. The phrase "possessed with devils" is the Greek word *daimonizomai*, a verb, and means, "to be demon possessed—possessed with devils."[14] That word *devils* in Matthew 8:31 is the Greek word *daimon*, a noun. The meaning of that word in the Greek is "demon, evil spirit—devils."[15] The two times the word *devils* is used are two different words, with two similar meanings, both meaning "devils." So we see that demons do enter and possess people, the same as devils do. Satan himself can also possess someone, as he did with Judas. Based on what the scholars have pointed out, there doesn't seem to be any difference.

CHAPTER 25

ARE SATAN AND HIS DEMONS ON THE EARTH AND IN SHEOL?

I BELIEVE SCRIPTURE INDICATES THAT SATAN AND THE DEMONS ARE ON the earth and also in Sheol. Below is a list of Scripture verses, some commentaries, and others' opinions on the subject.

> How art thou fallen from heaven, O Lucifer…cut down to the ground.…Yet thou shall be brought *down to hell*, to the *sides of the pit*.
>
> —Isaiah 14:12, 15, KJV

The word *hell* is the word *Sheol* and the word *pit* is the Hebrew word *bowr*. That is one of the three words that are most often synonymous with Sheol. (See Psalm 28:1; 30:3; 40:2; 88:4; Proverbs 1:12; Isaiah 38:18; Ezekiel 26:20; 31:14, 16; 32:18, 23–25.)

> The theme seems to expand from the fall of the king of Babylon to the fall of the one who energized him, Satan (Lucifer) himself. Ryrie writes that this is "evidently a reference to Satan…"[1]
>
> —*Believer's Bible Commentary*

Similarly, the reference to Satan having been cast out of heaven appears to be an allusion to Is. 14:3–21, where the reference is directed toward the King of Babylon but here is applied to Satan.[2]

—*Dictionary of Biblical Imagery*

Passages taken to refer to Satan (Is. 14:12–15; Ez. 28:11–19).[3]

—*Encyclopedia of Biblical Words*

Jesus' use of verse 12 to describe Satan's fall (Luke 10:18; cf. Rev. 12:8–10) has led many to see more than a reference to the king of Babylon. Just as the Lord addressed Satan in His words to the serpent (Gen. 3:14, 15), this inspired dirge speaks to the king of Babylon and to the devil who energized him. See Ezekiel 28:12–17 for similar language to the king of Tyre and Satan behind him.[4]

—*The MacArthur Bible Commentary*

This has been commonly alluded to (and it is a mere allusion) to illustrate the fall of the angels, who were as the morning stars (Job 38:7), but how have they fallen![5]

—*Matthew Henry's Commentary on the Whole Bible*

Two Old Testament passages—Isaiah 14:12–15 and Ezekiel 28:11–19—have held to furnish a picture of Satan's original condition and the reasons for his loss of that position. These passages were addressed originally to the Kings of Babylon and Tyre. But in their long-range implications, some scholars believe they refer to Satan himself.[6]

—*Nelson's New Illustrated Bible Dictionary*

How Lucifer (the daystar or the shining one) became Satan (the opposer of God) and how he fell and was cut down to the ground are revealed in verses 13 and 14.... The Church Fathers who saw Satan in this prophecy were correct, despite the denials of many modern commentators...

Instead of ascending into heaven (Matt. 11:23) his quick descent to Sheol, to the sides of the pit, is announced (v. 9) in contrast to the "sides of the North" (v. 13), an alternate designation of the underworld (Ezek. 31:15–18).[7]

—Unger's Commentary on the Old Testament

Ezekiel 28:13–17 further supports that Satan and his demons are both on the earth and in Sheol. It reads: "Thou hast been in Eden the garden of God.... Thou are the anointed cherub that covereth.... Thou wast upon the holy mountain of God.... Thou wast perfect in thy ways from the day that thou wast created, till iniquity was found in thee.... I will cast thee to the ground..." (KJV).

In regard to Ezekiel 28:11–19, the *Baker Commentary on the Bible* says, "Some commentators have suggested that verses 11–19 are indeed about Satan (Lucifer) who once walked among the angels of God but fell from paradise because of rebellion and insubordination."[8] Other commentaries agree as well.

For this reason many Bible students see in verses 11–19 a description of Satan and his fall from Heaven.... [Ezekiel] saw the work and activity of Satan, whom the king of Tyre was emulating in so many ways.[9]

—Believer's Bible Commentary

This refers to Satan.... This verse...was accurate of Satan before he sinned.... The description transitions to feature the king of Tyre, describing his demise, as he followed the pattern of Satan himself.[10]

—MacArthur Study Bible

The Prince of Tyre as a reflection of Satan...that the career of Satan is here reflected under the person of the king of Tyre is true.[11]

—*Unger's Commentary on the Old Testament*

It might be that they (demons) have access to regions below the earth's surface.[12]

—Lester Sumrall

Some have said that humans and demons are in separate areas in hell because of Jude 6 and 2 Peter 2:4. But that is a special place for only certain demons (could be the same ones in Revelation 9:2). The Scripture doesn't clearly specify of any other separate pits for the remainder of the demons. As I pointed out, in Isaiah 14:12–15, Satan was cast down to hell (which is the word *Sheol*), to the sides of the pit. If you'll notice, it uses that same verbiage in Ezekiel 32:23 regarding Egypt and Asshur (to the sides of the pit, with "pit" also being the same word *bowr*). This shows Satan and these kings, or kingdoms, in the same location. Isaiah 14:9–15 states, "Hell from beneath is moved for thee to meet thee at thy coming: it stirreth up the dead for thee, even all the chief ones of the earth; it hath raised up from their thrones all the kings of the nations. All they shall speak and say unto thee, Art thou also become weak as we? art thou become like unto us? Thy pomp is brought down to the grave [Sheol, NKJV], and the noise of thy viols: the worm [maggot, NKJV] is spread under thee, and the worms cover thee. How art thou fallen from heaven, O Lucifer, son of the morning! how art thou cut down to the ground....Yet thou shalt be brought down to hell [Sheol, NKJV] to the sides of the pit" (KJV).

Now let's look at Ezekiel 28:17: "Thine heart was lifted up because of thy beauty...I will cast thee to the ground, I will lay thee before kings, that they may behold thee" (KJV). Notice in Isaiah 14:9, it mentions "all the kings of the nations." And in Ezekiel 28:17, it mentions, "I will lay thee before kings." The commentaries agree that this is referring to Satan in both verses, and he is before kings. They both are in the same place. This also goes along with Isaiah 24:21–22. It says, "It shall come to pass in that day, that the LORD will punish on high the host of exalted ones, and on the earth, the kings of the earth. They will be gathered *together*, as prisoners gathered in the pit, and will be shut up in the prison; after many days they will be punished."

First of all, regarding "they," *John MacArthur's Study Bible* says, "Kings. In the climatic phase of the day of the Lord, He will strike against rebelling forces both angelic (Eph. 6:12) and human. 24:22 shut up in the prison. The N.T. teaches more about the imprisonment of fallen angels before their final assignment to the lake of fire (2 Pet. 2:4; Jude 6; Rev. 9:2–3, 11, 11:7, 17:8, 20:1–10). It does the same regarding unbelieving humans (Luke 16:19–31; Rev. 20:11–15)."[13]

The word *they* seems to refer to fallen angels and humans. They are shut up in the pit (*bowr*) and visited after many days (in the pit—*sheol*, until judgment day).

Some have said to me that men do not go to the pit. That is not true. Below is a partial list of verses that state he does.

1. Numbers 16:30—"...and they go down alive into the pit [*Sheol*]."

2. Numbers 16:33—"So they and all those with them went down alive into the pit [*Sheol*]."

3. Job 17:16—"They shall go down to the bars of the pit [*Sheol*]" (KJV).

4. Job 33:18—"He keepeth back his soul from the pit, and his life from perishing [*shachat*]" (KJV).

5. Psalm 28:1—"...If You are silent to me, I become like those who go down to the pit [*bowr*]."

6. Psalm 40:2—"He brought me up also out of an horrible pit [*bowr*]" (KJV).

7. Psalm 88:4—"I am counted with them that go down into the pit [*bowr*]" (KJV).

8. Psalm 88:6—"Thou hast laid me in the lowest pit [*bowr*], in darkness, in the deeps" (KJV).

9. Proverbs 1:12—"Let us swallow them up alive as the grave [*Sheol*]; and whole, as those that go down into the pit [*bowr*]" (KJV).

10. Isaiah 38:18—"They that go down into the pit cannot hope for thy truth [*bowr*]" (KJV).

I point more of this out in the chapter, "How Can Demons Torment When They Are in Torment?"

It is clear in Scripture that Sheol and the pit (several words for pit) are synonymous. Unrepented man is there, along with demons. It is a place you don't want to see. Their guests are permanent.

CHAPTER 26

DOES THE DEVIL RULE OVER HELL?

SOME SAY THAT IT IS THE DEVIL THAT HAS COMPLETE AUTHORITY in hell (Sheol). However, it is the Lord who is in control of everything. It is true that Satan has a kingdom (Matt. 12:26), and the demons are subject unto him, but it is the Lord who allows the devil to move and operate within God's orders and boundaries. According to W. E. Vine, the devil does preside over hell: "The abode of condemned souls and devils. The underworld place or state of torture and punishment for the wicked after death, presided over by Satan."[1]

> Hell is ruled by God....It is no wonder that, as the ruler of hell, God is to be revered....God rules over everything, including heaven and hell. The popular idea that hell is Satan's kingdom over which he rules is proved false by the passage we just studied (Matt. 25:41, 46)....Instead of reigning over hell, Satan will suffer the worst punishment there.[2]

Peterson states clearly that God is the one ruling over hell, not the devil. So which view is correct? There may be some differences between Satan's rule over Hades now and what takes place in the lake of fire later. No one seems to point out these possible differences. We know by the commentaries, and some Scripture verses, that Satan will then be in full torment after he is thrown into the lake of fire. He currently may not be in full torment, as some of these commentaries also point out in the next chapter. The demons say to Jesus in Matthew 8:29, "What have we to do with you, Jesus, you son of God? Have you come here to torment us *before the time*?" The verse points out that "the time" has not come yet. I believe the scripture is clear that "the time" is Revelation 20:10. So that could explain some of the verses about Satan's kingdom now and Satan's torment later.

Some have actually said that the devil is in charge of his kingdom because his kingdom has gates, which show his authority (for example, "the gates" of hell [death] referred to in Psalm 9:13, Isaiah 38:10, and Matthew 16:18). However, those are not gates indicating his authority, but rather his prison. Jesus has the keys of hell and death (Rev. 1:18). God gives the orders to Satan. God is the one who oversees hell and looks in upon it.

Revelation 14:10 states, "He shall be tormented with fire and brimstone in the presence of the holy angels *and in the presence of the Lamb*." God is also the one who assigns sinners their rightful place in hell and appoints them their due punishment.

> But rather fear Him who is able to destroy both soul and body in hell.
>
> —Matthew 10:28

> Then he shall reward every man according to his works.
>
> —Matthew 16:27, KJV

> He will cut him to pieces and *assign him a place* with the hypocrites.
>
> —Matthew 24:51, NIV

> ...will cut him in two and *appoint him his portion* with the unbelievers.
>
> —Luke 12:46

> ...of how much worse punishment...
>
> —Hebrews 10:29

They were judged, each one according to his works.

—Revelation 20:13

All liars shall have *their part* in the lake which burns with fire…

—Revelation 21:8

You can also read additional verses on this point: Job 20:29; 21:17; Psalms 86:13; 88:6; Proverbs 9:18; Zechariah 1:6; Matthew 10:15; 16:27; 23:14–15; Romans 2:5–6; 1 Peter 1:17.

The verses below show how God is the one who gives orders to the devil.

Then God sent an evil spirit….

—Judges 9:23, KJV

An evil spirit from the LORD troubled him.

—1 Samuel 16:14, KJV

The evil spirit from the LORD was upon Saul.

—1 Samuel 19:9, KJV

And there came forth a spirit, and stood before the LORD….And he said, I will go forth, and I will be a lying spirit in the mouth of all his prophets. And he [the Lord] said…Go forth, and do so.

—1 Kings 22:21–22, KJV

And the LORD said to Satan, "Behold, he is in your hand, but spare his life.

—Job 2:6

…by sending evil angels among them.

—Psalm 78:49, KJV

The LORD has mingled a perverse spirit in her midst.

—Isaiah 19:14

You can see by these verses that the Lord uses the devil as He pleases.

Matthew Henry says, "God does often, for wise and holy ends, permit the efforts of Satan's rage, and suffer him to do the mischief he would, and even by it serve his own purposes. The devils are not only Christ's captives, but his vassals."[3]

Whether the devil's kingdom includes hell or not is not clear in the Scriptures. We know Satan was thrown down into Sheol (Isa. 14:12–15; Ezek. 28:17) and onto the earth (Rev. 12:4–8). There were demons in Sheol tormenting people, and the many verses I list in the tormenting chapter indicate this, along with the many testimonies I have heard from others who state the same. I believe Satan has his part in hell, but it is God who gives all the orders and who oversees it (Rev. 14:10). As Matthew Henry pointed out above, God uses the devil for His purposes. And as I pointed out, Sheol and Gehenna are two different places, and there may be some differences. Satan will definitely be in full torment when thrown into the lake of fire. But until then, there seems to be some freedom as he torments people on the earth and is able to deceive them.

In Matthew 4:8–9 it reads, "Again, the devil taketh him up into an exceeding high mountain, and sheweth him all the kingdoms of the world, and the glory of them; and saith unto him, all these things will I give thee, if thou wilt fall down and worship me."

Notice it says that the devil offered Jesus all the kingdoms of the world. He must have had them to offer them. And Jesus didn't deny his ability to give them.

Second Corinthians 4:4 says the devil is the "god of this world." So as we can see, Satan has a kingdom, but how much rulership he has in Sheol is not clear.

The varying viewpoints on this subject could be because of the two locations of hell (Sheol and the lake of fire), which would explain why both could be correct. This is not a dogmatic position and is not a crucial point. These are questions people ask, but a definite Scriptural answer is not always possible.

CHAPTER 27

HOW CAN DEMONS TORMENT WHEN THEY ARE IN TORMENT?

SOME HAVE ASKED, "HOW COULD DEMONS TORMENT YOU WHEN THEY themselves are in torment?" I included some information on this in my first book, and some of that information will be repeated here, but with many additional verses and quotes from commentaries.

I am aware that Revelation 20:10 states, "The devil...was cast into the lake of fire...and...will be tormented day and night forever and ever." This is the verse some quote to me to back this belief that devils are in torment and cannot torment those in hell. However, that time has obviously not yet come, but takes place after the thousand years (millennium), according to the verse itself, and verse 7. We will look at many scriptures ahead that will show you that the time for the devil has not yet come. He *will* be in torment, along with his demons. But for now, he roams to and fro throughout the earth, and is also in Sheol. He may be in torment in Sheol, or partial torment, as some commentaries state.

First, can demons torment people in hell? "Where is that in the Bible?" some ask. We know through Scripture that there are demons on the earth *and* in hell (Sheol). Satan and his demons have been cast down to the earth and hell (Sheol) already (Isa. 14:12–15; Ezek. 28:17; Rev. 12:4–8). This is covered in the chapter, "Are Satan and His Demons on the Earth and in Sheol?" Let's first look at some of the verses and commentaries in regard to torment.

Matthew 18:34 says, "...delivered him to the tormentors" (KJV). Notice the next verse says, "So My heavenly Father also will do to you." The question is, Who are the tormentors?

According to *Matthew Henry's Commentary on the Whole Bible*, "Devils, the executioners of God's wrath, will be their tormentors forever."[1] John Wesley states, "His pardon was retracted, the whole debt required, and the offender *delivered to the tormentors forever.*"[2]

The word *tormentor* in the Greek is *basanistes*, which, in *Strong's Exhaustive Concordance*, means, "tormentor; a torturer."[3] It can mean, "one who elicits the truth by the use of the rack" or "an inquisitor, torturer also used as a jailer doubtless because the business of torturing was also assigned to him."

Walter Martin, in his book *The Kingdom of the Cults*, states, "The root meaning of the Greek word *basanizo* is 'to torment, to be harassed, to torture or to vex with grievous pain,' and is used throughout the New Testament to denote great conscious pain and misery, never annihilation or cessation of consciousness."[4]

Luke 12:47–48 says, "...beaten with many stripes... [or] beaten with few." In regard to this verse John Wesley states, "For the executioners of God's vengeance are at hand, and when he has once delivered you over to them, you are undone forever."[5] (See Psalm 50:22.)

Psalm 50:22 says, "Now consider this, ye that forget God, lest I tear you in pieces, and there be none to deliver" (KJV). Regarding this verse, Matthew Henry says, "Those that will not consider the warnings of God's word will certainly be torn to pieces *by the executioners.*"[6] Who are the "executioners"?

Matthew 25:41 says, "Then He will also say to those on the left hand, 'Depart from Me, you cursed, into the everlasting fire prepared for the devil and his angels.'" *Matthew Henry's Commentary on the Whole Bible* says in this regard that "if they must be doomed to such a state of endless misery, yet may they not have some good company there? No, none but the *devil and his angels*, their sworn enemies, that helped to bring them to this misery and *will triumph over them in it.* They served the devil while they lived, and therefore are justly sentenced to be where he is, as those that served closest are taken to be with him where he is. It is terrible to be in a house haunted with devils; what will it be then to be *companions with them forever*? If sinners make themselves associates with Satan by indulging in these lusts, they may thank themselves if they became sharers in that misery which was prepared for him and his associates."[7]

According to the *American Heritage Dictionary*, the definition of hell is "the abode of condemned souls and devils—The underworld place or state of *torture* and punishment for the wicked after death, *presided over by Satan*."[8]

There *will be* a piece of hell on Earth during the Great Tribulation period. In Revelation 9:2–11, it mentions that men will seek death, but death will flee, for a period of five months. That will be like hell, in that, no matter how bad off one would be, he won't be able to die. Can you imagine, say, someone who has fallen from a tall building and is crushed, but still living? Or someone who has been blown up, and can't die? Revelation 9:5–6 states, "And to them it was given that they should not kill them, but that they should be tormented five months: and their torment was as the torment of a scorpion, when he striketh a man. And in those days shall men seek death, and shall not find it; and shall desire to die, and death shall flee from them" (KJV). These demons come up from hell and torment men, and during that five-month period, men cannot die. That is just like hell: demons tormenting, just like in hell, and no death can occur, even though you would want death. Below are some of the commentaries' perspective on this verse.

> The tormented will find no relief. Even their unimaginable attempts to end their misery in suicide will be unsuccessful.[9]
> —*MacArthur Study Bible*

> These locusts were of a monstrous size and shape.... The king and commander of this hellish squadron is here described, [1.] As an angel; so he was by nature, an angel, once one of the angels of heaven.... His true name is Abbadon, Apollyon, a destroyer, for that is his business, his design, and employment, to which he diligently attends, in which he is very successful, and takes a horrid hellish pleasure.[10]
> —*Matthew Henry's Commentary on the Whole Bible*

John Bunyan, who wrote *The Pilgrim's Progress*, the most well-known book ever written, except for the Bible, was a very well-known and respected pastor and author in the mid-1600s. He also wrote another book called *Visions of Heaven and Hell*. In this book, he was escorted by an angel in a vision that he had of heaven and hell (Sheol). He saw people being tortured by demons, smelled the foul odor, heard the loud screams, saw the fire and brimstone, knew he was in the bowels of the earth, saw many terrible torments, and so on.

In the book he records the angel as saying, "The Devils are the Almighty's agents and just executioners of his deserved vengeance against sinners."[11] He also quotes the damned: "The pains we [people] suffer here are so extreme that it is impossible that they should be known by anyone but those who feel them. Excruciating pains, which *scarcely an Angel's strength could endure*."[12] John goes on to describe further torments:

> Among others, we saw one who had flaming sulfur forced down her throat by a tormenting spirit. He carried out this action with such horrid cruelty and insolence....And then the fiend tormented him afresh, which caused him to roar out so horribly....We saw a multitude of damned souls together, gnashing their teeth with extreme rage and pain, while the tormenting fiends with hellish fury poured liquid fire and brimstone continually on them.[13]

There are many pages where he described the demons tormenting people. His book is listed in the bibliography. I also possess what I believe is one of the very early copies of his book, published by Gospel Publishing House. It contains the same verbiage as the newer version published by Whitaker House.

John MacArthur even quotes Bunyan in his teaching on hell called, "Hell, the Furnace of Fire." He said, quoting Bunyan, "In hell, thou have none company but the company of damned souls with an innumerable company of devils....all those devils of hell will be with thee, howling, roaring and screaming in such a hideous manner that thou will be ever at thy wits end...and ready to run stark mad again for anguish and pain."[14]

John MacArthur goes on to say in his teaching, "One writer said, 'There is no way to describe hell. Nothing on earth can compare with it. No living person has any real idea of it. No madman in wildest flights of insanity ever beheld its horror. No man in delirium ever pictured a place so utterly terrible as this. No nightmare racing across a fevered mind ever produces a terror to match that of the mildest hell. No murder scene with splashed blood and oozing wound ever suggested a revulsion that could touch the border lands of hell. Let the most gifted writer exhaust his skill in describing this roaring cavern of unending flame, and he would not even brush in fancy the nearest edge of hell.'"[15]

> This region (Sheol) is allowed as a place of custody for souls in which *angels are appointed* or guardians to them, who distribute to them *temporary punishments*, agreeable to everyone's behavior and manners....But as to be unjust, they are dragged by force to the left hand, by the *angels allotted for punishment*...as prisoners driven by violence; to whom are sent the *angels appointed over them to reproach them and to threaten them with their terrible looks,* and to thrust them still downwards.[16]
>
> —Josephus

> The temporary spiritual bodies of these dead men and women will not be consumed in the fires of Hades, since they are not physical bodies. Nevertheless, their spirits are real (in fact a man's spirit and soul are more real than his body, and will continue to exist in this real world even after this body is dead), and will undoubtedly be subject to intense suffering. The tremendous heat and pressure of such depths will serve as a fitting environment...which will continually torment the occupants of Hades.[17]
>
> —Henry M. Morris and Martin E. Clark

Jesus said, "And whoever falls on this stone will be broken; but on whomever it falls, it will grind him to powder" (Matt. 21:44).

Christ is "a stone of stumbling and a rock of offence" to unbelievers (Is.8:14; 1Pet 2:9) The saying suggests that both enmity and apathy are wrong responses to Christ and those guilty of either are in danger of judgment.[18]

—*MacArthur Study Bible*

It will be more tolerable for the land of Sodom and Gomorrah in the day of judgment than for that city!

—Matthew 10:15

There are different degrees of punishment in that day. All the pains of hell will be intolerable, but some will be more so than others. Some sink deeper into Hell than others, and *are beaten with more stripes.*[19]

—*Matthew Henry's Commentary on the Whole Bible*

Weeping and gnashing of teeth speaks of inconsolable grief and unremitting torment. Jesus commonly uses the phrases in this verse to describe hell (cf. 13:42, 50; 24:51).[20]

—*The MacArthur Bible Commentary*

He shall be driven from light into darkness, and chased out of the world.

—Job 18:18, KJV

He is chased out of this world, hurried and dragged away by the messengers of death, sorely against his will.[21]

—*Matthew Henry's Commentary on the Whole Bible*

His soul draweth near to the grave [Sheol], and his life to the destroyers.

—Job 33:22, KJV

He says, *angels of death* commissioned by God to end man's life.[22]

—*Jamieson, Fausset, and Brown's
Commentary on the Whole Bible*

And the smoke of their torment ascends forever and ever, and they have no rest day or night.

—Revelation 14:11

The lost have no rest from sin and Satan, terror, torment and remorse.[23]

—*Jamieson, Fausset, and Brown's
Commentary on the Whole Bible*

God has not in His word represented his wrath more terrible than it really is, nay, what is felt in the other world is *infinitely worse that what is feared in this world.*[24]

—*Matthew Henry's Commentary on the Whole Bible*

It is understandable that demonic spirits would await those who enter eternity without God's forgiveness and acceptance.[25]

—Erwin Lutzer

Woe to you that desire the day of the LORD! to what end is it for you? the day of the LORD is darkness, and not light. As if a man did flee from a lion, and a bear met him…and a serpent bit him.

—Amos 5:18–19, KJV

We know that demons can torment people on the earth. *Vine's Expository Dictionary of Old and New Testament Words* states, "Acting under Satan, (cf. Rev. 16:13–14), 'demons' are permitted to afflict with bodily disease, Luke 13:16."[26]

Since they are also in hell (Sheol), why would they have to leave people alone? There are no angels to protect you, nor is God there to watch over you. God sometimes uses evil angels on the earth. Would hell be any less?

> He cast on them the fierceness of His anger, wrath, indignation, and trouble, by sending angels of destruction among them.
>
> —Psalm 78:49

> Then God sent an evil spirit...
>
> —Judges 9:23, KJV

> And there came forth a spirit, and stood before the LORD....And he said, I will go forth, and I will be a lying spirit in the mouth of all his prophets. And he [the Lord] said...Go forth, and do so.
>
> —1 Kings 22:21–22, KJV

> The LORD has mingled a perverse spirit in her midst.
>
> —Isaiah 19:14

Matthew Henry says, "God does often, for wise and holy ends, permit the efforts of Satan's rage, and suffer him to do the mischief he would, and even by it serve his own purposes. The devils are not only Christ's captives, but his vassals."[27]

Here are some verses and commentaries that state that the devil is not yet in torment, or at least full torment until after the millennium.

> Before the Millennium begins, Satan must be restrained....And the angel seized Satan and bound him for a thousand years during the millennium.[28]
>
> —*Believer's Bible Commentary*

> Being cast into the lake that was prepared for him and his angels is the *final judgment* on Satan.[29]
>
> —*Bible Knowledge Commentary*

...is followed by the binding of Satan himself for a thousand years...he is *now* to be made to feel himself the torment which he had inflicted on men, but his full torment is not *until* he is cast into the "lake of fire."[30]

—*Jamieson, Fausset, and Brown's*
Commentary on the Whole Bible

Satan and his demons were cast out of heaven at the time of their original rebellion, but still have access to it (Job 1:6, 2:1). That access will then be denied and they *will be* forever barred from heaven.[31]

—*MacArthur Study Bible*

The doom and punishment of the grand enemy, the devil, he is *now* cast into Hell.[32]

—*Matthew Henry's Commentary on the Whole Bible*

Satan *will be* consigned to hell.[33]

—*The Wiersbe Bible Commentary*

In Matthew 8:29, the demons ask Jesus, "Hast thou come hither to torment us *before the time?*"

The demons recognize Jesus as the one *destined* to destroy them.[34]

—*Baker Commentary on the Bible*

They knew who Jesus was, and that He would *finally* destroy them.[35]

—*Believer's Bible Commentary*

From the words of the demons, they believed in the existence of God and the deity of Christ, as well as the reality of *future* judgment.[36]

—*Bible Exposition Commentary*

His coming would ultimately mean doom.[37]

—*Bible Knowledge Commentary*

Themselves tormentors and destroyers of their victims, they discern in Jesus their own destined torments and destroyer anticipating and dreading what they know and feel to be awaiting them.[38]

—*Jamieson, Fausset, and Brown's*
Commentary on the Whole Bible

Judgment...great day. This refers to the final judgment when all demons and Satan are forever consigned to the "lake of fire" prepared for them (Matt 25:41; Rev. 20:10) and all the ungodly (Rev. 20:15).[39]

—*The MacArthur Bible Commentary*

The demons not only recognize the deity of Jesus, but also know that he will judge them at a divinely appointed time.[40]

—*The MacArthur Bible Commentary*

Not all demons are bound. Many roam the heavens and earth (cf Rev. 12:7–9). Some temporarily bound (see notes on Rev. 9:1–12). These were, because of their sin in Genesis 6, permanently bound in darkness, reserved for judgment. These permanently bound demons are like prisoners who are incarcerated awaiting final sentencing. Tartarus is only temporary in the sense that, in the day of judgment, the wicked angels confined there will be ultimately cast into the lake of fire (Rev. 20:10).[41]

—*The MacArthur Bible Commentary*

The last degree of torment is not till the day of judgment. The sinning angels, though in hell already, are yet reserved to the judgment of the great day.[42]

—*Matthew Henry's Commentary on the Whole Bible*

The devils, once angels in the best sense, are reserved.[43]
—*Matthew Henry's Commentary on the Whole Bible*

There is a time in which devils will be more tormented than they are, and they know it. The great assize at the *last day* is the time fixed for their complete torture...for the judgment of that day they are reserved....They will then be made close prisoners. They have now some ease; they *will then be* in torment without ease. It is their own enmity to God and man that puts them upon the rack, and torments them before the time.[44]
—*Matthew Henry's Commentary on the Whole Bible*

This is a Hebrew phrase, which signifies. Why do you concern yourself about us?...*Before the time*—The great day.[45]
—John Wesley

The fear of the demons that Christ *would* torment them "before the time" (v. 29) indicates that there is *a future judgment* for Satan and his armies.[46]
—*The Wiersbe Bible Commentary*

Many times in the Old Testament, God used the Philistines or other enemies to move against His people when they refused to listen. Psalm 106:40–41 says, "Therefore the wrath of the LORD was kindled against His people....And He gave them into the hand of the Gentiles [heathen], and those who hated them ruled over them." Now if God would permit the heathen to rule over His people on the earth, why would He not allow the devil to torment those in hell (Sheol)? The Israelites were abused and beaten by their enemies many times, and God arranged it because of their rebellion.

There have been many books written by others who have had a near-death experience, or a vision of hell (Sheol). I have listed some of the books in the bibliography. We have received many e-mails claiming that the writers too have seen devils tormenting people, and other horrifying sights. These have been consistent comments from all the other people's testimonies. Many tell us that they were afraid to mention their experience to anyone for fear of others thinking they were crazy or delusional. I can understand their concern. My point is, I am not the only one out there. There are several good books I have read of others' experiences. I cannot vouch for them, as I do not know them personally, but they do seem to be credible and legitimate. I have met some and spoken on the phone with several, and they seem to me as to have had a valid experience. Joel 2:28 mentions, "Your old men shall dream dreams, your young men shall see visions."

God's wrath is poured out full strength, or without measure, in hell (Rev. 14:10). I believe the scriptural evidence I have pointed out, along with the many commentaries' opinions stating that the devil can torment those in the current hell (Sheol), should be enough to convince anyone of the horrors of hell. I know I am so very grateful for what Jesus spared us from. God's great love for us is evident and overwhelming in the sending of His Son to die in our place and thereby keeping us out of hell. Again, it's your choice.

CHAPTER 28

WERE THE GIANTS A RESULT OF THE FALLEN ANGELS?

HERE HAVE BEEN SOME QUESTIONS REGARDING THE SIZE OF THE demons being twelve or thirteen feet tall in connection with the giants mentioned in Genesis 6:4. I briefly wrote of this on pages 125–126 in *23 Minutes in Hell*. The commentaries' remarks will hopefully further explain my comments and give a clearer biblical understanding.

I believe the giants were a direct result of the fallen angels having relations with women. The majority of commentaries agree. Some think they were a result of demons entering men, who then had relations with women. Others believe that it was the Sethites having intermarriage with the daughters of Cain. Among the three views, there is no conclusive answer. I have included some of the readings that helped me come to my conclusion. I hope they can shed some light on this question.

Many don't like to address these issues, as they are controversial. I think it is a good exercise in Scripture and has no harm in outlining the varying opinions.

> The term "sons of God" elsewhere in the Old Testament designates angels (see Job 1:6; 38:7; Ps. 29:1; 89:7)...the sons of God may be the Sethites...Whatever the correct interpretation, the union is illicit.[1]
>
> —*Baker Commentary on the Bible*

The next example is that of the fallen angels. Some take this as a reference to the "sons of God" (Gen. 6:1–7) who married the daughters of men.[2]

—Baker Commentary on the Bible

There are two principal interpretations of verse 2. One is that *the sons of God* were angels who left their proper sphere (Jude 6) and intermarried with women on earth, a form of sexual disorder that was most hateful to God. Those that hold this view point out that the expression "sons of God" in Job 1:6 and 2:1 means angels who had access to the presence of God. Also, "the sons of God" as a term for angels is a standard Semitic expression. The passage in Jude 6, 7 suggests that the angels who left their own abode were guilty of vile, sexual behavior. Notice the words "as Sodom and Gomorrah" at the beginning of verse 7, immediately after the description of the fallen angels. The main objective to this view is that angels don't reproduce sexually, as far as we know. Matthew 22:30 is used to prove that Jesus taught that the angels don't marry. What the verse actually says, however, is that the angels in heaven neither marry nor are given in marriage. Angels appeared in human form to Abraham (Gen. 18:1–5), and it seems from the text that the two who went to Sodom had human parts and emotions.

The other view is that the sons of God were the godly descendants of Seth, and the daughters of men were the wicked posterity of Cain. The argument is as follows: The preceding context deals with the descendants of Cain (chap. 4) and the descendants of Seth (chap 5). Genesis 6:1–4 describes the intermarriage of these two lines. The word *angels* is not found in the context. Verses 3 and 5 speak of the wickedness of man. If it was the angels who sinned, why was the race of man to be destroyed? Godly men are called "sons of God," though not in exactly the same Hebrew wording as in Genesis 6:2 (see Deut. 14:1; Ps. 82:6; Hos. 1:10; Matt. 5:9).

There are several problems with this view. Why were all the Sethite men godly and all the women of Cain's lineage ungodly? Also, there is no indication that Seth's line stayed godly. If they did, why should they be destroyed? Also, why should such a union between godly men and ungodly women produce giants?[3] 6:4–5 regarding the giants (Heb. Nephilim, "fallen ones") Unger explains the Nephilim are considered by many as giants, demi-gods, the unnatural offspring of "the daughters of men" (mortal women) in cohabitation with the "sons of God" (angels). This utterly unnatural union, violating God's created orders of being, was such a shocking abnormality as to necessitate the worldwide judgment of the Flood.[4]

—Believer's Bible Commentary

Angels are called sons of God in Job 1:6; 2:1. The inference in Gen. 6 is that these sons of God left the angelic position assigned to them, exchanged their dwellings in Heaven for one of the earth, and intermarried with human wives. The children born to them were Nephilim, which means "fallen ones," (Gen 6:4). It seems clear from Gen. 6:3 that God was extremely displeased with these abnormal sexual unions.

Against this view it is generally argued that angels are sexless and therefore cannot marry. But the Bible does not say this. All it says is that *in Heaven* they do not marry (Mark 12:25). Angels often appear in human form in the O.T. For example, the two angels whom Lot entertained in Sodom (Gen. 19:1) are described as men in verses 5, 10, 12. They had feet (v. 2) and hands (v. 10); they could eat (v. 3); they had physical strength (vv. 10, 16). It is obvious from the perverted desires of the men of Sodom that these angels had bodies that were capable of sexual abuse (v. 5).[5]

—Believer's Bible Commentary

They were giants...with their great bulk...with their great name...These made them the terror of the mighty in the land of the living.[6]

—*Matthew Henry's Commentary on the Whole Bible*

The reference underscores the huge size of Og.[7]

—*Baker Commentary on the Bible*

There is no Bible statement that angels are sexless....The Bible does not say that angels do not marry but only that in Heaven they neither marry nor given in marriage (Matt. 22:30).[8]

—*Believer's Bible Commentary*

Og is remembered as a giant, with a huge iron bedstead that was 9 cubits long and 4 cubits wide (about 13 or 14 feet by 6 feet).[9]

—*Believer's Bible Commentary*

The sons of God (Gen. 6:2) were the fallen angels (cf. Job 1:6) who somehow had impregnated human women and fathered the Nephilim? (giants, as it says in the New KJV.)[10]

—*Bible Teacher's Commentary*

Taking the cubit at half a yard, the bedstead of Og would measure 13½ feet, so that as beds are usually a little longer than the person who occupy them, the stature of the Amorite king may be estimated at about 11 or 12 feet.[11]

—*Jamieson, Fausset, and Brown's*
Commentary on the Whole Bible

The angelic host (cf. 38:7; Ps. 29:1; 89:7; Dan. 3:25) came to God's throne to render account of their ministry throughout the earth and Heaven (cf. 1 Kings 22:19–22). Like Judas among the apostles, Satan was with the angels.[12]

—*The MacArthur Bible Commentary*

The size of the bedstead, 13½ by 6 feet, emphasized the largeness of Og, who was a giant (the last of the Nephaim, a race of giants).[13]

—*The MacArthur Bible Commentary*

The angels attended God's throne and Satan among them.[14]

—*Matthew Henry's Commentary on the Whole Bible*

When the morning stars sang together, the blessed angels...they were the sons of God, who shouted for joy.[15]

—*Matthew Henry's Commentary on the Whole Bible*

Og...very strong, for he was of the remnant of the giants (v.11); his personal strength was extraordinary...he was three yards and a half high, double the stature of an ordinary man.[16]

—*Matthew Henry's Commentary on the Whole Bible*

This was the commingling of "divine beings" (lit., "sons of God," which inescapably denote "angels" Job 1:6; 2:1) with "daughters of men," "Here...the main stress is on 'immortals' as opposed to 'mortals'" (Speiser, AB, p.44). Scholarly efforts to make "sons of God" pious Sethites and "the daughters of men" ungodly Cainites simply do not come to grips with the difficulties of the passage.... It was far more serious than mixed marriages between believers and unbelievers. It was a catastrophic outburst of occultism.

The Nephilim "fallen ones," were the spirit-human angelic-demon offspring of the sons of God (angels) and daughters of men (human females)....The thought is of spirit beings (fallen angels, demonic powers) cohabiting with women of the human race producing what later became known in pagan mythologies as demigods, partly human and partly superhuman. This is not mythology but the truth of the intermixture of the human race with the angelic creation from which later mythology developed "The Titans," (giants, partly superhuman). The sons of

HELL

God came into the daughters of men. This means it was when the angelic beings had united with human daughters that the Nephilim appeared on earth.[17]

...The stars are figuratively said to sing God's praises (Psalms 19:1; 148:3) and here, in lofty poetry, are symbolic of the angels, answering to the sons of God or angels in the parallelism of this verse.[18]

—Unger's Commentary on the Old Testament

This passage indicates that there is a special part of Hell in which God imprisoned those fallen angels who chose to defile mankind in the ancient past before the Flood by having illicit sexual relations with the women of the earth (Genesis 6:1–5). Their great sin was the violation of God's prohibition by breaking the physical barrier between angels and mankind through forbidden illicit sexual relations. The book of Jude reveals the nature of these fallen angels' sins at the dawn of man's existence on the earth.[19]

—Grant Jeffrey

Dr. Chuck Missler also teaches that the sons of God of Genesis 6 are the fallen angels. This is in his series called "The Nephilim." He is considered one of the most credible, detailed, and scholarly teachers in our world today. He investigates all sides and does exhaustive reading on a subject. His ministry is called Koinonia House, at www.khouse.org.

Jude 6–7 states, "The angels who did not keep their proper domain, but left their own abode...as Sodom and Gomorrah...having given themselves over to sexual immorality and gone after strange flesh, are set forth as an example, suffering the vengeance of eternal fire." This passage compares Sodom and Gomorrah, as they went after strange flesh (men with men—an unnatural mix as in Romans 1), and the fallen angels, going after strange flesh (angels with women—not natural). The comparing of the two gives clarity that it was angels, and not just men and women commingling.

In my opinion, it seems clear from many of the commentaries and the Scripture, most importantly, that the fallen angels were the "sons of God" and did produce "giants in the earth." Whether the giants were a result of the actual fallen angels having relations with women, or whether the fallen angels entered men and they had the relations with women, cannot be determined for certain.

It doesn't matter one way or the other. You decide for yourself.

CHAPTER 29

WAS IT REALLY SAMUEL?

R EGARDING 1 SAMUEL 28:14, SOME HAVE ASKED, "WAS IT SAMUEL, or was it a demon?"

We will look at some of the most reputable commentaries and also some of the great leaders in the Christian faith. To answer this question up front, I believe that it was actually Samuel. I believe Scripture makes it clear by at least four points in the chapter. You read them and decide for yourself.

> In the instance it is possible that God allowed the communication from the departed Samuel to be more extensive than usual, for Saul was the King and a national crises had arisen.[1]
>
> —*Baker Commentary on the Bible*

> Commentators are disagreed as to what actually happened next. Some feel that an evil spirit impersonated Samuel, while others believe that God interrupted the séance unexpectedly by allowing the real Samuel to appear. The latter is preferred for the following reasons: The medium was startled by the sudden appearance of Samuel in place of the familiar spirits with whom she was used to dealing. Also, the text specifies that it was Samuel. Finally, the spirit prophesied accurately what would happen the following day.[2]
>
> —*Believer's Bible Commentary*

On the other hand, many eminent writers (considering that the apparition came before her arts were put in practice; that she herself was surprised and alarmed; that the prediction of Saul's own death and the defeat of his forces was confidently made), are of opinion that Samuel really appeared.[3]

—*Jamieson, Fausset, and Brown's*
Commentary on the Whole Bible

Though questions have arisen as to the nature of Samuel's appearance, the text clearly indicates that Samuel, not an apparition, was evident to the eyes of the medium. God miraculously permitted the actual spirit of Samuel to speak (vv 16–19). Because she understood her inability to raise the dead in this manner, she immediately knew (1) that it must have been by the power of God and (2) that her disguised inquirer must be Saul.[4]

—*The MacArthur Bible Commentary*

It seems best to follow the early view that this was a genuine appearance of Samuel which God Himself brought about. Several points favor this interpretation: (1) The medium was surprised (v. 12). (2) Saul identified the figure as Samuel (v. 14). (3) The message Samuel spoke was clearly from God (vv. 16–19). (4) The text says that the figure was Samuel (vv. 12, 15, 16). There is no inherent difficulty with God bringing back the spirit of Samuel from heaven and allowing him to appear to Saul, in spite of the women's evil profession.[5]

—*Nelson's New Illustrated Bible Commentary*

The sudden and totally unexpected appearance of the spirit of Samuel. Transfixed with terror, the woman screamed out with shock as she perceived that God had stepped in. By God's power and special permission, Samuel's actual spirit was presented to pronounce final doom upon Saul. Ecclesiasticus 46:20 agrees on Samuel's actual appearance: "After death he [Samuel] prophesied and showed the king his latter end." The medium's terrified conduct at the appearance of a real spirit of a deceased person constitutes a complete scriptural disclosure of the fraudulency of all spiritistic mediumship.... The women's divining demon had nothing whatsoever to do with Samuel's sudden appearance. She and her spirit accomplice were completely side-tracked. God stepped in and brought up Samuel, who pronounced doom upon Saul. Samuel's pointed and stinging rebuke to Saul is added evidence that his spirit had actually appeared and that it was not an impersonating demon.

When Samuel said, "Tomorrow shalt thou and thy sons be with me," it meant that at the time of their death Saul and his sons would go to be where Samuel was, that is, to the paradise section of Hades, where all the spirits of the righteous dead went in Old Testament times (Luke 16:19–31).[6]

—*Unger's Commentary on the Old Testament*

...but when is faced with such concrete Old Testament instances as Samuel's appearance to Saul (1 Sam. 28:18–19)...[7]

—Walter Martin

Again, to reemphasize, since the scripture says, "And Samuel said to Saul" (1 Sam. 28:15), it says it was Samuel. If it was a demon spirit it would have said, and "evil spirit," or, a "familiar spirit."

Also, since Samuel foretold the events of the very next day with accuracy, a demon spirit wouldn't have known, and only God knows the future.

I would conclude, it was the real Samuel.

CHAPTER 30

WHAT IS SOUL SLEEP?

HERE ARE THOSE WHO BELIEVE IN SOUL SLEEP AFTER DEATH. THIS is not in the Scriptures, and the most reputable commentaries, great leaders of the past and present, and churches clearly do not support soul sleep. I will list comments and scriptures that clearly refute this belief.

So what is soul sleep? According to Dr. Erwin W. Lutzer, it's "...the belief that no one is conscious at death because the soul sleeps until the resurrection of the body. Although this view has had some able defenders, it suffers from the difficulty of having to reinterpret many clear passages of Scripture in order to make this doctrine fit."[1]

There are several verses that those who support soul sleep quote, but quote mistakenly. The first verse is:

> Then also those who have *fallen asleep* in Christ have perished.
> —1 Corinthians 15:18

> As for those who had died believing *in Christ*, their case would be absolutely hopeless. If Christ did not rise, then their faith was just a worthless thing. The expression fallen asleep refers to the bodies of believers. Sleep is never used of the soul in the N.T. The soul of the believer departs to be with Christ at the time of death, while the body is spoken of as sleeping in the grave.[2]
> —*Believer's Bible Commentary*

If Jesus was raised, how can some say, "There is no resurrection of the dead"? If there is no resurrection, then Christ could not have been raised, and in that case "your faith is futile; you are still in your sins."[3]

—*Bible Teacher's Commentary*

…a common euphemism for death. This is not soul sleep, in which the body dies and the soul, or spirit, supposedly rests in unconsciousness.[4]

—*The MacArthur Bible Commentary*

The term *sleep* is always applied to the body, since in death the body takes on the appearance of one who is asleep, but the term *soul sleep* or the *sleep of the soul* is never found in Scripture, and nowhere does it state that the soul ever sleeps or passes into a state of unconsciousness.[5]

—Walter Martin

John 11:11–14 is another verse some use to support the idea of soul sleep, but again it is used mistakenly. The passage reads, "Our friend Lazarus sleepeth; but I go, that I may awake him out of sleep. Then said his disciples, Lord, if he sleep, he shall do well. Howbeit Jesus spake of his *death*: but they thought that he had spoken *of taking a rest* in sleep. Then Jesus said unto them plainly, Lazarus is *dead*" (KJV). It is obvious when Jesus used the word *sleep* He meant "dead."

It should be noticed that in the N.T. sleep is never applied to the soul but only to the body. There is no teaching in the Scripture that at the time of death, the soul is in the state of sleep. Rather, the believer's soul goes to be with Christ.[6]

—*Believer's Bible Commentary*

Sleep is the death of the saints in the language of heaven. The symbol of sleep for death is common to all languages.[7]

—Jamieson, Fausset, and Brown's
Commentary on the Whole Bible

The death of Lazarus was in a peculiar sense a sleep,...because he was to be raised again speedily; and why should not the believing hope of that resurrection to eternal life make it as easy to us to put off the body and die as it is to put off our clothes and go to sleep...he rests from the labors of the day past and is refreshing himself for the next morning. Death has the advantage as sleep. The *soul does not sleep but becomes more active*; but the body sleeps without any toss, without any terror; not distempered nor disturbed. The grave to the wicked is a prison...but to the godly it is a bed, and all its bands as the soft and downy fetters of an easy quiet sleep.[8]

—Matthew Henry's Commentary on the Whole Bible

This next verse supporters of soul sleep quote is Ecclesiastes 9:5, which says, "The dead know nothing." Those who believe in soul sleep state that, when you are dead, you don't know anything because you are asleep.

Seizing upon such texts as Ecclesiastes 9:5–6, 10; Ps. 13:3; Daniel 12:2, etc., the Witnesses loudly contend that until the resurrection, the dead remain unconscious and inactive in the grave, thus doing away in one fell swoop with the doctrine of hell and the true biblical teaching regarding the soul of man.... The simplest refutation of Jehovah's Witnesses' perverted terms such as death can be found in the scriptures themselves, where it easily can be shown that death does not mean "termination of existence" and "utter cessation of conscious intellectual...activity" as the *Watchtower* desperately attempts to establish. The interested reader is referred to the following references: Ephesians 2:1–5; John 11:26; Philippians 1:21, 23 and Romans 8:10. The usage of "death" in these passages clearly indicates a state of existence solely in opposition to the definition that the *Watchtower* assigns to the word *death,* and the reader need only substitute the *Watchtower's* definition in each one of these previously enumerated passages to see how utterly absurd it is to believe that the body has experienced "the loss of life" or "termination of existence" in such a context where Paul writes, "If Christ be in you, the body is dead because of sin" (Romans 8:10). The inspired apostle here obviously refers to a spiritual condition of separation—certainly not to "termination of existence," as the *Watchtower's* definition states. We see, therefore, that death is a separation of the soul and spirit from the body, resulting in physical inactivity and a general appearance of sleep; however, in the spiritual sense death is the separation of the soul and spirit from God as the result of sin, and in no sense of the term can it ever be honestly translated "unconsciousness" or "termination of existence" as Jehovah's Witnesses would like to have it.[9]

—Walter Martin

This verse is constantly used by false teachers to prove that the soul sleeps in death, that consciousness ceases when the last breath is taken. But it is senseless....Once a person has died, there is no more love, hatred, envy, or any other human emotion. Never again will he have a share in any of this world's activities and experiences.[10]

—Believer's Bible Commentary

The dead know they are dead, and it is too late. When life is gone, all this world is gone with it, as to us. It does not appear that they know anything of what is done by those they left behind. Abraham is ignorant of us; they are removed into darkness—Job 10:22.[11]

—Matthew Henry's Commentary on the Whole Bible

...dead know not anything—i.e., so far as their bodily senses and worldly affairs are concerned (Job 14:21; Is. 63:16).[12]

—Jamieson, Fausset, and Brown's
Commentary on the Whole Bible

But the dead (insofar as life in this world is concerned) *know not anything* (Job 14:2; Psalms 6:5; 88:10–11). Death terminates all enjoyments in this world.[13]

—Unger's Commentary on the Old Testament

Below is a list of men who were not sleeping after they died. Since these were not, then it stands to reason that no one else will be sleeping either.

- *1 Samuel 28:13–15*: When the witch of Endor brought up Samuel, he talked to Saul. He was not sleeping. Samuel said to Saul, "Why have you disturbed me?" He didn't say, "Why have you awakened me?" Most commentaries believe it was actually Samuel and not an evil spirit.

- *Isaiah 14:9–10*: "Hell from beneath is moved for thee to meet thee at thy coming....All they shall speak and say unto thee, Art thou also become weak as we?" (KJV). How can one "say" if they're asleep, or how can they "meet thee" if they are asleep? "They that see thee shall narrowly look upon thee, and consider thee, saying, Is this the man..." (v. 16, KJV). How can one look upon someone who is sleeping and "say"?

- *Ezekiel 32:21–27*: "The strong among the mighty shall *speak* to him out of the midst of *hell* with them that help him. [How can they *speak* if sleeping?]...Yet have they borne their shame with them that go down to the pit. [How could one bare shame if he is sleeping?]...He is put in the midst of them [Are they all sleeping?]...which are gone down to hell...and they have laid their swords under their heads, but their iniquities shall be upon their bones [All just sleeping?]" (KJV).

- *Jonah 2:2*: "Out of the belly of Sheol I *cried*." Many commentaries (Tyndale, New International) believe he was in Sheol. How could he "cry" out if he was sleeping?

- *Matthew 17:3*: Moses and Elijah appeared to Jesus and *talked* with Him, and the disciples saw them. (Moses and Elijah talked—they were not asleep.)

- *Luke 16:22–30*: Abraham talking to the rich man in Sheol. The rich man said many things, one being, "For I am tormented in this flame" (v. 24). (Doesn't sound like he's getting his beauty sleep!)

- *Luke 23:43*: Jesus told the thief on the cross he would be with Him today in Paradise. Jesus wasn't going down there to sleep. He preached to the spirits in prison (1 Pet. 3:19), and He led captivity captive (Eph. 4:8).

- *Revelation 5:5*: John *talks* to an elder in heaven; the elder was not sleeping.

- *Acts 7:59*: When Stephen was about to die, he did not ask the grave to receive him, but he said, "Lord Jesus, receive my spirit."

- *Philippians 1:23*: "...to depart and to be with Christ." Paul expected to be with Christ.

As for this expression of "falling asleep," Dr. Erwin W. Lutzer states in his book *One Minute After You Die*, "For those who die in the Lord need not fear the unknown, for they fall asleep to awaken in the arms of God."[14]

That which survives of the deceased is not simply the spiritual component of the human being, but a shadowy image of the whole person, complete with head and skeleton. The inhabitants of Sheol are not asleep, but fully conscious. They are not only aware of one another and their relative positions; they also know that their conduct during their tenure in the "land of the living" has determined their respective positions in Sheol. This description agrees with Israelite burial practices, which suggest that the tomb was not considered the permanent resting place of the deceased. While the physical flesh decomposed, the person was thought to descend to the vast subterranean mausoleum in which the dead continued to live in a remarkably real sense as living corpses.[15]

—Daniel Block

The souls of OT saints are already with the Lord.[16]

—*The MacArthur Bible Commentary*

Those who support soul sleep also claim that the verses below show that you are dead until the resurrection day. This also is completely false.

Colossians 2:20 says, "If ye be *dead* with Christ from the rudiments of the world…" (KJV). This verse "refers to the believer's union with Christ in His death and resurrection (Rom. 6:1–11) by which he has been transformed to new life from all worldly folly."[17]

In referring to Ephesians 2:4–5, "…even when we were dead in sins" (KJV), the *MacArthur Bible Commentary* says, "A spiritually dead person needs to be made alive by God. This verse is not talking about being dead as, 'cease to exist' or as 'soul sleep in Sheol' as some say. It is talking about the need of sinners to be made alive in Christ.[18]

Another euphemism is found in Luke 15:32: "For this thy brother was dead, and is alive again; and was lost, and is found." The brother was not actually dead, but was lost, or had gone astray. Yet the term "dead" was used to describe his "lost state."

A third euphemism would be in Psalm 44:23, where God is spoken of as "sleeping." "Awake, why sleepest thou, O Lord? Arise, cast us not off forever." Psalm 95, Isaiah 51:9, and Isaiah 52:1 state the same. We know that the Lord does not sleep, as it says in Psalm 121:4: "He that keepeth Israel shall neither slumber nor sleep." This is a form of expression, or an idiom. Sleep was simply an expression for the body, not the soul, after death.

It is also seen that there is no "sleep of the soul." The body may sleep, but consciousness exists after death.[19]

—Charles R. Erdman

In the Bible, sleep is a common metaphor for death.[20]

—*Nelson's New Illustrated Bible Dictionary*

If death is viewed as sleep, we need to interpret this not as "soul sleep" in Sheol, as understood by Seventh-Day Adventists, but that the state of dying is a falling asleep to awake in another world.[21]

—Daniel I. Block

This view of soul sleep should easily be seen as false, even with the limited information I have provided. There are many scholarly books on the subject with much more conclusive proof as to the falsity of this belief. Hopefully there are enough facts here to settle this issue.

CHAPTER 31

DO PEOPLE IN HELL "CEASE TO EXIST"?— ANNIHILATIONISM

THERE IS A GROWING NUMBER OF CHRISTIANS WHO BELIEVE IN annihilationism. This teaching has come about because many people cannot accept the fact that God would allow a person to suffer in hell for all eternity. However, eternal punishment is taught by Jesus, Paul, and the apostles all throughout the New Testament. W. G. T. Shedd said, "The strongest support of the doctrine of Endless Punishment is the teaching of Christ."[1]

Christopher W. Morgan writes, "Annihilationism is the belief that those who die apart from saving faith in Jesus Christ will be ultimately destroyed. Thus, annihilationists reject the historic view of hell as conscious, endless punishment." He also stated that the words "from John Stott ignited the worldwide debate about hell in contemporary evangelism. Stott's reputation as an evangelical statesmen brought instant credibility to this nontraditional view called *annihilationism* (sometimes known as *conditionalism*)." Morgan continues with the words from John Stott: "Well, emotionally I find the concept [i.e., the historic view of an endless hell] intolerable and do not understand how people can live with it without either cauterizing their feelings or cracking under the strain.... We need to survey the biblical material afresh and to open our minds (not just our hearts) to the possibility that Scripture points in the direction of annihilationism, and that 'eternal conscious torment' is a tradition which has to yield to the supreme authority of Scripture." Morgan goes on to say, "Annihilationism is not new. Its advocates existed in the patristic, post-Reformation, and modern periods."[2]

Randy Alcorn says, "A growing number of Christians are embracing Annihilationism which postulates that unbelievers don't exist forever in hell as believers live forever in heaven."[3]

There have been several influential people who were Christian leaders and were proponents of annihilationism. Dr. R. Albert Mohler Jr. said, "John Wesham, vice principal of Tyndale Hall, Bristol, and a well-known figure among British evangelicals said...'unending torment speaks to me of sadism, not justice. It is a doctrine which I do not know how to preach without negating the loveliness and glory of God.'"[4] Mohler goes on to mention another proponent: "John Stott constructed an argument for annihilationism....By the mid-1980s, the number of evangelicals promoting annihilationism had reached the point that Anglican evangelical Peter Toon reflected, 'In conservative circles there is a seeming reluctance to espouse publicly a doctrine of hell, and where it is held there is a seeming tendency toward a doctrine of hell or annihilationism.'...Such erosion was evident in 1995 when the Church of England Doctrine Commission released *Mystery of Salvation*, an official report commended by the House of Bishops. The report embraced a hope for universal salvation, arguing that it is incompatible with the essential Christian affirmation that God is love to say that God brings millions into the world to damn them."[5]

Dr. Albert Mohler Jr. writes, "In an article published in 1990, [Clark] Pinnock rejected the traditional doctrine of hell as a monstrous concept: "I consider the concept of hell as endless torment in body and mind an outrageous doctrine...and needs to be changed."[6]

Robert W. Yarbrough says, "Edward W. Fudge has become well-known as a leading advocate of the view that when the wicked die, their punishment is 'eternal' in the sense that its consequences last forever, not in the sense that the wicked experience unending torment. This view is called conditional immorality, conditionalism, or annihilationism." Fudge said, "The fact is that the Bible does not teach the traditional view of final punishment....It never says the damned will writhe in ceaseless torment.... The idea of conscious everlasting torment was a grievous mistake."[7]

If someone believes in annihilationism, they would then dismiss the eternal suffering of hell, which would lessen the fear of the Lord and the final judgment. After all, what's the big concern if you simply "cease to exist"? I would like to hear the answer of the annihilationist as to why they think Jesus died. What did Jesus save us from, if there is no hell to suffer? Why did He go through all that pain and suffering if those who reject Him don't exist after death?

> When John the Baptist warned people to "flee from the wrath" (Matt. 3:7)—arguably the first message of the New Testament, and eternal punishment was exactly what he meant—his warning made sense. I doubt people would run from coming wrath with much concern if they knew in advance it meant only annihilation.[8]
>
> —R. T. Kendall

DEBUNKING ANNIHILATIONISM

I would like to look at the next six verses that the annihilationists believe support their view. However, it is just the opposite. Nothing could be further from the truth. The verses they believe support their claims are actually some of the strongest verses to refute this belief of annihilationism.

1. MATTHEW 25:46

This is actually one of the clearest verses in the Bible. Jesus talks about the wicked in "everlasting punishment" and "the righteous into eternal life." The same identical word is used for both *everlasting* and *eternal*. The word in the Greek is *aionios*.[9] If eternal life does, in fact, last forever, then it stands to reason that hell also would last forever, since Jesus used it as a comparison.

> The Lord Jesus spoke of eternal (same word as "everlasting") fire (v. 41), eternal punishment (v. 46), and eternal life (v. 46). The same one who taught eternal life taught eternal punishment.

Since the same word for eternal is used to describe each, it is inconsistent to accept one without the other. If the word translated *eternal* does not mean everlasting, there is no word in the Greek language to convey the meaning. But we know that it does mean *everlasting* because it is used to describe the eternality of God (1 Tim. 1:17).[10]

—Believer's Bible Commentary

The word [*everlasting*] in both clauses, being in the original the same, should have been the same in the translation also. Thus the decision of this awful day will be final, irreversible, unending.[11]

—Jamieson, Fausset, and Brown's
Commentary on the Whole Bible

The same Greek word is used in both instances. The punishment of the wicked is as never ending as the bliss of the righteous. The wicked are not given a second chance, nor are they annihilated. The punishment of the wicked dead is described throughout scripture as "everlasting fire" (v. 41); "unquenchable fire" (3:12); "shame and everlasting contempt" (Dan. 12:2); a place where "their worm does not die, and the fire is not quenched" (Mark 9:44–49); a place of "torments" and "flame" (Luke 16:23, 24); "everlasting destruction" (2 Thes. 1:9); a place of torment with "fire and brimstone" where "the smoke of their torment ascends forever and ever" (Rev. 14:10–11); and a "lake of fire and brimstone" where the wicked are tormented day and night forever and ever" (Rev. 20:10). Here Jesus indicates that the punishment itself is everlasting—not merely the smoke and flames. The wicked are forever subjected to the fury and wrath of God. They consciously suffer.[12]

—The MacArthur Bible Commentary

Matthew 25:46 is one of the two most explicit New Testament texts affirming permanent penal pain for some after death. Quick's other passage is Revelation 20:10–15.[13]

—O. C. Quick

The same word for *eternal* that is used in Matthew 25:46 is also used in these next verses. If eternal doesn't mean eternal, then these verses wouldn't either. If hell was not eternal, then the "King" would not be eternal, and the "Spirit," and so on. We know that is not the case. All are eternal.

...the blood of Christ, who through the *eternal* Spirit offered Himself without spot to God.

—Hebrews 9:14

What shall I do to inherit *eternal* life?

—Luke 18:18

...*eternal* salvation...

—Hebrews 5:9

...to the King *eternal*...

—1 Timothy 1:17

...*eternal* in the heavens.

—2 Corinthians 5:1

...things which are not seen are *eternal*.

—2 Corinthians 4:18

God...who called us to His *eternal* glory by Christ Jesus...

—1 Peter 5:10

...hath never forgiveness, but is in danger of *eternal* damnation.

—Mark 3:29, KJV

...*eternal* judgment...

—Hebrews 6:2

...*eternal* fire...

—Jude 7

2. MATTHEW 10:28

This is another verse that the annihilationists stand on. It reads: "Fear Him who is able to *destroy* both soul and body..." What is the definition of that word *destroy*? In *Strong's Exhaustive Concordance*, the Greek word is *appollymi*, meaning "to kill, cause to lose. To die or perish."[14] Annihilationists comment that the word *destroy* means "annihilate." Not true.

> In Matthew 10:28, he coupled Gehenna with *apolesai*, which *Thayer's Greek Lexicon* defines as "to be delivered up to eternal misery. Gehenna, then, symbolizes eternal separation and conscious punishment for the spiritual nature of the unregenerate man.[15]
>
> —Walter Martin

> A decisive proof that there is a hell for the body, as well as the soul.... The torment that awaits the lost will have elements of suffering adopted to the material as well as the spiritual part of our nature, both of which, we are assured, will exist forever.[16]
>
> —*Jamieson, Fausset, and Brown's Commentary on the Whole Bible*

In Jesus' usage "destroy" can also mean to inflict enduring torment. That is, unclean spirits who ask whether Jesus will "destroy" them (*apollymi*; Mark 1:24; Luke 4:34) understand that destruction in terms of unending torment (*basanizo*; Math. 8:29; Mark 5:7; Luke 8:28). The spirits were not afraid of being "destroyed" or "tormented" by Jesus on this earth, as if He might take time now and then to inflict pain on them when it suited Him and at worst even terminate their conscious existence. They rather feared the pain of the "forever and ever" torment that the Spirit of Jesus later revealed to John as the destiny of the devil and all those loyal to him (Rev. 14:11)—such as the unclean spirits.[17]

—Dr. Robert W. Yarbrough

3. JOHN 3:16

Their view on this verse is that the word *perish* means to annihilate. This is not true.

> Regarding the Greek word *apollumi*, which is translated "perish" in John 3:16, there is no use of the word in the New Testament that clearly indicates annihilation....If the New Testament writers wanted to make it clear that they meant annihilation they should have used the Greek word *ekmedenisis* (which clearly means "annihilation) or *ekmedenizo* ("to annihilate")— words that were in use then. Furthermore, there are times when *apollumi* (or the noun form, *apoleia*) could not mean "annihilation." For example, when some complained about the expensive perfume being poured on Jesus, they asked, "Why this waste?" (*apoleia*, the noun form of *apollumi*). "The perfume was wasted," they said. That is hardly annihilation. A modern equivalent is when an insurance company regards a wrecked car as a write-off. It is now waste.[18]

—R. T. Kendall

4. 2 THESSALONIANS 1:8–9

In this passage the words *everlasting destruction* come into question. This is what it says: "In flaming fire taking vengeance on those who do not know God, and those who do not obey the gospel of our Lord Jesus Christ. These shall be punished with everlasting *destruction* from the presence of the Lord and from the glory of His power."

> The Greek word *olethros* used here has the clear meaning of "ruining." Any N.T. Greek Lexicon bears out the meaning presented here. Many people who are not well versed in Greek try

263

to make "destruction" synonymous with "annihilation." This does violence to the N.T. Greek, which supports no such concept.

Dr. Francis Pieper, the great Lutheran scholar and author of the monumental 'Christian Dogmatics' states: Holy Scripture teaches the truth of an eternal damnation so clearly and emphatically that one cannot deny it without, at the same time, rejecting the authority of Scripture. Scripture parallels the eternal salvation of the believers, and the eternal damnation of the unbelievers. Whoever therefore denies the one must, to be consistent, deny the other (Matt. 25:46).[19]

—Walter Martin

Their punishment will be no less than destruction…both as to body and soul. This destruction will be everlasting. They shall be always dying, and yet never die. Their misery will run parallel with the line of eternity. The chains of darkness are everlasting chains, and the fire is everlasting fire.[20]

—*Matthew Henry's Commentary on the Whole Bible*

5. REVELATION 14:11

"And the smoke of their torment ascends *forever and ever*; and they have no rest day or night."

In his book *Hell on Trial*, Robert Peterson says, "John does not distinguish fire and smoke. Rather, when he says, 'The smoke of their torment rises for ever and ever,' he means that the torment of the damned with 'burning sulfur' is endless. Indeed, the perpetually rising smoke bears witness to the continual suffering of the lost."[21]

The definition of the word *aion*, the Greek word used for "forever," is, "eternity, age, time period."[22] If *aion* does not mean forever, and only a limited time period as some claim, then we can look at some other verses that use the same word and observe their meaning.

…Christ, and He shall reign *forever and ever*!

—Revelation 11:15

...swore by Him who lives *forever and ever*...

—Revelation 10:6

(see also Revelation 1:6; 4:9; 5:14; 15:7)

...lake of fire...day and night *forever and ever.*

—Revelation 20:10

...throne of God...they shall reign *forever and ever.*

—Revelation 22:1–5

...Mount Zion, which cannot be removed, but abides *forever.*

—Psalm 125:1

You can see that *forever and ever* is used in these verses in regard to the "throne," "Mount Zion," "Him who lives," and by "Christ" Himself. If it doesn't mean "forever," then nothing else is "forever." This is clearly not the case.

6. JOHN 3:36

This is another verse they twist. It states, "He who believes in the Son has everlasting life; and he who does not believe the Son shall not see life, but the wrath of God abides on him."

Dr. Walter Martin points out regarding this verse that the word *abides* is the Greek word *menei.* It "appears several times in the New Testament. It carries the idea of continuous action (see John 1:33; 2:12; 8:31; 15:9). Thus, in John 3:36 The Holy Spirit says that the wrath of God continually abides on the one who 'believeth not the Son.' Comparing this with Romans 2:8–9, we see that those who do not obey the truth but do evil are the objects of God's wrath, which Revelation 14:10–11 describes as eternal."[23]

In the New Testament, the torment is described as continuous and eternal (Mt. 3:12; 25:41; 2 Thes.1:9; Jude 7).[24]

—*Dictionary of Biblical Imagery*

Saved and unsaved will exist forever as self-conscious, aware individuals.[25]

—*Encyclopedia of Biblical Words*

The Word of God teaches that the suffering of the lost in hell is eternal (Is. 66:24; Matt. 25:46; Mark 9:44, 46, 48; Rev. 14:11). The assertion that God would be unfair to punish eternally a temporary sin underestimates the seriousness of sin, the spiritual nature of sin, and the supreme holiness of God.[26]

—*Holman Illustrated Bible Dictionary*

Dr. Whilby shows that the eternity of the torments of hell was not only the constant faith of the Christian Church, but had been so of the Jewish Church. Josephus saith, the Pharisees held that the souls of wicked were to be punished with perpetual punishments; and that there was appointed to them a perpetual prison. And Philo saith, the punishment of the wicked is to live forever dying, and to be forever in pains and griefs that never cease.[27]

—*Matthew Henry's Commentary on the Whole Bible*

...for those that are cast into hell, will find the fire to have not only the corroding quality of salt, but its preserving quality; whence it is used to signify that which is lasting: a covenant of salt is a perpetual covenant, and Lot's wife being turned into a pillar of salt, made her a remaining monument of divine vengeance.[28]

—*Matthew Henry's Commentary on the Whole Bible*

The punishment of the wicked in the future state will be an everlasting punishment, for that state is an unalterable state.[29]

—*Matthew Henry's Commentary on the Whole Bible*

Two groups will arise from Death; they constitute the "many," meaning all, as in John 5:29. Those of faith will rise to eternal life, the rest of the unsaved to eternal torment.[30]

—*The MacArthur Bible Commentary*

...anticipation of eternal punishment for the impenitent pervades the whole New Testament. The fire of God's wrath will be an everlasting fire; a fire that, fastening and preying upon immortal souls, can never go out for want of fuel; and being kindled and kept burning by the wrath of an immortal God, can never go out...[31]

—J. I. Packer

Like the teaching of Eternal Punishment, it conflicts with the dictates of the carnal mind and is repugnant to the sentiments of the unregenerate heart.[32]

—A. W. Pink

As to the theory of annihilation...this idea has to be read into the texts; it cannot be read out of them, since the fire is pictured not of destruction but of ongoing pain, as Luke 16:24 makes unambiguously clear. Also the Greek words that express destruction...signify functional ruination (as when one totals a car, thereby reducing it to a heap of wreckage) rather than ontological abolition.[33]

—J. I. Packer

Though the Church has traditionally taught that the fate of the lost is eternal punishment, fewer and fewer people are willing to think seriously about that dreadful prospect. Can the future of unbelievers really be that bad? Today a growing number of scholars are answering no.[34]

—Robert A. Peterson

These next verses would be hard to explain if you believe in annihilationism.

And you shall go to your fathers in peace...

—Genesis 15:15

How does one go to his fathers if they don't exist?

> Behold, thou shall sleep with thy fathers...
>   —Deuteronomy 31:16, KJV

How does one sleep with his fathers if they are gone? This is also not soul sleep, but an expression, a euphemism.

> ...for I shall go down into the grave [Sheol] to my son in mourning.
>   —Genesis 37:35

If his son ceased to exist, how could he say that he would go to him?

> I shall go to him, but he shall not return to me.
>   —2 Samuel 12:23

Regarding John 15:6 Matthew Henry says, "They will not be consumed in a moment, like thorns under a pot (Ecc. 7:6), but *kaietai*, they are burning forever in a fire, which not only cannot be quenched, but will never spend itself."[35] The word *destruction* is used in these next verses, and it is obvious that it could not mean "cease to exist."

> Deliver such a one to Satan for the *destruction* of the flesh, that his spirit may be saved.
>   —1 Corinthians 5:5

Satan does not have the ability to annihilate someone's soul.

> But those who desire to be rich fall into temptation and a snare, and into many foolish and harmful lusts which drown men in *destruction* and perdition.
>   —1 Timothy 6:9

As I said above, the word *destruction* does not mean "cease to exist." The word *everlasting* is another word annihilationists state doesn't really mean everlasting. These next verses use the same word, and it is obvious it means "everlasting" or "forever," just as the *kingdom* is everlasting.

> ...having the *everlasting* gospel to preach to those...
> —Revelation 14:6

> ...into the *everlasting* kingdom of our Lord.
> —2 Peter 1:11

> ...and believes in Him may have *everlasting* life...
> —John 6:40

If *everlasting* does not mean "eternal," then neither is the "gospel" or the "kingdom" or "eternal life" eternal.

These next verses show that the same word for "destroy" is used in these verses and obviously does not mean annihilate, as annihilationists claim.

> Art thou come to *destroy* us? [demon speaking]
> —Mark 1:24, KJV

This verse cannot be talking about annihilation since a fallen angel, or demon, cannot die or cease to exist. As Luke 20:36 says, "Nor can they die anymore, for they are equal to the angels."

> The leaders of the people sought to *destroy* Him.
> —Luke 19:47

In the verse above, *destroy* obviously means to kill, not to cause Him to cease to exist.

> I will *destroy* the wisdom of the wise.
> —1 Corinthians 1:19

> ...to steal, and to kill, and to *destroy* [Satan cannot destroy a soul].
> —John 10:10

Herod will seek the young child to *destroy* him.

—Matthew 2:13, KJV

Herod did not mean to cause Jesus to be annihilated, but simply to kill Him.

But if thy brother be grieved with thy meat...*destroy* [does not mean to cause your brother to cease to exist] not him with thy meat.

—Romans 14:15, KJV

Look at Revelation 19:20. This is proof that these two people still exist after being in the lake of fire for one thousand years. The annihilationist cannot twist this one. In this verse the beast and the false prophet are cast into the lake of fire after the tribulation. Then at the end of the thousand years, John sees Satan being thrown into the lake of fire where the beast and the false prophet *are* (Rev. 20:10). They still exist after the thousand years—they are not "annihilated."

Some say that Psalm 92:7 is proof that people are annihilated: "They [the wicked] shall be *destroyed* for ever" (KJV). The same word used in these next verses:

For we are sold, I and my people, to *be destroyed*, to be slain, and to perish [means "to die"].

—Esther 7:4, KJV

And the LORD was very angry with Aaron and would have *destroyed* [killed] him.

—Deuteronomy 9:20

He did not leave to Jeroboam any that breathed, until he had *destroyed* [killed] him.

—1 Kings 15:29

This next word for *destruction* does not mean annihilation. It is the Hebrew word *baddon*, meaning "place of destruction, realm of the dead."[36] It is used in the following verses.

...a fire that consumes to *destruction*...

—Job 31:12

Hell and *Destruction* are before the LORD.

—Proverbs 15:11

In Psalm 92:7, "destroyed" does not mean "annihilate," as annihilationists state. The Hebrew word is *samad*, and it means, "demolish; bring to nought."[37] Here is another verse where the same word is used.

...that we should be *destroyed* from remaining in any of the territories of Israel [does not mean annihilate, but "bring to nought]...

—2 Samuel 21:5

Below is a partial list of the great leaders of the past, and present, who believe that hell is eternal and eternal torment for the individual. In my first book, *23 Minutes in Hell*, we also listed some of the major denominations' beliefs, which stated the same. If you are one who does not believe in an eternal hell, you are in opposition to not only the scriptures, but also to almost all of the well-known and highly respected leaders of the past and present, and the major church denominations. You virtually stand almost alone and with no credible support. Jesus made it so very clear. I don't know how anyone could miss the clear teachings of Jesus. He mentioned hell in forty-six separate verses, which we have listed in Appendix A. But first, here are some of the well-known leaders, present and past, and some of the churches' views on this matter.

If Christ's crucifixion and resurrection didn't deliver us from an eternal Hell, his work on the cross is less heroic, less potent, less consequential, and thus less deserving of our worship and praise. As theologian William G.T. Shedd put it, "The doctrine of Christ's vicarious atonement logically stands or falls with that of eternal punishment."[38]

—Randy Alcorn

We set aside the error of those who say that the punishment of the wicked are to be ended at some time....Now a sin that is against God is infinite; the higher the person against whom it is committed, the graver the sin—it is more criminal to strike a head of state than a private citizen—and God is of infinite greatness. Therefore an infinite punishment is deserved for a sin committed against Him.[39]

—Thomas Aquinas

Hence, because the eternal life of the saints will be endless, the eternal punishment also, for those condemned to it, will assuredly have no end.[40]

—Augustine

Impenitent sinners in hell shall have end without end, death without death, night without day, mourning without mirth, sorrow without solace, and bondage without liberty. The damned shall live as long in hell as God Himself shall live in Heaven.[41]

—Thomas Brooks

Everlasting destruction and the torment of the flesh await all those whom he will drive from his presence at the last day....We ought to represent to our minds the future vengeance of God against the wicked, which, being more grievous than all earthly torments, ought rather to excite horror than a desire to know it. But we must observe the eternity of this fire...[42]

—John Calvin

It is eternal punishment and death which has no end. The perpetual duration of this death is proved from the fact that its opposite is the glory of Christ.[43]

—John Calvin

An eternity in hell will not begin to exhaust God's anger. Yet it is all deserved. Sin against an infinite God demands an infinite and everlasting penalty.[44]

—Edward Donnelly

Concerning the endless punishment of those who will die impenitent, "Eternal punishment is not eternal annihilation. Surely they will not be raised to life at the last day only to be annihilated."[45]

—Jonathan Edwards

There is the realization that this separation is permanent....Thus, hopelessness comes over the individual.[46]

—Millard J. Erickson

O what an eternity is this for the sinner, lost forever.[47]

—Charles Finney

The scriptures, however, clearly state that those who reject Christ's mercies during this life will endure an eternity in hell while fully conscious forever.[48]

—Grant Jeffrey

The fiery oven is ignited merely by the unbearable appearance of God and endures eternally....Constantly, the damned will be judged, constantly they will suffer pain, and constantly they will be a fiery oven, that is, they will be tortured.[49]

—Martin Luther

Since the same word eternal describes both the destiny of the righteous and the wicked, it seems clear that Christ taught that both groups will exist forever, albeit in different places. The same eternal fire that Satan and his host experience will be the lot of unbelievers.... Finally, the occupants of hell are clearly said to experience eternal misery.... Perpetually burning lusts never subside and the tortured conscience burns but is never sated or oppressed.[50]

—Erwin Lutzer

We find Scripture is clear in its teaching that those who reject God's salvation will suffer throughout eternity in outer darkness.... There is conscious punishment after death... it still remains a scriptural doctrine substantiated by God's Word.[51]

—Walter Martin

The agents of suffering never end because those in hell experience conscious suffering forever.[52]

—Christopher W. Morgan

Hell entails eternal punishment, utter loss, rejection by God, terrible suffering, and unspeakable sorrow and pain.[53]

—Robert A. Peterson

Startling as it may sound, it is nevertheless a fact, that the Scriptures speak much more frequently of God's anger and wrath, than they do of His love and compassion. To argue, then, that because God is love, He will not inflict eternal torment on the wicked, is to ignore the fact that God is light, and is to asperse His holiness.... Moreover, to deny the justice of eternal punishment is to fly in the face of Christian consciousness.[54]

—A. W. Pink

Regius Professor of Theology at Oxford stated that Matt. 25:46 is one of the two most explicit New Testament texts offering permanent penal pain for some after death... "The strain of anti-universalist teaching in the New Testament can hardly be regarded by an impartial mind as other than conclusive."[55]

—O. C. Quick

...We speak of the wrath to come, and everlasting punishment which God apportions to the unrepentant, with fear and trembling, but we speak of it because we cannot escape from correction that it is taught in the Word of God.[56]

—C. H. Spurgeon

...the fire of hell is eternal—expressly announced as an everlasting penalty, and let him then admit that it is from this circumstance that this never-ending "killing" is more formidable than a merely human murder, which is only temporal.[57]

—Tertullian

The time must come when repentance and the acceptance of the Savior become impossible, then one becomes eternally confirmed in his separation from God, and eternal torment must necessarily follow.[58]

—R. A. Torrey

Because the word "everlasting" is sometimes used by the sacred writers to mean no more than long-lasting (as "the everlasting hills"), some persons have argued that the concept of unending existence was not in the minds of the writers when they used the word but was supplied by the theologians. This is of course a serious error, and, as far as I can see, has no ground in serious scholarship. It has been used by certain teachers as an escape from the doctrine of eternal punishment. These reject the eternity of moral retribution, and to be consistent they are forced to weaken the whole idea of endlessness.... Indeed I know of no tenet of the Christian creed that could retain its significance if the idea of eternity were extracted from it.[59]

—A. W. Tozer

There cannot be one argument urged, why God should reward his saints with everlasting happiness, which will not equally prove that he ought to punish sinners with eternal misery.[60]

—George Whitefield

Jesus is at conspicuous pains to underscore the unending nature of Hell's affliction. He does this first by speaking of the "Fire that never goes out." Then he does it by quoting Is. 66:24.... That clearly teaches "The notion of eternal punishment." (Dan. 12:2)...Then Jesus teaches that Hell's agonies are on going and never ending.[61]

—Robert W. Yarbrough

The Roman Catholic Church officially believes in the traditional doctrine of hell, as is evidenced by the statement of the Fourth Lateran Council in 1215: "Those (the rejected) will receive a perpetual punishment with the devil."[62]

—Catholic Church

It is also taught among us that our Lord Jesus Christ will return on the last day for judgment and will raise up all the dead...to condemn ungodly men and the devil to hell and eternal punishment.[63]

—The Lutheran Church's Augsburg Confession (1530)

The wicked...shall be cast into eternal torments, and be punished with everlasting destruction from the presence of the Lord, and from the glory of His power.[64]

—Presbyterian Westminster Confession of Faith

Christ will judge all men in righteousness. The unrighteous will be consigned to hell, the place of everlasting punishment.[65]

—The Baptist Faith and Message of 1963

There will be a final judgment in which the wicked dead will be raised and judged according to their works. Whosoever is not found written in the Book of Life, together with the devil and his angels, the beast and the false prophet, will be consigned to everlasting punishment in the lake which burneth with fire and brimstone, which is the second death (Matt. 25:46; Mark 9:43–48; Rev. 19:20, 20:11–15, 21:8).[66]

...The punishment will be as eternal as the eternal life...The punishment is as eternal as the fire. If the fire brought an annihilation of the wicked, there would be no reason for the fire being eternal."[67]

—Assemblies of God

These next verses show that there are people still existing after death.

- *1 Samuel 28:13–15*: When the witch of Endor brought up Samuel, he talked to Saul. He existed after death. Samuel said to Saul, "Why have you disturbed me?" He had to exist to talk with Saul. (Commentaries believe it was actually Samuel and not an evil spirit. He was not in the torment side of Sheol, but Abraham's bosom.)

- *Isaiah 14:9–10*: "Hell from beneath is moved for thee to meet thee at thy coming....All they shall *speak* and *say* unto thee, Art thou become weak as we?" (KJV). How can one "say" if they don't exist, or how can they "meet thee" if they are annihilated? Verse 16 continues, "They that see thee shall narrowly look upon thee, and consider thee, saying, Is this the man...?" (KJV). How can one look upon someone who doesn't exist and "say" anything? And then in verse 18, "...every one in his own house" (KJV). Why have a house?

277

- *Ezekiel 32:21–27*: "The strong among the mighty shall *speak* to him out of the midst of *hell* with them that help him. [How can they *speak* if nonexistent?]...Yet have they borne their shame with them that go down to the pit. [How could one bare shame if he doesn't exist?]...He is put in the midst of them [he must exist]...which are gone down to hell...and they have laid their swords under their heads, but their iniquities shall be upon their bones [still have heads and bones; therefore, they must still exist]" (KJV).

- *Jonah 2:2*: "Out of the belly of Sheol I cried." Many commentaries (Tyndale, New International) believe he was in Sheol. How could he "cry" out if he was annihilated?

- *Matthew 17:3*: Moses and Elijah appeared unto Jesus and *talked* with Him, and the disciples saw them. (Moses and Elijah talked—they were not annihilated. They were not in Sheol but in Abraham's bosom.)

- *Luke 16:22–30*: Abraham talking to the rich man in Sheol. The rich man said many things, one being, "For I am tormented in this flame" (v. 24). (Doesn't sound like he's annihilated.)

- *Luke 23:43*: Jesus told the thief on the cross he would be with Him today in Paradise. Jesus wasn't going down there to cease to exist. He preached to the spirits in prison (1 Pet. 3:19), and He led captivity captive (Eph. 4:8). The thief was taken to paradise, not to the torment side of Sheol.

- *Revelation 5:5*: John *talks* to an elder in heaven. (The elder existed; he was not annihilated.)

- *Acts 7:59*: When Stephen was about to die, he did not ask the grave to receive him, but he said, "Lord Jesus, receive my spirit."

- *Philippians 1:23*: "…to depart and to be with Christ." Paul expected to be with Christ.

Look at Luke 16, where Jesus gives the account of the rich man "being in torments" (v. 23) and saying in verse 24, "For I am tormented in this flame." The rich man still existed after death. Some say this is only a parable. But it is not, as you will see. But even if it were, why would that change the entire meaning of the story to the point where the rich man was not really in torment at all? That he really didn't even exist? How does one draw that conclusion even if it were a parable? As for it supposedly being a parable, let's look at a few commentaries:

> It should be noted that this is not spoken of as a parable.[68]
> —*Believer's Bible Commentary*

> Some regard this account to be a parable, but if it is, it is the only parable in which a character is actually named. There is no reason to doubt that Jesus was speaking about a genuine historical experience.[69]
> —*New Testament Survey*

> The beggar was the only character in any of Jesus' parables ever given a name. Some, therefore, have speculated that this was no imaginary tale, but an actual incident that really took place. Either way, Christ employs it in the same fashion, as all his parables, to teach a lesson.[70]
> —*The MacArthur Bible Commentary*

If you still choose to believe in annihilationism, you are choosing to ignore one of the principles of the doctrine of Christ, one of the six foundational teachings found in Hebrews 6:1–2. Verse 2 says, "…and of eternal judgment." It is your choice, but Scripture is clear. Hell and eternal punishment are forever (John 3:36; 2 Thess. 1:9; Rev. 14:10–11; 20:10). See Appendix A where Jesus spoke about hell. You can see He mentioned it on forty-six separate occasions. I think that is significant. Edward Donnelly says, "Jesus Christ has been described as the theologian of hell, because he has more to say about it than anyone else."[71] As Jesus is our Savior, we would be wise to pay attention to His warnings.

CHAPTER 32

ARE PEOPLE EVENTUALLY SAVED OUT OF HELL?— UNIVERSALISM

J. I. PACKER, IN THE BOOK *HELL UNDER FIRE*, STATES THAT "A *UNIVERSALIST* is someone who believes that every human being whom God has created or will create will finally come to enjoy the everlasting salvation into which Christians enter here and now. *Universalism* is the recognized name for this belief....Most universalists (granted, not all) concede that universalism is not clearly taught in the Bible; what then is the warrant for the universalist confidence? It seems plain that the deepest motivation in their minds has always been revolt against mainstream belief in endless punishment in hell for some people. It is argued that the biblical revelation of God's love to his world entails a universal salvific intention, that is, a purpose of saving everybody, and that sooner or later God must achieve that purpose."[1]

Robert A. Peterson says, "British evangelist John Blanchard has some hard words for the view that everyone eventually will be saved....All the ways to hell are one-way streets. The idea that those who go there will eventually be released and join the rest of humanity in heaven has not a shred of biblical evidence to support it."[2] Peterson goes on to mention John Hick, the British philosopher of religion, as saying, "God will eventually succeed in His purpose of winning all men to Himself in faith and love."[3]

Many of the supporters of universalism do so by building their case on a moral ground issue. They appeal to others of God's goodness and desire to want to save everyone. And of course, that is true. God's desire is to save all, but that doesn't mean all will be saved. They try to make the point that if God's desire is for all men to be saved (1 Tim. 2:4), then how could God not achieve His goal? After all, He is God and would eventually get what He wants.

That sounds rational, but they fail to take into account man's free will. Man can choose to reject God's offer of salvation. Because God is a God of love, He gives man a choice, a free will to decide for himself. Unfortunately, man many times chooses wrongly. Jesus said in Matthew 7:13–14, "Enter ye in at the strait gate: for wide is the gate, and broad is the way, that leadeth to destruction, and many there be which go in thereat: Because strait is the gate, and narrow is the way, which leadeth unto life, and few there be that find it" (KJV). Jesus said few will find eternal life. So you can see that their premise of God getting His way, in that all will get saved, is wrong.

This whole belief of universalism came about because some think that to suffer for all eternity is too long in comparison with the sin, and it would be heartless for God to allow this. The scriptures are clear as to the support of eternal punishment, but people can twist anything if they want to. The previous chapter refutes universalism also, as it proves eternal torment for the unrepentant. We will not repeat the same verses, as you can read all those we listed.

Other books, some listed in the bibliography, have addressed this topic rather conclusively. This book is not intended to be an extensive work on this issue, as the others have done so already. This was intended to simply answer briefly. I will only list a few of the verses again, as they are so clear a child could get it.

Matthew 25:46 states, "And these will go away into everlasting punishment, but the righteous into eternal life." The same word is used here for "everlasting" and "eternal." It is the Greek word *aionios*, and it means "eternal, long ago, forever world began." If eternal life is eternal, then punishment is also eternal.

Second Thessalonians 1:8–9 says, "In flaming fire taking vengeance on those who do not know God, and on those who do not obey the gospel of our Lord Jesus Christ. These shall be punished with everlasting *destruction* from the presence of the Lord and from the glory of His power." The word *everlasting* is the same word used in these next verses. You can see that just as the gospel, kingdom, and life are everlasting, so is destruction.

If the punishment is not everlasting, then neither would be the gospel, kingdom, and life in the verses below. We know that is not the case. So how could some of these people miss the obvious?

> ...having the *everlasting* gospel to preach to those...
>
> —Revelation 14:6

> ...into the *everlasting* kingdom of our Lord.
>
> —2 Peter 1:11

> ...and believes in Him may have *everlasting* life.
>
> —John 6:40

> And many of these who sleep in the dust of the earth shall awake, some to *everlasting life*, some to shame and *everlasting contempt*.
>
> —Daniel 12:2

The word *contempt* in this verse comes from the Hebrew word *deraown*, which means "loathing, aversion, abhorring."[4]

The word *everlasting* is also used in these following verses. If everlasting does not mean everlasting, then these next verses would also not mean everlasting. See also Numbers 25:13; Psalm 41:13; 103:17.

> You are from *everlasting*.
>
> —Psalm 93:2

> Even from *everlasting* to everlasting, You are God.
>
> —Psalm 90:2

...to bring in *everlasting* righteousness...

—Daniel 9:24

...the *Everlasting* God.

—Genesis 21:33

...the *everlasting* arms.

—Deuteronomy 33:27

As J. I. Packer points out in *Hell Under Fire*, "Universalism is making great strides today, both among the church's leaders and among its rank and file."[5] Universalists claim, as Packer goes on to say, "They claim, any belief in the eternal loss and unending torment of any of God's rational creatures makes God out to be a failure and something of a devil'" Packer quotes Nels Ferré saying, "We must preach hell and having also a school and a door in it."[6] Packer goes on to say, "'Ferré was the most exuberant expositor of this line of thought that the twentieth century produced.'" He quotes Ferré again saying, "'God has no permanent problem children,' and in hell he will, 'put on the screws tighter and tighter until we come to ourselves and are willing to consider the good he has prepared for us.' This is typical mainstream universalist thinking." How this belief is packaged and sold is primarily on the basis that God is love, and He would never allow anyone to suffer for eternity. But the fact that "God is love" is the very reason He gives man a free will to choose to love Him. If Ferré's concept of God "putting the screws tighter and tighter" were true, then that is just the opposite of having a free will. If God has to force us into loving Him and seeing things His way, then that is obviously tyrannical and not in any way loving.

No, God gives us that choice, and He warns us of the impending danger that lies ahead if we ignore His ways and choose to disobey Him. Some have said, "Oh, it's your God's way, or the highway." That would be a twisted way to look at it, because His way is not only the correct way, but also the way that will bless us and lead us to heaven. He endeavors to lead us to truth throughout our entire lives, just as a loving parent leads their child.

Many times the child thinks the parent is mean in their direction, but later to find out it was only for their best interest.

God's love for us is not nullified because He allows eternal punishment. This is why Jesus came and died for us to save us from the eternal hell. He warned why Jesus came and died for us, to save us from the eternal hell. He warned us over and over of, "The fire that never shall be quenched" (Mark 9:43–48). Why would the fire continue on forever if no one is in that fire?

The fact is there are people in that fire. Revelation 14:10–11 reads, "…And he shall be tormented with fire and brimstone…and the smoke of their torment ascendeth up forever and ever and they have no rest day nor night." Notice it says, "And they have no rest day nor night." It is not just the smoke ascending up, but "they" have no rest. "They" would mean there are people there. Remember the beast and false prophet are thrown into the lake of fire at the beginning of the thousand-year period, and then at the end of the thousand years they are still there (Rev. 19:20; 20:10).

Man is already condemned and on his way to hell. Jesus came to get us off the road that leads to destruction (Isa. 38:17; Ps. 40:2; 103:4; Matt. 7:13–14).

John 3:18 says, "He that believeth on him is not condemned: but he that believeth not is condemned already, because he hath not believed in the name of the only begotten son of God."

Man tries to fashion a god to suit himself, and that is why he creates a god that would let everyone out of hell. But the true God of the Bible makes it clear that hell is eternal for all those who reject Jesus as the Son of God and Savior (Luke 13:3; John 3:36; 14:6; Acts 4:12; Rom. 10:9–10; 2 Thess. 1:8–9; 1 Tim. 2:5; 1 John 5:12). If you choose to believe in universalism, you stand against the Scriptures and almost all mainstream Christianity. Do as the Bereans did in Acts 17:11: "Searched the scriptures daily, whether those things were so." We are to walk as children of the light (Eph. 5:8).

CHAPTER 33

WHAT IS "BORN AGAIN"?

E MENTIONED EARLIER WHAT SPIRITUAL DEATH IS, AS THERE ARE many misconceptions about it. Again, spiritual death means to be separated from God. It does not mean "cease to exist," because the soul of man is eternal. Dr. Walter Martin says, "This brings us to the scriptural teaching of the eternal existence of the soul. First of all, there is much evidence that the soul does exist as a conscious entity after it departs from the body, and there is no scriptural evidence to the contrary.... They should heed the teaching of the Word of God that the soul of man, whether regenerate or unregenerate, exists after the death of the body."[1]

The soul of man needs to be born again, which simply means born of the Spirit of God. We are born once physically, of water, and we are born "again" by the Spirit of God (John 3:3). Jesus said, "Most assuredly I say to you, unless one is born again, he cannot see the kingdom of God." Notice it is Jesus who said that we must be born again. Our spirit needs to be made alive unto God. To be dead spiritually is to be separated from God. Through Jesus dying on the cross for us and redeeming us from sin, He has placed us back to the state He first intended for us in the garden—to coexist with Him for all eternity.

He died for all men to be saved (1 Tim. 2:4; 2 Pet. 3:9). He doesn't want a single person to go to hell. Justice has been served once and for all at the cross of Calvary. God took out His anger for sin on Jesus at the cross. That was painful for God to punish His own Son, but yet the Bible says, "It pleased the LORD to bruise Him" (Isa. 53:10). This is because, by His Son's death, all mankind could now be saved and stand before Him, if they would repent. It took a sinless God (Jesus) to pay that price. Charles Stanley stated it so well by saying, "God made a swap. Actually, the correct term is imputation. He imputed our sin to Christ and His righteousness to us. To impute something to people is to credit them with it. Christ credited us with His righteousness, including all its rights and privileges. But there was still the problem of our sin. God could not remain just and ignore sin. There was a penalty to be paid. So Christ was credited with our sin. Consequently, He suffered death in our place and in doing so paid the penalty we had incurred."[2]

Second Corinthians 5:21 says, "For He made Him [Jesus] who knew no sin to be sin for us, that we might become the righteousness of God in Him." We need to recognize that we are sinners and cannot get to heaven on our own. It takes some humility to admit we are not good enough. But we are to trust in Jesus, who died in our place. We deserved the punishment, but He took it for us. That is awesome! God took our place, suffered, and died. He shed His blood for us (1 John 1:7; Col. 1:12–14; Heb. 9:11–12, 14, 22, 28; 13:12–20; 1 Pet. 1:2, 18–19). His blood is what washes away our sins. He rose again the third day and lives forevermore.

If we repent of our sin (as Luke 13:3 tells us), ask forgiveness, and confess with our mouth and believe in our heart that God has raised Jesus from the dead, we will be saved (Rom. 10:9–10). It is not by our works. Titus 3:5 says, "Not by works of righteousness which we have done, but according to His mercy He saved us." (See also Romans 3:12, 20, 28; Ephesians 2:8–9). We can't earn it. He paid for it, and we accept it as a free gift. That is it. There is no other way. Jesus said in John 14:6, "I am the way, the truth, and the life. No one comes to the Father except through Me." Likewise, Deuteronomy 30:19 says, "I have set before you life and death, blessing and cursing: therefore, choose life..." We all have to make that choice.

PRAYER

If you want to receive Him today, then say this prayer from your heart:

> *Dear God in heaven, I know that I am a sinner, and I cannot save myself. I believe You sent Your Son, Jesus, to die on a cross for me. I believe He was crucified on a cross at Calvary, died, and was buried. He rose again from the dead on the third day. I believe He shed His blood for my sins. I ask You to forgive me of my sins. I repent, which means I turn away from my sins. I ask You to come into my heart. I receive You now as my Lord and Savior. It is not my works but Your shed blood that washes away my sins. Take me to heaven with You. I give You my life completely. Thank You for saving me now, in Jesus's name, amen.*

If you said that prayer, it is the wisest decision you will ever make. Go and tell someone what you have done. Find a Bible-believing church to attend, and read your Bible daily and pray. Get yourself baptized at your new church, which means to be emerged in water. This is an outward sign of dying to self and resurrecting to a new life in Christ. It is in obedience to His Word. (See Matthew 3:6; Mark 1:5, 8; Luke 3:7, 12; John 3:22–23; 4:1; Acts 16:15, 33; 18:8; 22:16; Romans 6:3; 1 Corinthians 1:13–16.) Also renounce any sin you might have been involved in. Don't look back, but only ahead, and keep your eyes focused on Him. Make some new friends who are also Christians. Your life will never be the same. You are now a member of God's family, and you are going to heaven. The Lord is having a party for you in heaven, celebrating your birth. Praise the Lord! May the Lord bless, direct, and guide your life as you serve Him. Thank you for your new commitment to Him.

APPENDIX A

JESUS SPEAKS ON HELL AND DESTRUCTION— FORTY-SIX VERSES

1. *Matthew 5:22:* "But whosoever shall say, Thou fool, shall be in danger of hell fire" (KJV).

2. *Matthew 5:29:* "...and not that thy whole body should be cast into hell" (KJV).

3. *Matthew 5:30:* "...and not that thy whole body should be cast into hell" (KJV).

4. *Matthew 7:13:* "For wide is the gate, and broad is the way, that leadeth to destruction, and many there be which go in thereat" (KJV).

5. *Matthew 7:19:* "Every tree that bringeth not forth good fruit is hewn down, and cast into the fire" (KJV).

6. *Matthew 8:12:* "But the children of the kingdom shall be cast out into outer darkness: there shall be weeping and gnashing of teeth" (KJV).

7. *Matthew 10:15:* "Verily I say unto you, It shall be more tolerable for the land of Sodom and Gomorrha in the day of judgment, than for that city" (KJV).

8. *Matthew 10:28:* "...but rather fear him which is able to destroy both soul and body in hell" (KJV).

9. *Matthew 11:23:* "And thou, Capernaum, which are exalted unto heaven, shalt be brought down to hell" (KJV).

10. *Matthew 13:30:* "And in the time of harvest I will say to the reapers, Gather ye together first the tares, and bind them in bundles to burn them: but gather the wheat into my barns" (KJV).

11. *Matthew 13:40:* "As therefore the tares are gathered and burned in the fire; so shall it be in the end of this world" (KJV).

12. *Matthew 13:42:* "And shall cast them into a furnace of fire: there shall be wailing and gnashing of teeth" (KJV).

13. *Matthew 13:49–50:* "So shall it be at the end of the world: the angels shall come forth, and sever the wicked from among the just, and shall cast them into the furnace of fire: there shall be wailing and gnashing of teeth" (KJV).

14. *Matthew 16:18:* "And the gates of hell shall not prevail against it" (KJV).

15. *Matthew 18:8:* "...to be cast into everlasting fire" (KJV).

16. *Matthew 18:9:* "It is better for thee to enter into life with one eye, rather than having two eyes to be cast into hell fire" (KJV).

17. *Matthew 18:34:* "And his lord was wroth, and delivered him to the tormentors" (KJV).

18. *Matthew 22:13:* "Then said the king to the servants, Bind him hand and foot, and take him away, and cast him into outer darkness; there shall be weeping and gnashing of teeth" (KJV).

19. *Matthew 23:14:* "Ye shall receive the greater damnation" (KJV).

20. *Matthew 23:15:* "Ye make him twofold more the child of hell than yourselves" (KJV).

21. *Matthew 23:33:* "Ye serpents, ye generation of vipers, how can ye escape the damnation of hell?" (KJV).

22. *Matthew 24:51:* "And shall cut him asunder, and appoint him his portion with the hypocrites: there shall be weeping and gnashing of teeth" (KJV).

23. *Matthew 25:30:* "And cast ye the unprofitable servant into outer darkness: there shall be weeping and gnashing of teeth" (KJV).

24. *Matthew 25:41:* "Then shall he say also unto them on the left hand, Depart from me, ye cursed, into everlasting fire, prepared for the devil and his angels." (KJV).

25. *Matthew 25:46:* "And these shall go away into everlasting punishment: but the righteous into life eternal" (KJV).

26. *Mark 3:29:* "But he that shall blaspheme against the Holy Ghost hath never forgiveness, but is in danger of eternal damnation" (KJV).

27. *Mark 9:43:* "...than having two hands to go into hell, into the fire that never shall be quenched" (KJV).

28. *Mark 9:44:* "Where their worm dieth not, and the fire is not quenched" (KJV).

29. *Mark 9:45:* "...than having two feet to be cast into hell, into the fire that never shall be quenched" (KJV).

30. *Mark 9:46:* "Where their worm dieth not, and the fire is not quenched" (KJV).

31. *Mark 9:47:* "...than having two eyes to be cast into hell fire" (KJV).

32. *Mark 9:48:* "Where their worm dieth not, and the fire is not quenched" (KJV).

33. *Mark 12:40:* "These shall receive greater damnation" (KJV).

34. *Luke 3:17:* "But the chaff he will burn with fire unquenchable" (KJV). (John the Baptist speaking of Jesus)

35. *Luke 10:15:* "And thou, Capernaum, which art exalted to heaven, shalt be thrust down to hell" (KJV).

36. *Luke 12:5:* "But I will forewarn you whom ye shall fear: Fear him, which after he hath killed hath power to cast into hell; yea, I say unto you, Fear him" (KJV).

37. *Luke 12:46:* "And will cut him in sunder, and will appoint him his portion with the unbelievers" (KJV).

38. *Luke 12:47:* "...shall be beaten with many stripes" (KJV).

39. *Luke 12:48:* "But he that knew not, and did commit things worthy of stripes, shall be beaten with few stripes" (KJV).

40. *Luke 16:23:* "And in hell he lift up his eyes, being in torments..." (KJV).

41. *Luke 16:24:* "...for I am tormented in this flame" (KJV).

42. *Luke 16:25:* "...and thou art tormented" (KJV).

43. *Luke 16:26:* "And besides all this, between us and you there is a great gulf fixed: so that they which would pass from hence to you cannot; neither can they pass to us, that would come from thence" (KJV).

44. *Luke 20:47:* "...the same shall receive greater damnation" (KJV).

45. *John 5:29:* "And shall come forth; they that have done good, unto the resurrection of life; and they that have done evil, unto the resurrection of damnation" (KJV).

46. *John 15:6:* "If a man abide not in me, he is cast forth as a branch, and is withered; and men gather them, and cast them into the fire, and they are burned" (KJV).

APPENDIX B

JESUS SAID HE WAS THE SON OF GOD

HERE IS A LIST OF SCRIPTURES IN WHICH JESUS CLAIMED TO BE THE Son of God. Also included are verses where several others called Him the Son of God.

- *Matthew 8:29* (demons speaking to Jesus): "And suddenly they cried out, saying, 'What have we to do with You, Jesus, You Son of God? Have You come here to torment us before the time?'"

- *Matthew 14:33* (Jesus rescues Peter, who began sinking after walking on the water): "Then those who were in the boat came and worshiped Him, saying, 'Truly You are the Son of God.'"

- *Matthew 16:16:* "Simon Peter answered and said, 'You are the Christ, the Son of the living God.'"

- *Matthew 16:20:* "He commanded His disciples that they should tell no one that He was Jesus the Christ."

- *Matthew 26:63–64:* "And the high priest answered and said to Him, 'I put You under oath by the living God: Tell us if

You are the Christ, the Son of God!' Jesus said to him, 'It is as you said.'"

- *Matthew 27:43* (the chief priest mocking Jesus on the cross): "…for He said, 'I am the Son of God.'"

- *Matthew 27:54* (centurion at the cross speaking): "Truly this was the Son of God!"

- *Mark 1:1:* "The beginning of the gospel of Jesus Christ, the Son of God."

- *Mark 3:11:* "And the unclean spirits, whenever they saw Him, fell down before Him and cried out, saying, 'You are the Son of God.'"

- *Mark 5:7* (demon speaking): "And he cried out with a loud voice and said, 'What have I to do with You, Jesus, Son of the Most High God? I implore You by God that You do not torment me.'"

- *Mark 14:61–62:* "Again the high priest asked Him, saying to Him, 'Are You the Christ, the Son of the Blessed?' Jesus said, 'I am.'"

- *Mark 15:39* (centurion at the cross speaking): "Truly this Man was the Son of God!"

- *Luke 1:31–32* (angel speaking to Mary): "…and shall call His name Jesus. He will be great, and will be called the Son of the Highest."

- *Luke 1:35* (angel speaking to Mary): "…that Holy One who is to be born will be called the Son of God."

- *Luke 4:41:* "And demons also came out of many, crying out and saying, 'You are the Christ, the Son of God!'"

- *Luke 8:28:* "When he saw Jesus, he cried out, fell down before Him, and with a loud voice said, 'What have I to do with You, Jesus, Son of the Most High God? I beg You, do not torment me!'"

- *Luke 22:70* (Jesus to the Sanhedrin): "Then they all said, 'Are You then the Son of God?' So He said to them, 'You rightly say that I am.'"

- *Luke 23:42* (thief on the cross speaking): "Then he said to Jesus, 'Lord, remember me when You come into Your kingdom.'"

- *John 1:1–5* (John testifies of Jesus as God): "In the beginning was the Word, and the Word was with God, and the Word was God. He was with God in the beginning. Through him all things were made; without him nothing was made that has been made. In him was life, and that life was the light of men. The light shines in the darkness, but the darkness has not understood it" (NIV).

- *John 1:10–14* (John testifies of Jesus as God): "He was in the world, and though the world was made through him, the world did not recognize him. He came to that which was his own, but his own did not receive him. Yet to all who received him, to those who believed in his name, he gave the right to become children of God—children born not of natural descent, nor of human decision or a husband's will, but born of God. The Word became flesh and made his dwelling among us. We have seen his glory, the glory of the One and Only, who came from the Father, full of grace and truth" (NIV).

- *John 1:34:* "And I have seen and testified that this is the Son of God."

- *John 1:17–18:* "Grace and truth came through Jesus Christ. No one has ever seen God at any time. The only begotten Son, who is in the bosom of the Father, He has declared Him."

- *John 1:49:* "Nathanael answered and said to Him, 'Rabbi, You are the Son of God!'"

- *John 3:16–18:* "For God so loved the world that He gave His only begotten Son, that whoever believes in Him should not perish but have everlasting life. For God did not send His Son into the world to condemn the world, but that the world through Him might be saved. He who believes in Him is not condemned; but he who does not believe is condemned already, because he has not believed in the name of the only begotten Son of God."

- *John 3:36:* "He who believes in the Son has everlasting life; and he who does not believe the Son shall not see life, but the wrath of God abides on him."

- *John 4:10, 13* (Jesus at the well speaking to the Samaritan woman): "Jesus answered her, 'If you knew the gift of God and who it is that asks you for a drink, you would have asked him and he would have given you living water.' . . . Jesus answered, 'Everyone who drinks this water will be thirsty again, but whoever drinks the water I give him will never thirst. Indeed, the water I give him will become in him a spring of water welling up to eternal life'" (NIV).

- *John 4:25–26:* "The woman said, 'I know that Messiah' (called Christ) 'is coming. When he comes, he will explain everything to us.' Then Jesus declared, 'I who speak to you am he'" (NIV).

- *John 4:42* (other Samaritans speaking): "They said to the woman, 'We no longer believe just because of what you said; now we have heard for ourselves, and we know that this man is really the *Savior of the world*'" (NIV).

- *John 5:16–27* (Jesus speaks of Himself): "So, because Jesus was doing these things on the Sabbath, the Jews persecuted him. Jesus said to them, 'My Father is always at his work to this very day, and I, too, am working.' For this reason the Jews tried all the harder to kill him; not only was he breaking the Sabbath, but he was even calling God his own Father, making himself equal with God.

"Jesus gave them this answer: 'I tell you the truth, the Son can do nothing by himself; he can do only what he sees his Father doing, because whatever the Father does the Son also does. For the Father loves the Son and shows him all he does. Yes, to your amazement he will show him even greater things than these. For just as the Father raises the dead and gives them life, even so the Son gives life to whom he is pleased to give it. Moreover, the Father judges no one, but has entrusted all judgment to the Son, that all may honor the Son just as they honor the Father. He who does not honor the Son does not honor the Father, who sent him.

"'I tell you the truth, whoever hears my word and believes him who sent me has eternal life and will not be condemned; he has crossed over from death to life. I tell you the truth, a time is coming and has now come when the dead will hear the voice of the Son of God and those who hear will live. For as the Father has life in himself, so he has granted the Son to have life in himself. And he has given him authority to judge because he is the Son of Man'" (NIV).

- *John 5:30:* "I do not seek My own will but the will of the Father *who sent Me.*"

- *John 5:36:* "I have testimony weightier than that of John. For the very work that the Father has given me to finish, and which I am doing, *testifies that the Father has sent me*" (NIV).

- *John 5:37–40:* *"And the Father who sent me* has himself testified concerning me. These are the Scriptures *that testify about me*, yet you refuse to come to me to have life" (NIV).

- *John 5:46:* "If you believed Moses, you would believe me, *for he wrote about me*" (NIV).

- *John 6:69* (Peter speaking): "Also we have come to believe and know that You are the Christ, the Son of the living God."

- *John 8:54–58:* "Jesus replied, 'If I glorify myself, my glory means nothing. My Father, whom you claim as your God, is the one who glorifies me. Though you do not know him, I know him. If I said I did not, I would be a liar like you, but I do know him and keep his word. Your father Abraham rejoiced at the thought of seeing my day; he saw it and was glad.'

  "'You are not yet fifty years old,' the Jews said to him, 'and you have seen Abraham!'

  "'I tell you the truth,'" Jesus answered, 'before Abraham was born, I am!'" (NIV).

- *John 9:35–37* (Jesus and the man born blind): "'Do you believe in the Son of God?'

  "He answered and said, 'Who is He, Lord, that I may believe in Him?'

  "And Jesus said to him, 'You have both seen Him and it is he who is talking with you.'"

- *John 10:33:* "The Jews answered Him, saying, 'For a good work we do not stone You, but for blasphemy, and because *You*, being a Man, *make Yourself God.*'"

- *John 10:36, 38:* "Do you say of Him whom the Father sanctified and sent into the world, 'You are blaspheming,' because I said, 'I am the Son of God?' . . . Believe the works, that you may know and believe that the Father is in Me, and I in Him."

- *John 11:4* (Jesus speaking about raising Lazarus from the dead): " . . . that the Son of God may be glorified through it."

- *John 11:25–27:* "Jesus said to her, 'I am the resurrection and the life. He who believes in me will live, even though he dies; and whoever lives and believes in me will never die. Do you believe this?'

  "'Yes, Lord," she told him, 'I believe that you are the Christ, the Son of God, who was to come into the world'" (NIV).

- *John 17:3, 5* (Jesus praying to the Father): "And this is eternal life, that they may know You, the only true God, and Jesus Christ whom You have sent. . . . with the glory which I had with You before the world was."

- *John 17:24:* " . . . for You loved Me before the foundation of the world."

- *John 19:7* (Religious leaders speaking): "He ought to die, because He made Himself the Son of God."

- *John 20:31:* "But these are written that you may believe that Jesus is the Christ, the Son of God, and that believing you may have life in His name."

APPENDIX C

ALL VERSES ON HELL AND DESTRUCTION

Location	
Ezekiel 26:20, KJV	When I shall bring thee down with them that descend into the pit, with the people of old time, and shall set thee in the *low parts of the earth*, in places desolate of old, with them that go down to the pit...
Numbers 16:32–33	And the earth opened up its mouth and swallowed them up...they...went *down* alive into the pit, and the earth closed over them, and they perished from among the congregation.
Ephesians 4:9	He [Jesus]...descended into the lower parts on the earth.
Matthew 12:40	...so will the Son of Man be three days and three nights in the *heart* of the earth.
1 Samuel 28:13–15	"I saw a spirit ascending out of the earth..." An old man is coming up... "Why have you disturbed me by bringing me up?" (This is Samuel speaking from the paradise side of Sheol.)
Psalm 63:9, KJV	But those that seek my soul, to destroy it, shall go into *the lower parts* of the earth.

Isaiah 26:19, KJV	...and the earth shall cast out the dead
Ezekiel 31:14, KJV	For they are all delivered unto death, to the *nether parts* of the earth...with them that go down to the pit.
Psalm 139:15, KJV	...in the lowest parts of the earth
Proverbs 9:18, AMP	...and that her invited guests are (already sunk) in the depths of Sheol (the lower world, Hades, the place of the dead.)
Psalm 55:15, KJV	...let them go down quick into hell.
Psalm 88:6	You have laid me in the lowest pit, in darkness, in the depths.
Isaiah 14:15, KJV	Yet thou shalt be brought down to hell, to the sides of the pit.
Isaiah 38:18	For Sheol cannot thank You, death cannot praise You; those who go down to the pit cannot hope for Your truth.
Isaiah 57:9	...and even *descended* to Sheol.
Ezekiel 31:16, KJV	...when I cast him down to hell with them that descend into the pit.
Ezekiel 31:17, KJV	They also went down into hell...
Ezekiel 31:18, KJV	Yet shalt thou be brought down...unto the nether parts of the earth.
Ezekiel 32:18, KJV	...cast them down...unto the nether parts of the earth...with them that go down into the pit.
Ezekiel 32:23, KJV	...whose graves are set in the sides of the pit.

Ezekiel 32:24, KJV	...are gone down...into the nether parts of the earth...yet have they borne their shame with them that go down to the pit.
Ezekiel 32:25, KJV	...yet have they borne their shame with them that go down to the pit.
Ezekiel 32:27, KJV	...which are gone down to hell.
Ezekiel 32:29, KJV	...with them that go down to the pit.
Ezekiel 32:30, KJV	...and bear their shame with them who go down to the pit.
Ezekiel 32:21, KJV	...speak to him out of the midst of hell...they are gone down
Deuteronomy 32:22, KJV	For a fire is kindled in mine anger, and shall burn unto the lowest hell.
Isaiah 14:19	...hell from *beneath*...
Ezekiel 31:15	In the day when he went down to the grave [Sheol]...
Matthew 11:23, KJV	...shalt be brought down to hell...
Proverbs 7:27	Her house [the harlot] is the way to hell, descending to the chambers of death.
Revelation 9:1	...bottomless pit.
Psalm 55:23	But you, O God, shall bring them down to the pit of destruction.
Psalm 40:2	He also brought me up also out of a horrible pit, out of the miry clay...
Ezekiel 32:20, AMP	...draw her down (to her judgment)

Psalm 30:3	...not go down to the pit.
Job 11:8, KJV	It is as high as heaven...deeper than hell.
Job 33:24	Deliver him from going down to the Pit.
Job 33:28	He will redeem his soul from going down into the Pit, and his life shall see the light.
Psalm 9:15, KJV	The heathen are sunk down in the pit.
Psalm 28:1, KJV	...that go down into the pit.
Psalm 30:9	...down to the pit?
Psalm 143:7	Lest I be like those who go down into the pit.
Proverbs 1:12, KJV	Let us swallow them up alive as the grave [Sheol]; and whole, as those that go down into the pit.
Psalm 73:18	You cast them down to destruction.
Ezekiel 28:8	They shall throw you down into the Pit...
2 Peter 2:4	...but cast them down to hell.
Psalm 49:17	For when he dies he shall carry nothing away; His glory shall not *descend* after him.
Amos 9:2	Though they *dig* into hell...
Lamentations 3:55	From the lowest pit [dungeon]...
Revelation 9:1–2; 17:8; 20:1, 3	...bottomless pit...
Luke 10:15, KJV	...shalt be thrust *down* to hell...
Job 21:13	...and in a moment, go down to the grave [Sheol in original Hebrew]
Pit	
Psalm 30:3	...that I should not go down to the pit.

Psalm 30:9	...when I go down to the pit?
Psalm 40:2	He also brought me up out of a horrible pit.
Psalm 55:23	But you, O God, shall bring them down to the pit of destruction.
Psalm 143:7	Do not hide Your face from me, lest I be like those who go down into the pit.
Job 33:24	Deliver him from going down to the Pit.
Job 33:28, KJV	He will deliver his soul from going into the pit.
Job 33:30, KJV	To bring back his soul from the pit, to be enlightened with the light of the living.
Job 33:18	He keeps back his soul from the Pit.
Isaiah 38:17	But You have lovingly delivered my soul from the pit of corruption...
Isaiah 38:18	For Sheol cannot thank you, death cannot praise You; those who go down to the pit cannot hope for Your truth.
Psalm 89:48	...shall he deliver his soul from the hand of the grave [Sheol]
Ezekiel 32:23	Her graves are set in the recesses of the Pit.
Ezekiel 32:25	Yet they bear their shame with those who go down to the Pit.
Ezekiel 32:29	...and with those who go down to the Pit.
Ezekiel 32:30	And bear their shame with those who go down to the Pit.
Revelation 9:1	To him was given the key to the bottomless pit.
Revelation 9:2	And he opened the bottomless pit, and smoke arose out of the pit like the smoke of a great furnace.

Revelation 11:7	…the beast that ascends out of the bottomless pit…
Revelation 20:1	…having the key to the bottomless pit…
Revelation 20:3	…and he cast him into the bottomless pit…
Revelation 17:8	The beast…will ascend out of the bottomless pit.

Fire/Burning

Psalm 140:10	Let burning coals fall upon them; let them be cast into the fire; into deep pits, that they rise not up again.
Job 18:15, KJV	…brimstone shall be scattered upon his habitation.
Psalm 11:6, KJV	Upon the wicked he shall rain snares, fire and brimstone, and an horrible tempest: this shall be the portion of their cup.
Luke 3:9	Every tree which does not bear good fruit is cut down and thrown into the fire.
Job 31:12, KJV	For it is a fire that consumeth to destruction.
Deuteronomy 32:22, KJV	For a fire is kindled in mine anger, and shall burn unto the lowest hell.
Revelation 14:10, KJV	He shall be tormented with fire and brimstone.
Revelation 20:10, KJV	…cast into the lake of fire and brimstone…and shall be tormented day and night for ever and ever.
Revelation 21:8	…shall have their part in the lake which burns with fire and brimstone.
Jude 7, KJV	…suffering the vengeance of eternal fire.
James 3:6, KJV	…on fire of hell.
Matthew 13:30	First gather together the tares and bind them in bundles to burn them.

Matthew 13:42, KJV	And shall cast them into a *furnace of fire*: there shall be wailing and gnashing of teeth.
Matthew 18:9, KJV	…cast into hell fire.
Matthew 18:8, KJV	…cast into *everlasting* fire.
Mark 9:43, KJV	…than having two hands to go into hell, into the fire that never shall be quenched.
Mark 9:45, KJV	…than having two feet to be cast into hell, into the fire that never shall be quenched.
Mark 9:46	…where "Their worm does not die, And the fire is not quenched."
Mark 9:47	…than having two eyes, to be cast into hell fire.
Mark 9:48	…where "Their worm does not die, And the fire is not quenched."
Mark 9:44	…where "Their worm does not die, And the fire is not quenched."
Matthew 5:22, KJV	Whosoever shall say, Thou fool, shall be in danger of hell fire.
Luke 3:17	But the chaff He will burn with unquenchable fire.
Psalm 37:20, KJV	They shall consume; into smoke shall they consume away.
Isaiah 66:24	And their fire is not quenched.
John 15:6	And they gather them and throw them into the fire and they are burned.
Matthew 3:12	But He will burn up the chaff with unquenchable fire.

Matthew 13:50, KJV	…and shall cast them into the furnace of fire.
Matthew 25:41, KJV	Depart from me, ye cursed, into everlasting fire.
Zechariah 3:2, KJV	Is not this a brand plucked out of the fire?
Amos 4:11, KJV	…and ye were as a firebrand plucked out of the burning.
Jude 23	Others save with fear, pulling them out of the fire.
Matthew 7:19, KJV	…and cast into the fire.
Matthew 13:49	…and cast them into a furnace of fire.
Hell	
Proverbs 5:5, KJV	Her steps take hold of hell.
Proverbs 9:18, KJV	Her guests are in the depths of hell.
Isaiah 5:14, KJV	Hell hath enlarged herself.
Proverbs 27:20, KJV	Hell and destruction are never full.
Psalm 88:3, KJV	My life draweth nigh unto the grave [sheol].
Psalm 55:15, KJV	Let them go down quick into hell.
Psalm 139:8	If I make my bed in hell, behold, You are there.
Luke 12:5	But I will show you whom you should fear: Fear Him who, after He has killed, has power to cast into hell; yes, I say to you, fear Him!

Revelation 20:14, KJV	...death and hell...
Habakkuk 2:5, KJV	...who enlargeth his desire as hell...
Matthew 23:33, KJV	How can ye escape the damnation of hell?
Matthew 16:18, KJV	...gates of hell shall not prevail...
Acts 2:27, KJV	Because thou wilt not leave my soul in hell...
Acts 2:31, KJV	His soul was not left in hell.
Revelation 6:8, KJV	Death, and Hell followed with him.
Psalm 49:15	But God will redeem my soul from the power of the grave [Sheol].
Destruction	
Isaiah 1:28	The destruction of transgressors and the sinners shall be together,
2 Peter 2:9, KJV	...reserve the unjust unto the day of judgement to be punished.
2 Thessalonians 1:9, KJV	Who shall be punished with *everlasting* destruction from the presence of the Lord, and from the glory of his power.
Romans 3:16, KJV	Destruction and misery are in their ways.
Matthew 7:13	Wide is the gate...that leads to destruction.
Matthew 23:33, KJV	How can ye escape the damnation of hell?

Matthew 25:30, KJV	There shall be weeping and gnashing of teeth.
Luke 13:3, KJV	Except ye repent, ye shall all likewise perish.
Luke 16:23, KJV	And in hell he lifted up his eyes, being in torments…
Psalm 9:17, KJV	The wicked shall be turned into hell, and all the nations that forget God.
Psalm 16:10, KJV	For thou wilt not leave my soul in hell; neither wilt thou suffer thine Holy One to see corruption.
Proverbs 10:29, KJV	Destruction shall be to the workers of iniquity.
Proverbs 11:21, KJV	The wicked shall not be unpunished.
Proverbs 15:11, KJV	Hell and Destruction are before the LORD.
Proverbs 21:15, KJV	Destruction shall be to the workers of iniquity.
Proverbs 31:8, KJV	…appointed to destruction.
Psalm 32:10, KJV	Many sorrows shall be to the wicked.
Psalm 139:19, KJV	Surely thou wilt slay the wicked.
Job 31:3	Is it not destruction for the wicked, and disaster for the workers of iniquity?
Job 31:23, KJV	For destruction from God was a terror to me.
Psalm 88:11, KJV	Shall thy lovingkindness be declared in the grave? or thy faithfulness in destruction?

Job 21:30, KJV	...that the wicked is reserved to the day of destruction?
Psalm 103:4, KJV	...who redeemeth thy life from destruction...
Matthew 25:30, KJV	There shall be weeping and gnashing of teeth.
Matthew 24:51, KJV	There shall be weeping and gnashing of teeth.
Matthew 13:42, KJV	There shall be wailing and gnashing of teeth.
Matthew 13:50, KJV	There shall be wailing and gnashing of teeth.
Matthew 23:14, KJV	Ye shall receive the greater damnation.
Mark 3:29, KJV	...in danger of eternal damnation.
Mark 12:40, KJV	These shall receive greater damnation.
John 5:29, KJV	...the resurrection of damnation.

Torment in Hell

Matthew 18:34, KJV	...delivered him to the tormentors.
Luke 12:46	...cut him in two...
Luke 12:47–48, KJV	...beaten with many stripes...beaten with few...
Psalm 50:22, KJV	...ye that forget God, lest I tear you in pieces.
Matthew 24:51	...and will cut him in two.... There shall be weeping and gnashing of teeth.

1 Corinthians 10:10, KJV	Neither murmur ye … [and be] destroyed of the destroyer.
Job 33:22, KJV	His soul draweth near unto the grave [Sheol], and his life to the destroyers.
1 Samuel 2:10, KJV	The adversaries of the LORD shall be broken to pieces.
2 Samuel 22:6, KJV	The sorrows of hell compassed me about.
Psalm 116:3	And the pangs of Sheol laid hold of me; I found trouble and sorrow.
Psalm 74:20, KJV	For the dark places of the earth are full of the habitations of cruelty.
Psalm 18:5, KJV	The sorrows of hell compassed me about.
Song of Solomon 8:6, KJV	Jealousy is cruel as the grave [Sheol].
Job 24:19	Drought and heat consume the snow waters: so doeth the grave [sheol] those who have sinned.
Psalm 49:14	…and their beauty shall consume in Sheol from their dwelling.
Revelation 9:2–11	…locust [demons] came [out of the pit] … to torment [men]…. Men will seek death and will not find it.
Darkness	
Job 18:18, KJV	He shall be driven from light into darkness, and chased out of the world.
Proverbs 20:20	Whoever curses his father or his mother, his lamp will be put out in deep darkness.

Psalm 88:6	You have laid me in the lowest pit, in darkness, in the depths.
Job 10:21–22	Before I go to the place from which I shall not return, to the land of darkness and the shadow of death, a land as dark as darkness itself, as the shadow of death, without any order, where even the light is like darkness...
Job 33:28, KJV	He will deliver his soul from going into the pit, and his life shall see the light.
1 Samuel 2:9, KJV	And the wicked shall be silent in darkness.
Nahum 1:8, KJV	And darkness shall pursue his enemies.
Revelation 16:10, KJV	And his [the beast] kingdom was full of darkness.
2 Peter 2:17, KJV	...to whom the midst of darkness is reserved for ever.
Jude 13	...blackness of darkness forever.
Psalm 49:19, KJV	They shall never see the light.
Job 33:30, KJV	...to bring back his soul from the pit, to be enlightened with the light of the living.
Matthew 25:30, KJV	...into outer darkness...
Lamentations 3:6, KJV	He hath set me in dark places, as they that be dead of old.
2 Peter 2:4, KJV	...delivered them into chains of darkness...
Matthew 8:12, KJV	...outer darkness...
Matthew 22:13, KJV	Cast him into outer darkness; there shall be weeping and gnashing of teeth.

Levels	
Matthew 23:14, KJV	Therefore ye shall receive the greater damnation [inferring a lesser].
Matthew 10:15, KJV	It shall be more tolerable for the land of Sodom…
Luke 12:42–48, KJV	Servant…beaten with many stripes…or few…
Matthew 23:15, KJV	Ye make him twofold more the child of hell than yourselves.
Hebrews 10:28, KJV	He that despised Moses' law died without mercy under two or three witnesses: Of how much sorer punishment, suppose ye, shall he be thought worthy, who hath trodden under foot the Son of God?
Proverbs 9:18, KJV	…the depths of hell…
Lamentations 3:35, KJV	…out of the low dungeon…
Psalm 86:13, KJV	Thou hast delivered my soul from the lowest Hell.
Psalm 88:6	You have laid me in the lowest pit, in darkness in the deeps.
Mark 12:40, KJV	These shall receive greater damnation.
Luke 20:47, KJV	The same shall receive greater damnation.
Matthew 16:27, KJV	And then he shall reward every man, according to his works.
Revelation 20:13, KJV	And they were judged every man according to their works.

Romans 2:5–6, KJV	…who will render to every man according to his deeds.
Revelation 21:8, KJV	…and all liars shall have their part in the lake which burneth with fire.
Job 21:17, KJV	God distributeth sorrows in His anger.
Job 20:29, KJV	This is the portion of the wicked man from God, and the heritage appointed unto him by God.
Zechariah 1:6	Just as the LORD of hosts determined to do to us, According to our ways and according to our deeds, So He has dealt with us.
Appointed or Assigned—God Assigns	
Matthew 24:51	…and will cut him in two and *appoint him his portion* with the hypocrites.
Revelation 21:8	All liars shall have *their part* in the lake which burns with fire.
Luke 12:46, KJV	…will cut him in sunder, and will *appoint him his portion* with the unbelievers.
Proverbs 31:8, KJV	…all such as are *appointed* to destruction.
Job 21:17, KJV	God *distributeth* sorrows in his anger.
1 Kings 20:42, KJV	Thus saith the LORD…a man whom I *appointed* to utter destruction.

Ezekiel 32:21–30	The strong among the mighty shall speak to him out of the midst of hell with them that help him. ("These heroic personages speak from the midst on Sheol, which may suggest that they are located in the heart of the netherworld, perhaps a more honorable assignment than 'remotest recesses of the pit.'"[1])
Job 20:29, KJV	This is the portion of the wicked man from God, and the heritage *appointed* unto him by God.

Prison Cell

Proverbs 7:27, KJV	…down to the chambers of death [chamber is an inner room]…
Isaiah 24:22, KJV	And they shall be gathered together, as prisoners are gathered in the pit, and shall be shut up in the prison.
Lamentations 3:55, KJV	…out of the low dungeon.
Isaiah 14:17, KJV	…that opened not the house of his prisoners?

Bars

Job 17:16, KJV	They shall go down to the bars of the pit.
Jonah 2:6, KJV	The earth with her bars was about me for ever: yet hast thou brought up my life from corruption.
Psalm 9:13, KJV	Thou liftest me up from the gates of death.
Psalm 107:18, KJV	…gates of death.
Job 38:17, KJV	Have the gates of death been opened unto thee?
Isaiah 38:10, KJV	I shall go to the *gates* of the grave [sheol; gates would be composed of bars].

Revelation 1:18, KJV	…keys of hell and of death.
Revelation 20:1, KJV	…key…

Stones

Lamentations 3:6–9, KJV	He hath set me in dark places, as they that be dead of old. He hath hedged me about, that I cannot get out: he hath made my chain heavy.…He hath inclosed my ways with hewn stone [despondent state of prophet while alive, could be prophetic of hell also].

Body in Hell

Matthew 10:28, KJV	Fear him which is able to destroy both soul and body in hell.
Proverbs 1:12, KJV	Let us swallow them up as the grave [Sheol]; and *whole*, as those that go down into the pit.
Matthew 5:29, KJV	…whole body should be cast into hell.
Ezekiel 32:27, KJV	…their iniquities shall be upon their bones. [They have bones in Sheol.]

Fear

Proverbs 10:24, KJV	The fear of the wicked, it shall come upon him.
Hebrews 10:31, KJV	It is a fearful thing to fall into the hands of the living God.
Psalm 73:18–19	You cast them down to destruction. Oh, how they are brought to desolation, as in a moment! They are utterly consumed with terrors.
Psalm 55:4, KJV	The terrors of death are fallen upon me.

Job 18:14, KJV	It shall bring him to the king of terrors.
Job 31:23, KJV	For destruction from God was a terror to me.

No Hope

Isaiah 38:18, KJV	They that go down into the pit cannot hope for thy truth.
1 Thessalonians 4:13, KJV	...as others, who have no hope.
Job 8:13, KJV	The hypocrite's hope shall perish.
Proverbs 11:7, KJV	The hope of unjust men perisheth.
Ecclesiastes 9:4, KJV	For to him that is joined to all living there is hope.
Ephesians 2:12, KJV	...having no hope, and without God in the world...
Lamentations 3:18, KJV	My strength and my hope is perished from the LORD.

Life Is Short

Psalm 102:3, KJV	For my days are consumed like smoke...
James 4:14, KJV	...vapour...
Psalm 39:5, KJV	Thou hast made my days as a handbreadth.
Psalm 103:15–16, KJV	As for man, his days are as grass....For the wind passeth over it, and it is gone.

Hell Desolate (No Life of Any Kind)

Ezekiel 26:20, KJV	...and shall set thee in the low parts of the earth, in places desolate of old, with them that go down into the pit.

Isaiah 59:10, KJV	We are in desolate places as dead men.
No Purpose	
Ecclesiastes 9:10	There is no work or device or knowledge or wisdom in the grave [Sheol]...
Psalm 31:17	Let them be silent [nothing to say—guilty—no one to talk to] in the grave [Sheol].
Psalm 88:12, KJV	...the land of forgetfulness?
Proverbs 10:28, KJV	The expectation of the wicked shall perish.
Job 10:22, KJV	A land...without any order...
Ecclesiastes 6:4, KJV	His name shall be covered in darkness.
Psalm 88:5, KJV	...whom thou rememberest no more.
Psalm 6:5, KJV	For in death there is no remembrance of thee
No Peace	
Isaiah 57:21, KJV	There is no peace, saith my God, to the wicked.
Ezekiel 7:25, KJV	Destruction cometh; and they shall seek peace, and there shall be none.
No Rest (From Torment, Also No Physical Rest or Sleep)	
Revelation 14:11, KJV	And the smoke of their torment ascendeth up for ever and ever: and they have no rest day nor night. [There is no rest from the torments and no sleep. Psalm 127:2 says, "He gives His beloved sleep." But they are not His beloved in hell.]

Isaiah 57:20, KJV	The wicked are like the troubled sea, when it cannot rest.
Thirst	
Zechariah 9:11, KJV	Thy prisoners out of the pit wherein is no water...
Luke 16:24, KJV	...that he may dip the tip of his finger in water, and cool my tongue; for I am tormented in this flame.
Odors/Stench	
Mark 9:25, KJV	When Jesus saw that the people came running together, he rebuked the foul spirit.
Revelation 18:2, KJV	...every foul spirit...
Profanity	
Ezekiel 22:26, KJV	I am profaned among them [vulgar and blasphemous language].
Ezekiel 28:14–16, KJV	You were the anointed cherub who covers.... Therefore I cast you as a profane thing. [Satan is profane, which means blasphemy and contempt against God.]
James 2:7, KJV	Do not they blaspheme that worthy name?
No Mercy	
Psalm 36:5, KJV	Thy mercy, O LORD, is in the heavens [not in hell].
Psalm 103:17, KJV	The mercy of the LORD is...upon them that fear him. [Those in hell do not fear.]
Psalm 103:4, KJV	Who redeemeth thy life from destruction; who crowneth thee with lovingkindness and tender mercies [tender mercies are connected with life].

Psalm 62:12, KJV	Also unto thee, O Lord, belongeth mercy.
Humiliation and Shame (Endured in Hell)	
Isaiah 5:14, KJV	Therefore hell hath enlarged herself, and opened her mouth without measure...and the mighty man shall be humbled.
Ezekiel 32:24, KJV	Yet have they borne their shame with them that go down into the pit.
Isaiah 5:15, KJV	And the mean man shall be brought down, and the mighty man shall be humbled.
Isaiah 57:9, KJV	...debase thyself even unto hell.
Worms	
Isaiah 14:11, KJV	The worm [maggot] is spread under thee, and the worms cover thee.
Isaiah 66:24	...for their worm does not die.
Mark 9:44, KJV	Where their worm dieth not...
Mark 9:46, KJV	Where their worm dieth not...
Mark 9:48, KJV	Where their worm dieth not...
Job 21:26, KJV	They shall lie down alike in the dust, and the worms shall cover them.
Job 24:20, KJV	The worm shall feed sweetly on him.
Eternal Separation	
2 Thessalonians 1:9, KJV	...who shall be punished with everlasting destruction from the presence of the Lord.
Proverbs 15:29, KJV	The LORD is far from the wicked.

No Strength	
Isaiah 14:9–10, KJV	Hell from beneath is moved to meet thee at thy coming....All they shall speak and say unto thee, Art thou become *weak* as we? [The word *weak* is the same word used in Judges 16:7 where Samson became weak when his hair was cut. It also means "ill" or "faint."]
Psalm 88:4, KJV	I am counted with them that go down into the pit: I am as a man that hath no strength.
Proverbs 10:29, KJV	The way of the LORD is strength to the upright. [They are not the upright in hell.]
Wrath	
John 3:36, KJV	The wrath of God abides on him.
Psalm 90:7–11, KJV	We are consumed by thine anger, and by thy wrath we are troubled. Who knoweth the power of thine anger?
2 Thessalonians 1:8, KJV	...taking vengeance on them that know not God.
Romans 1:18, KJV	For the wrath of God is revealed from heaven against all ungodliness.
Jeremiah 25:37, KJV	...fierce anger of the LORD.
1 Thessalonians 1:10, KJV	Jesus who delivers us from the wrath to come...
Romans 5:9	We shall be saved from wrath through Him.
Isaiah 66:15	...to render His anger with fury...
2 Thessalonians 1:9, KJV	...who shall be punished with everlasting destruction...

Psalm 73:27	For indeed, those who are far from You shall perish; You have destroyed all those who desert You for harlotry.
Hebrews 10:31	It is a fearful thing to fall into the hands of the living God.
Exodus 15:7	You sent forth Your wrath.
Lamentations 4:11	The Lord has fulfilled His fury, He has poured out His fierce anger.
Job 31:23, KJV	Destruction from God was a terror to me.
Proverbs 11:23, KJV	The expectation of the wicked is wrath.
Job 21:30, KJV	...the wicked is reserved to the day of destruction? they shall be brought forth to the day of wrath.
2 Peter 2:9	...to reserve the unjust under punishment for the day of judgment.
Jeremiah 4:4	...lest my fury come forth like fire, and burn so that no one can quench it.
Hebrews 10:27, KJV	...but a certain fearful looking for of judgment and fiery indignation, which shall devour the adversaries.

Righteous Judge

Zechariah 8:16, KJV	Execute the judgment of truth and peace in your gates.
Deuteronomy 16:18, KJV	...and they (judges) shall judge the people with just judgment.
Deuteronomy 16:20, KJV	That which is altogether just shalt thou follow.
Deuteronomy 32:4, KJV	For all his ways are judgment: a God of truth and without iniquity, just and right is he.

Proverbs 11:1, KJV	A just weight is his delight.
Proverbs 17:26, KJV	To punish the just is not good...
Isaiah 45:21, KJV	...a just God and a Savior...
Acts 17:31, KJV	He will judge the world in righteousness.
Psalm 7:9, KJV	For the righteous God trieth the hearts and reins.
Psalm 96:10, KJV	He [God] shall judge the people righteously.
Psalm 96.13, KJV	He shall judge the world with righteousness and the people with his truth.
Ecclesiastes 3:17, KJV	God shall judge the righteous and the wicked.

NOTES

Introduction

1. As quoted in Ted Koppel, "Lulling Viewers Into a State of Complicity," *Nieman Reports*, vol. 54, no. 3, Fall 2000, http://www.nieman.harvard.edu/reports/00-3NRfall/Lulling-Viewers.html (accessed May 13, 2008).

2. As quoted in R. T. Kendall, *In Pursuit of His Glory* (Lake Mary, FL: Charisma House, 2004), 1.

2—How Can a Loving God Send People to Hell?

1. Erwin Lutzer, *Where Was God* (n.p.: n.d.), 100.

2. Walter Ralston Martin and Jill Martin Rische, *Through the Windows of Heaven* (n.p.: Broadman and Holman Publisher, 1999), 103.

3. Billy Graham, *The Classic Writings of Billy Graham* (New York: Inspirational Press, 2005), 60.

4. Ibid., 56–57.

5. A. W. Pink, *The Doctrine of Election* (Pensacola, FL: Chapel Library, n.d.), 8.

6. Keith Morrison, "Hell, You Say?" Dateline NBC, MSNBC.com, http://www.msnbc.msn.com/id/14274572/ (accessed June 17, 2008).

7. Lutzer, *One Minute After You Die* (Chicago: Moody Publishers, 1997), 99.

8. Chuck and Nancy Missler, *Tomorrow May Be Too Late* (Coeur d'Alene, ID: The King's Highway Ministries, 2004), 61.

3—Don't All Roads Lead to God?

1. Erwin Lutzer, *Where Was God?* (Wheaton, IL: Tyndale House Publishers, 2006), 74–75.

2. Chuck Missler, *Prophecy 20/20* (Nashville, TN: Thomas Nelson, 2006), 263.

4—Am I Good Enough to Enter Heaven?

1. The Barna Group, "Beliefs: Heaven or Hell," http://www.barna.org/FlexPage.aspx?Page=Topic&TopicID=3 (accessed May 1, 2008).

2. Ray Comfort, *Hell's Best Kept Secret* (Springdale, PA: Whitaker House, 1989), 29.

3. Ray Comfort and Kirk Cameron, *The Way of the Master* (Wheaton, IL: Tyndale House Publishers, 2004), 48–49.

4. Graham, *The Classic Writings of Billy Graham*, 61.

5. Walter Martin, *The Kingdom of the Cults*, revised and updated (Grand Rapids, MI: Bethany House, 2003), 132.

5—Can't God Just Overlook My Sins?

1. Charles Stanley, *Charles Stanley's Handbook for Christian Living* (Nashville, TN: Thomas Nelson Publishers, 1996), 246.

2. Hal Lindsey, *Planet Earth—2000 AD* (Palos Verdes, CA: Western Front, Ltd., 1994), 301.

3. Graham, *The Classic Writings of Billy Graham*, 277.

7—Why Did God Create Such a Horrible Place?

1. Henry M. Morris and Martin E. Clark, *The Bible Has the Answer* (Green Forest, AR: Master Books, Inc., 1976, 1987), 311.

2. Charles Spurgeon, "The Holy Spirit and the One Church," sermon no. 167, delivered December 13, 1857, at the Music Hall, Royal Surrey Gardens, http://www.spurgeon.org/sermons/0167.htm (accessed May 13, 2008).

8—Does the Crime Fit the Punishment?

1. Lutzer, *One Minute After You Die*, 107.

2. Ibid., 108.

3. Christopher W. Morgan and Robert A. Peterson, eds., *Hell Under Fire* (Grand Rapids, MI: Zondervan, 2004), 223. Permission applied for.

4. R. T. Kendall, *Out of Your Comfort Zone* (New York: FaithWords, 2006), 85.

9—Hell by Default

1. Morris and Clark, *The Bible Has the Answer*, 311.

10—How Does God Warn Us?

1. Lutzer, *One Minute After You Die*.

2. Chuck Missler, "The Nature of Our Reality," *Personal Update*, March 2008, http://www.khouse.org/articles/2008/766/ (accessed May 19, 2008).

3. Jonathan Henry, *The Astronomy Book* (n.p.: n.d.), 16.

4. John Bunyan, *Visions of Heaven and Hell* (New Kensington, PA: Whitaker House, 1998), 36.

5. John MacArthur, *The MacArthur Bible Commentary* (Nashville, TN: Thomas Nelson, 2005), 1857. Permission applied for.

11—We Wouldn't Want to Offend Anyone

1. Holly McClure, *Death by Entertainment* (n.p.: Lions Head Press, 2001), 43, 131–132.

2. Franklin Graham, *The Name* (Nashville, TN: Nelson Books, 2002), 47, 51.

3. Missler, *Prophecy 20/20*, 248.

4. C. S. Lewis, *Mere Christianity* (New York: HarperOne, 2001), 38.

5. MSNBC.com, "Belief in Hell Boosts Economic Growth, Fed Says," July 27, 2004, http://www.msnbc.msn.com/id/5529195/ or for full text see: http://www.kaleochurch.net/viewtopic.php?t=293&sid=9250dea65aef990ebf0afded12b97d50 (accessed May 9, 2008).

6. Jeffress, *Hell? Yes!* 80.

7. Ibid., 29.

8. Morris and Clark, *The Bible Has the Answer*, 14.

9. A. W. Tozer, *Jesus, Our Man in Glory* (Camp Hill, PA: Christian Publications, 1988), 68.

10. Reinhard Bonnke, *Faith: The Link with God's Power* (Nashville, TN: Thomas Nelson, 1998), 75.

11. Kendall, *Out of Your Comfort Zone*, 15, 84.

12—What Makes Christianity Unique?

1. Graham, *The Classic Writings of Billy Graham*, 254.

2. Harrison House Publishers, *Powerful Faith-Building Quotes From Leading Charismatic Ministers of All Times* (Tulsa, OK: Harrison House, 1996), 151.

3. Graham, *The Classic Writings of Billy Graham*, 182.

4. Ibid., 183.

5. Ibid.

6. Henry Morris, *Defending the Faith* (Green Forest, AR: Master Books, Inc., 1999), 37.

7. John G. Lake, *His Life, His Sermons, His Boldness of Faith*, Kenneth Copeland, compiler (Fort Worth, TX: Kenneth Copeland Ministries, 1995), 5.

8. Josh McDowell, *Evidence That Demands a Verdict* (Nashville, TN: Nelson Reference, 1999), 20.

9. Ibid., 21.

10. Ibid., 19.

11. Ibid., 22.

12. Morris and Clark, *The Bible Has the Answer*, 2.

13. As quoted in McDowell, *Evidence That Demands a Verdict*, 30.

13—How Can a Christian See Hell?

1. Phil Pringle, *Moving in the Spirit* (n.p.: n.d.), 85.

2. Lutzer, *One Minute After You Die*, 25.

3. Ibid., 69.

4. *Strong's Exhaustive Concordance*, PC Study Bible V3.2F (www.biblesoft.com: BibleSoft, 1998), s.v. "*etsem*."

5. Morgan and Peterson, eds., *Hell Under Fire*, 58.

6. Morris and Clark, *The Bible Has the Answer*, 312–313.

7. Josh McDowell, *A Ready Defense* (Nashville, TN: Thomas Nelson, Inc., 1993), 417.

8. Martin, *The Kingdom of the Cults*, 582.

9. Lester Sumrall, *Run With the Vision* (South Bend, IN: Sumrall Publishing, 1986), 105.

10. David W. Baker, T. Desmond Alexander, and Bruce K. Waltke, *Obadiah, Jonah, Micah: Tyndale Old Testament Commentaries* (Downers Grove, IL: InterVarsity Press, 1988), 114, 116.

11. Leslie C. Allen, *The Books of Joel, Obadiah, Jonah, and Micah: New International Commentary on the Old Testament* (Grand Rapids, MI: Wm. B. Eerdmans Publishing Co., 1976), 216–217.

12. Franklin S. Page and Billy K. Smith, *Amos, Obadiah, Jonah: New American Commentary* (Nashville, TN: B&H Publishing Group, 1995), 251.

13. Morris and Clark, *The Bible Has the Answer*, 75–76.

14. MacArthur, *The MacArthur Bible Commentary*, 1335.

15. Matthew Henry, *Matthew Henry's Commentary on the Whole Bible* (Hendrickson Publishers, 2005), 1439. Public domain.

16. Robert Jamieson, A. R. Fausset, and David Brown, *Jamieson, Fausset, and Brown's Commentary on the Whole Bible* (Grand Rapids, MI: Zondervan, 1999), 1023. Permission applied for.

17. Wayne Grudem, *Systematic Theology: An Introduction to Biblical Doctrine* (Grand Rapids, MI: Zondervan, 1995), 609.

18. Randy Alcorn, *Heaven* (Wheaton, IL: Tyndale House Publishers, Inc., 2004), 115.

19. MacArthur, *The MacArthur Bible Commentary*, 1424.

20. Henry, *Matthew Henry's Commentary on the Whole Bible*, 1439.

21. Kendall, *Out of Your Comfort Zone*, 36.

14—Expounding on *23 Minutes in Hell*

1. John MacArthur, "Hell—the Furnace of Fire," Tape #GC2304 http://www.jcsm.org/StudyCenter/john_macarthur/sg2304.htm (accessed May 15, 2008).

2. Times Online, "Pope: Hell Is a Real Place Where Sinners Burn in Everlasting Fire," *The Times*, March 27, 2007, http://www.timesonline.co.uk/tol/news/world/europe/article1572646.ece (accessed May 15, 2008).

3. Robert Jeffress, *Hell? Yes!* (Colorado Springs, CO: Waterbrook Press, 2004), 76.

4. Morgan and Peterson, eds., *Hell Under Fire*, 28

5. John Calvin, *Commentary of the Harmony of the Evangelists, Matthew, Mark, and Luke*, William Pringle, trans. (Edinburgh, Scotland: The Calvin Translation Society, 1846), 182.

6. John Piper, "Behold the Kindness and the Severity of God," a sermon delivered June 14, 1992, at Bethlehem Baptist Church, http://www.soundofgrace.com/piper92/06-14-92.htm (accessed May 15, 2008).

7. Quoted in Robert Peterson, *Hell on Trial* (Phillipsburg, NJ: Presbyterian and Reformed Publishing Co., 1995), 113–114.

8. *Strong's Exhaustive Concordance*, s.v. "*chalah*."

9. Lester Sumrall, *101 Questions and Answers on Demon Powers* (South Bend, IN: Sumrall Publishing, 1983), 45.

10. Alcorn, *Heaven*, 292.

11. Grudem, *Systematic Theology*, 612.

12. *Strong's Exhaustive Concordance*, s.v. "*arowm.*"

13. United Methodist Church, "The Sermons of John Wesley: Sermon 73, Of Hell," http://new.gbgm-umc.org/umhistory/wesley/sermons/73/ (accessed May 15, 2008).

14. MacArthur, "Hell—the Furnace of Fire."

15. Trent C. Butler et al., eds., *Holman Illustrated Bible Dictionary* (Nashville, TN: B&H Publishing Group, 2003), 1488, s.v. "Commentary on Isaiah 14:10–11." Permission applied for.

16. W. E. Vine, *Vine's Expository Dictionary of Old and New Testament Words* (Grand Rapids, MI: Fleming H. Revell & Co., 1981), 286.

17. Lutzer, *One Minute After You Die*, 39.

18. Morgan and Peterson, eds., *Hell Under Fire*, 58.

19. Paul J. Achtemeier, ed. *Harper's Bible Dictionary* (New York: HarperCollins, 1985), 365.

20. Henry, *Matthew Henry's Commentary on the Whole Bible*, 2346.

21. Morgan and Peterson, eds., *Hell Under Fire*, 58.

15—Why Does a Christian Need to Know About Hell?

1. Edward Donnelly, *Heaven and Hell* (Carlisle, PA: Banner of Truth, 2002), 55.

2. Grant R. Jeffrey, *Journey Into Eternity* (Minneapolis, MN: Waterbrook Press, 2000), 219.

3. Graham, *The Classic Writings of Billy Graham*, 278.

4. Donnelly, *Heaven and Hell*, 56.

5. Alcorn, *Heaven*, 27.

6. John Calvin, *Calvin's Commentaries, Vol. 33: Matthew, Mark and Luke, Part III*, trans by John King, Sacred-Texts.com, http://www.sacred-texts.com/chr/calvin/cc33/cc33024.htm (accessed May 19, 2008).

7. Barna.org, "Barna Lists the 12 Most Significant Religious Findings from 2006 Surveys," *The Barna Update*, December 20, 2006, http://www.barna .org/FlexPage.aspx?Page=BarnaUpdateNarrow&BarnaUpdateID=252 (accessed May 9, 2008).

8. Ibid.

9. Solomon Stoddard, *The Fear of Hell Restrains Men From Sin*, ed. Don Kistler (Morgan, PA: Soli Deo Gloria Publications, 2003), 9.

10. Peterson, *Hell on Trial*, 42.

11. R. T. Kendall, *Total Forgiveness* (Lake Mary, FL: Charisma House, 2002, 2007), 23.

12. Comfort and Cameron, *The Way of the Master*, 79.

13. Mike Anton and William Lobdell, "Hold the Fire and Brimstone," *Los Angeles Times*, June 19, 2002, A1.

14. As quoted in Peterson, *Hell on Trial*, 81.

15. CBNNews.com, "Most Don't Believe in Hell," March 28, 2007, http://www.cbn.com/cbnnews/127721.aspx (accessed May 19, 2008).

16. Times Online, "Pope: Hell Is a Real Place Where Sinners Burn in Everlasting Fire."

17. Jeffrey, *Journey Into Eternity*, 212.

18. As quoted in Morgan and Peterson, eds., *Hell Under Fire*, 68.

19. *Strong's Exhaustive Concordance*, s.v. "arats."

20. John Bevere, *The Fear of the Lord* (Lake Mary, FL: Charisma House, 1997, 2006), 78–80.

21. William MacDonald, *Believer's Bible Commentary* (Nashville, TN: Thomas Nelson Publishers, Inc., 1989, 1990, 1992, 1995), 1839. Permission applied for.

22. Robert G. Gromacki, *New Testament Survey* (Grand Rapids, MI: Baker Academic, 1974), 104, 222.

23. Jamieson, Fausset, and Brown, *Jamieson, Fausset, and Brown's Commentary on the Whole Bible*, 1240.

24. Charles Spurgeon, John Wesley, and Matthew Henry, *Parallel Commentary on the New Testament* (Chattanooga, TN: AMG Publishers, 2003), 605.

25. Ray Comfort on TBN

26. Comfort and Cameron, *The Way of the Master*, 267.

27. Ibid.

28. As quoted in Morgan and Peterson, eds., *Hell Under Fire*, 233.

29. Ibid.

30. Norvel Hayes, *Rescuing Souls from Hell* (Tulsa, OK: Harrison House, 1983), 9.

31. Comfort, *Hell's Best Kept Secret*, 96.

32. C. H. Spurgeon, *The Soulwinner* (New Kensington, PA: Whitaker House, 1995), 110.

33. Donnelly, *Heaven and Hell*, 60.

34. Sumrall, *Run With the Vision*, 34.

35. Spurgeon, *The Soulwinner*, 9.

36. Donnelly, *Heaven and Hell*, 58.

37. Hayes, *Rescuing Souls From Hell*, 43.

38. Jeffress, *Hell? Yes!* 73.

39. As quoted in Comfort, *Hell's Best Kept Secret*, 23.

40. Ibid., 24.

41. Comfort and Cameron, *The Way of the Master*, 85.

42. Ibid.

43. Ibid., 86.

44. Ibid., 87.

45. Henrietta C. Mears, *What the Bible Is All About* (San Bernardino, CA: Regal Books, 1983), 473.

46. Spurgeon, *The Soulwinner*, 19, 77.

47. As quoted in Comfort and Cameron, *The Way of the Master*, 89.

48. Ibid., 78.

49. Comfort and Cameron, *The Way of the Master*, 122.

50. Donnelly, *Heaven and Hell*, 56.

51. As quoted in Jeffress, *Hell? Yes!* 92.

52. Ibid., 91.

53. Sumrall, *Run With the Vision*, 163.

17—True Stories and Testimonies

1. Pastor Phil Clements, Victory Vision, P.O. Box 284, Barnsdall, OK 74002; Revphil@barnsdallag.com.

18—An Overall Perspective

1. Lake, *His Life, His Sermons, His Boldness of Faith*, 62.

2. Morris, *Defending the Faith*, 75.

3. Graham, *The Classic Writings of Billy Graham*, 54.

4. Ibid., 55–56.

5. Morris, *Defending the Faith*, 74.

6. Graham, *The Classic Writings of Billy Graham*, 54.

7. McDowell, *A Ready Defense*, 412.

8. Chuck Smith, *What the World Is Coming To* (Costa Mesa, CA: Word for Today, 1993), 56.

9. Graham, *The Classic Writings of Billy Graham*, 60, 195.

10. Lake, *His Life, His Sermons, His Boldness of Faith*, 5.

11. Martin, *The Kingdom of the Cults*, 585.

12. Missler, *Prophecy 20/20*, 262.

19—Hell, Hades, Sheol, Gehenna—What Is the Difference?

1. *Strong's Exhaustive Concordance.*

2. MacArthur, *John MacArthur Study Bible*, 803, s.v. "Psalm 69:15."

3. Henry, *Matthew Henry Commentary on the Whole Bible*, 823, s.v. "Ps. 55:23."

4. MacDonald, *Believer's Bible Commentary*, 2366, s.v. "Revelation 9:1, 2."

5. Butler et al., eds., *Holman Illustrated Bible Dictionary*, 15.

6. Jamieson, Fausset, and Brown, *Jamieson, Fausset, and Brown's Commentary on the Whole Bible*, 1552, s.v. "Revelation 9:2."

7. MacArthur, *The MacArthur Bible Commentary*, 2010, s.v. "Revelation 9:1–2."

8. Ronald F. Youngblood, ed., *Nelson's New Illustrated Bible Dictionary* (Nashville, TN: Thomas Nelson Publishers, Inc., 1995), 13. Permission applied for.

9. Vine, *Vine's Complete Expository Dictionary of Old and New Testament Words.*

10. MacDonald, *Believer's Bible Commentary*, 1433.

11. Taken from Leland Ryken et al., eds., *Dictionary of Biblical Imagery* (Downers Grove, IL: InterVarsity Christian Fellowship/USA, 1998), 198, 647. Used with permission of InterVarsity Press, P. O. Box 1400, Downer's Grove, IL 60515. ivpress.com.

12. William Evans, *The Great Doctrines of the Bible* (Chicago, IL: Moody Publishers, 1992), 297.

13. Butler et al., eds., *Holman Illustrated Bible Dictionary*, 699, 1482–1483, 745.

14. Jamieson, Fausset, and Brown, *Jamieson, Fausset, and Brown's Commentary on the Whole Bible*, 1477, 1013.

15. M. Mills, *The Life of Christ: A Study Guide to the Gospel Record* (Dallas, TX: 3E Ministries, 1999).

16. Lutzer, *One Minute After You Die*, 35.

17. MacArthur, *The MacArthur Bible Commentary*, 1438, s.v. "Acts 2:27."

18. Ibid., 1313, 1332, s.v. "Luke 16:23."

19. Paul Enns, *The Moody Handbook of Theology* (Chicago, IL: Moody Publishers, 2008), 393.

20. Youngblood, ed., *Nelson's New Illustrated Bible Dictionary*, 1164, 996.

21. I. Howard Marshall et al., eds., *New Bible Dictionary* (Downers Grove, IL: InterVarsity Press, 1996), 1092.

22. Merrill F. Unger, *Unger's Commentary on the Old Testament* (Chattanooga, TN: AMG Publishers, 2003), 765. Permission applied for.

23. Vine, *Vine's Complete Expository Dictionary of Old and New Testament Words*, 900, 300.

24. Smith, *What the World Is Coming To*, 195, 92.

25. Jeffress, *Hell? Yes!* 76.

26. Jeffrey, *Journey Into Eternity*, 217.

27. Taken from Ryken et al., eds., *Dictionary of Biblical Imagery*, 376.

28. Butler et al., eds., *Holman Illustrated Bible Dictionary*, 631.

29. John MacArthur, ed., *MacArthur Study Bible* (Nashville, TN: Thomas Nelson, 2006), 1001, regarding Isaiah 30:33.

30. Henry, *Matthew Henry's Commentary on the Whole Bible*, 1136.

31. Youngblood, ed., *Nelson's New Illustrated Bible Dictionary*, 556, 568.

32. Unger, *Unger's Commentary on the Old Testament*, 1226, s.v. "Isaiah 30:33."

33. Vine, *Vine's Complete Expository Dictionary of Old and New Testament Words*, 300.

34. As quoted in Morgan and Peterson, eds., *Hell Under Fire*, 227.

35. Houghton Mifflin, *The American Heritage Dictionary of the English Language*, 4th edition (Boston, MA: Houghton Mifflin, 2006), s.v. "hell."

36. Taken from Ryken et al., eds., *Dictionary of Biblical Imagery*, 376.

37. Lawrence O. Richards, *Encyclopedia of Biblical Words* (Grand Rapids, MI: Zondervan, 1985, 1991), 337.

38. Youngblood, ed., *Nelson's New Illustrated Bible Dictionary*, 556.

39. Vine, *Vine's Complete Expository Dictionary of Old and New Testament Words*, 300.

40. Butler et al., eds., *Holman Illustrated Bible Dictionary*, 745.

41. Jeffrey, *Journey Into Eternity*, 218.

42. Lutzer, *One Minute After You Die*, 110.

43. MacArthur, *The MacArthur Bible Commentary*, 1934.

44. Vine, *Vine's Complete Expository Dictionary of Old and New Testament Words*, 300.

45. Walter A. Elwell, ed., *Baker Commentary on the Bible* (Grand Rapids, MI: Baker Academic, 2001), 495.

46. MacDonald, *Believer's Bible Commentary*, 960.

47. Jamieson, Fausset, and Brown, *Jamieson, Fausset, and Brown's Commentary on the Whole Bible*, 546.

48. MacArthur, *The MacArthur Bible Commentary*, 795.

49. Henry, *Matthew Henry's Commentary on the Whole Bible*, 1136.

50. Youngblood, ed., *Nelson's New Illustrated Bible Dictionary*, 1269.

51. Taken from Ryken et al., eds., *Dictionary of Biblical Imagery*, 198, 647.

52. Butler et al., eds., *Holman Illustrated Bible Dictionary*, 699, 1482.

53. Youngblood, ed., *Nelson's New Illustrated Bible Dictionary*, 1164, 966.

54. Marshall et al., eds., *New Bible Dictionary*, 1092.

55. Chuck Missler, "Heaven and Hell," tape two, available as an audio CD, VHS video, or DVD from Koinonia House Online, http://www.khouse.org.

56. Morris and Clark, *The Bible Has the Answer*, 312.

57. Maurice Rawlings, *Beyond Death's Door* (Nashville, TN: Thomas Nelson, 1978), 85.

20—Is the Fire Real or Metaphorical?

1. MacDonald, *Believer's Bible Commentary*, 2366, s.v. "Revelation 9:1–2."

2. Henry, *Matthew Henry's Commentary on the Whole Bible*, 2475, s.v. "Revelation 9:2."

3. Butler et al., eds., *Holman Illustrated Bible Dictionary*, 745–746.

4. Ibid., 567.

5. Morris and Clark, *The Bible Has the Answer*, 74.

6. As quoted in Morgan and Peterson, eds., *Hell Under Fire*, 226–227.

7. Richards, *Encyclopedia of Biblical Words*, 280.

8. Times Online, "Pope: Hell Is a Real Place Where Sinners Burn in Everlasting Fire."

9. Henry, *Matthew Henry's Commentary on the Whole Bible*, 1885, 2018.

10. As quoted in Robert Jeffress, *Hell? Yes!* 76.

11. As quoted by R. Albert Mohler Jr., *Hell Under Fire*, 28.

12. Henry, *Matthew Henry's Commentary on the Whole Bible*, 1834.

13. Donnelly, *Heaven and Hell*, 37.

14. Jamieson, Fausset, and Brown, *Jamieson, Fausset, and Brown's Commentary on the Whole Bible*, 373.

15. Henry, *Matthew Henry's Commentary on the Whole Bible*, 759.

16. Ibid., 1136.

17. Ibid., 1752.

21—Who Were the "Spirits in Prison"?

1. Elwell, ed., *Baker Commentary on the Bible*, 1168.
2. MacDonald, *Believer's Bible Commentary*, 2272.
3. Grudem, *Systematic Theology*, 591.
4. MacArthur, *The MacArthur Bible Commentary*, 1915.
5. Ibid., 1739.
6. Henry, *Matthew Henry's Commentary on the Whole Bible*, 2430.
7. Youngblood, ed., *Nelson's New Illustrated Bible Dictionary*, 1198–1199.
8. Jamieson, Fausset, and Brown, *Jamieson, Fausset, and Brown's Commentary on the Whole Bible*, 1477.

22—What Is the Significance of the Number 23?

1. Henry, *Matthew Henry's Commentary on the Whole Bible*, 1632.
2. Smith, *What the World Is Coming To*, 71–72.

23—Who Were the "Captivity Captive"?

1. MacArthur, *The MacArthur Bible Commentary*, 1693, s.v. "Ephesians 4:8–9."
2. Jamieson, Fausset, and Brown, *Jamieson, Fausset, and Brown's Commentary on the Whole Bible*, 1289.
3. Ibid., 1290.
4. Ibid., 948, s.v. "Matthew 27:52."
5. Ibid., 1437, s.v. "Hebrews 11:39."
6. Henry, *Matthew Henry's Commentary on the Whole Bible*, 2313, s.v. "Ephesians 4:8–9."
7. Ibid., 1770, s.v. "Matthew 27:52–53."
8. Youngblood, ed., *Nelson's New Illustrated Bible Dictionary*, 247.
9. Vine, *Vine's Complete Expository Dictionary of Old and New Testament Words*, 88.
10. Smith, *What the World Is Coming To*, 91–93.

24—Demons and Fallen Angels—Is There a Difference?

1. Taken from Ryken et al., eds., *Dictionary of Biblical Imagery*, 202.
2. Richards, *Encyclopedia of Biblical Words*, 218.

3. Ibid., 219.

4. Graham, *The Classic Writings of Billy Graham*, 39, 57.

5. MacArthur, *The MacArthur Bible Commentary*, 2015, s.v. "Revelation 12:4."

6. Henry, *Matthew Henry's Commentary on the Whole Bible*, 2461.

7. Youngblood, ed., *Nelson's New Illustrated Bible Dictionary*, 346.

8. Sumrall, *101 Questions and Answers on Demon Powers*, 14.

9. *Strong's Exhaustive Concordance*, s.v. "*daimonion.*"

10. MacArthur, *MacArthur Study Bible*, 1559.

11. Vine, *Vine's Complete Expository Dictionary of Old and New Testament Words*, 166.

12. *The American Heritage Dictionary of the English Language*, s.v. "demon."

13. Vines, *Vine's Complete Expository Dictionary of Old and New Testament Words*, 157.

14. *Strong's Exhaustive Concordance*, s.v. "*daimonizomai.*"

15. Ibid., s.v. "*daimon.*"

25—Are Satan and His Demons on the Earth and in Sheol?

1. MacDonald, *Believer's Bible Commentary*, 950. s.v. "Isaiah 14:12–17."

2. Taken from Ryken et al., eds., *Dictionary of Biblical Imagery*, 761, s.v. "Isaiah 14:3–21."

3. Richards, *Encyclopedia of Biblical Words*, 543.

4. MacArthur, *The MacArthur Bible Commentary*, 777, s.v. "Isaiah 14:12–14."

5 Henry, *Matthew Henry's Commentary on the Whole Bible*, 1106, s.v. "Isaiah 14:11–12."

6. Youngblood, ed., *Nelson's New Illustrated Bible Dictionary*, 1131.

7. Unger, *Unger's Commentary on the Old Testament*, 1182, s.v. "Isaiah 14:13–17."

8. Elwell, ed., *Baker Commentary on the Bible*, 578.

9. Charles L. Feinberg, *The Prophecy of Ezekiel* (n.p.: Wipf & Stock Publishers, 2003), as quoted in MacDonald, *Believer's Bible Commentary*, 1058.

10. MacArthur, ed., *MacArthur Study Bible*, 1191, s.v. "Ezekiel 28:14–16."

11. Unger, *Unger's Commentary on the Old Testament*, 1552–1553, s.v. "Ezekiel 28:11–19."

12. Sumrall, *101 Questions and Answers on Demon Powers*, 18–19.

13. MacArthur, *MacArthur Study Bible*, 990.

26—Does the Devil Rule Over Hell?

1. Vine, *Vine's Expository Dictionary of Old and New Testament Words*, 300.

2. Peterson, *Hell on Trial*, 44–45, 47.

3. Henry, *Matthew Henry's Commentary on the Whole Bible*, 165.

27—How Can Demons Torment When They Are in Torment?

1. Henry, *Matthew Henry's Commentary on the Whole Bible*, 1709, s.v. "Matthew 18:34."

2. Spurgeon, Wesley, and Henry, *Parallel Commentary on the New Testament*, 72, s.v. "Matthew 18:34."

3. *Strong's Exhaustive Concordance*, s.v. "*basanistes*."

4. Martin, *The Kingdom of the Cults*, 583.

5. Spurgeon, Wesley, and Henry, *Parallel Commentary on the New Testament*, 76.

6. Henry, *Matthew Henry's Commentary on the Whole Bible*, 816.

7. Ibid., 1452. s.v. "Matthew 25:41."

8. Mifflin, *The American Heritage Dictionary of the English Language*, s.v. "hell."

9. MacArthur, ed., *MacArthur Study Bible*, 2004.

10. Henry, *Matthew Henry's Commentary on the Whole Bible*, 2475.

11. Bunyan, *Visions of Heaven and Hell*, 140.

12. Ibid., 136.

13. Ibid., 127, 139–140.

14. MacArthur, "Hell—the Furnace of Fire."

15. Ibid.

16. Josephus, "An Extract Out of Josephus's Discourse to the Greeks Concerning Hades," Wesley Center Online, http://wesley.nnu.edu/biblical_studies/josephus/hades.htm (accessed May 21, 2008).

17. Morris and Clark, *The Bible Has the Answer*.

18. MacArthur, ed., *MacArthur Study Bible*, 1433.

19. Henry, *Matthew Henry's Commentary on the Whole Bible*, 1661.

20. MacArthur, *The MacArthur Bible Commentary*, 1166, s.v. "Matthew 22:13, 'weeping and gnashing of teeth.'"

21. Henry, *Matthew Henry's Commentary on the Whole Bible*, 692, s.v. "Job 18:18."

22. Jamieson, Fausset, and Brown, *Jamieson, Fausset, and Brown's Commentary on the Whole Bible*, 395, s.v. "Job 33:22."

23. Ibid., 1569.

24. Henry, *Matthew Henry's Commentary on the Whole Bible*, 876.

25. Lutzer, *One Minute After You Die*, 25.

26. Vine, *Vine's Expository Dictionary of Old and New Testament Words*, 158.

27. Henry, *Matthew Henry's Commentary on the Whole Bible*, 165.

28. MacDonald, *Believer's Bible Commentary*, 2377.

29. John F. Walvoord, *Bible Knowledge Commentary: Old Testament and New Testament* (n.p.: Victor, 1985).

30. Jamieson, Fausset, and Brown, *Jamieson, Fausset, and Brown's Commentary on the Whole Bible*, 1583, s.v. "Revelation 20:1–2."

31. MacArthur, ed., *MacArthur Study Bible*, 2008.

32. Henry, *Matthew Henry's Commentary on the Whole Bible*, 165, s.v. "Revelation 20:10."

33. Warren W. Wiersbe, *The Wiersbe Bible Commentary: The Complete New Testament* (Colorado Springs, CO: David C. Cook, 2007), 1082.

34. Elwell, ed., *Baker Commentary on the Bible*, 732.

35. MacDonald, *Believer's Bible Commentary*, 1233.

36. Warren W. Wiersbe, *Bible Exposition Commentary* (Colorado Springs, CO: David C. Cook, 2004).

37. Walvoord, *Bible Knowledge Commentary*.

38. Jamieson, Fausset, and Brown, *Jamieson, Fausset, and Brown's Commentary on the Whole Bible*, 952, s.v. "Luke 4:34."

39. MacArthur, *The MacArthur Bible Commentary*, 1982, s.v. "Jude 6."

40. Ibid., 1137.

41. Ibid., 1935, s.v. "2 Peter 2:4."

42. Henry, *Matthew Henry's Commentary on the Whole Bible*, 2437.

43. Ibid., 2461.

44. Ibid., 1652–1653.

45. As quoted in Spurgeon, Wesley, and Henry, *Parallel Commentary on the New Testament*, 28.

46. Wiersbe, *The Wiersbe Bible Commentary: The Complete New Testament*.

28—Were the Giants a Result of the Fallen Angels?

1. Elwell, ed., *Baker Commentary on the Bible*, 16.

2. Ibid., 1191.

3. MacDonald, *Believer's Bible Commentary*, 39, s.v. "Jude 6."

4. Merrill F. Unger, *Unger's Bible Dictionary* (Chicago, IL: Moody Press, 1986), 788, as quoted in MacDonald, *Believer's Bible Commentary*, 40.

5. Ibid., 2295.

6. Henry, *Matthew Henry's Commentary on the Whole Bible*, 22, s.v. "Genesis 6:4."

7. Elwell, ed., *Baker Commentary on the Bible*, 113, s.v. "Deuteronomy 3:11."

8. MacDonald, *Believer's Bible Commentary*, 2341.

9. Ibid., 205.

10. Larry Richards, *Bible Teacher's Commentary* (Colorado Springs, CO: David C. Cook, 2002), 42.

11. Jamieson, Fausset, and Brown, *Jamieson, Fausset, and Brown's Commentary on the Whole Bible*, 143, s.v. "Deuteronomy 3:11."

12. MacArthur, *The MacArthur Bible Commentary*, 569, s.v. "Job 1:6."

13. Ibid., 201.

14. Henry, *Matthew Henry's Commentary on the Whole Bible*, 658, s.v. "Job 2."

15. Ibid., 732, s.v. "Job 38:7."

16. Ibid., 239, s.v. "Deuteronomy 3:11."

17. *Unger's Commentary on the Old Testament*, 36, s.v. "Genesis 6:4."

18. Ibid., 733.

19. Jeffrey, *Journey Into Eternity*, 218.

29—Was It Really Samuel?

1. Elwell, ed., *Baker Commentary on the Bible*, 211.

2. MacDonald, *Believer's Bible Commentary*, 319.

3. Jamieson, Fausset, and Brown, *Jamieson, Fausset, and Brown's Commentary on the Whole Bible*, 227.

4. MacArthur, *The MacArthur Bible Commentary*, 343.

5. Youngblood, ed., *Nelson's New Illustrated Bible Dictionary*, 381.

6. Unger, *Unger's Commentary on the Old Testament*, 405–406.

7. Martin, *The Kingdom of the Cults*, 582.

30—What Is Soul Sleep?

1. Lutzer, *One Minute After You Die*, 48.

2. MacDonald, *Believer's Bible Commentary*, 1805, s.v. "1 Corinthians 15:18."

3. Richards, *Bible Teacher's Commentary*, 872, s.v. "1 Corinthians 15:18."

4. MacArthur, *The MacArthur Bible Commentary*, 1606, s.v. "1 Corinthians 15:18."

5. Martin, *The Kingdom of the Cults*, 143.

6. Richards, *Bible Teacher's Commentary*, 1530, s.v. "John 11:11."

7. Jamieson, Fausset, and Brown, *Jamieson, Fausset, and Brown's Commentary on the Whole Bible*, 1052.

8. Henry, *Matthew Henry's Commentary on the Whole Bible*, 1989, s.v. "John 11:11–12."

9. Martin, *The Kingdom of the Cults*, 143–144.

10. Richards, *Bible Teacher's Commentary*, 907, s.v. "Ecclesiastes 9:5."

11. Henry, *Matthew Henry's Commentary on the Whole Bible*, 1048, s.v. "Ecclesiastes 9:5."

12. Jamieson, Fausset, and Brown, *Jamieson, Fausset, and Brown's Commentary on the Whole Bible*, 484.

13. Unger, *Unger's Commentary on the Old Testament*, 1096.

14. Lutzer, *One Minute After You Die*, 50.

15. Morgan and Peterson, eds., *Hell Under Fire*, 53–58, s.v. "Ezekiel 32."

16. MacArthur, *The MacArthur Bible Commentary*, 968.

17. Ibid., 1740.

18. Ibid., 1686, "s.v. Ephesians 2:4–5."

19. As quoted in MacDonald, *Believer's Bible Commentary*, 1456, s.v. "Luke 23:43."

20. Youngblood, ed., *Nelson's New Illustrated Bible Dictionary*, 1187.

21. Morgan and Peterson, eds., *Hell Under Fire*, 54.

31—Do People in Hell "Cease to Exist"?—Annihilationism

1. As quoted in Peterson, *Hell on Trial*, 77.

2. As quoted in Morgan and Peterson, eds., *Hell Under Fire*, 196–197.

3. Jeffress, *Hell? Yes!* 77.

4. Morgan and Peterson, eds., *Hell Under Fire*, 30.

5. Ibid., 30–32.

6. Ibid., 34.

7. Ibid., 78.

8. Kendall, *Out of Your Comfort Zone*, 84.

9. *Strong's Exhaustive Concordance*, s.v. "aionios."

10. MacDonald, *Believer's Bible Commentary*, 1300, s.v. "Matthew 25:41–46."

11. Jamieson, Fausset, and Brown, *Jamieson, Fausset, and Brown's Commentary on the Whole Bible*, 946, s.v. "life everlasting."

12. MacArthur, *The MacArthur Bible Commentary*, 1176, s.v. "Matthew 25:46."

13. As quoted in Morgan and Peterson, eds., *Hell Under Fire*, 183.

14. *Strong's Exhaustive Concordance*, s.v. "appollumi."

15. Martin, *The Kingdom of the Cults*, 582.

16. Jamieson, Fausset, and Brown, *Jamieson, Fausset, and Brown's Commentary on the Whole Bible*, 863, s.v. "Matthew 10:28."

17. As quoted in Morgan and Peterson, eds., *Hell Under Fire*, 81.

18. Kendall, *Out of Your Comfort Zone*, 81.

19. Martin, *The Kingdom of the Cults*, 582–584.

20. Henry, *Matthew Henry's Commentary on the Whole Bible*, 2346, s.v. "2 Thessalonians 1:9."

21. Peterson, *Hell on Trial*, 88.

22. *Strong's Exhaustive Concordance*, s.v. "aion."

23. Martin, *The Kingdom of the Cults*, 584.

24. Taken from Ryken et al., eds., *Dictionary of Biblical Imagery*, 377.

25. Richards, *Encyclopedia of Biblical Words*, 335.

26. Butler et al., eds., *Holman Illustrated Bible Dictionary*, 745.

27. Henry, *Matthew Henry's Commentary on the Whole Bible*, 1799.

28. Ibid.

29. Ibid., 1752.

30. MacArthur, *The MacArthur Bible Commentary*, 968, s.v. "Daniel 12:2."

31. As quoted in Morgan and Peterson, eds., *Hell Under Fire*, 184.

32. Pink, *The Doctrine of Election*, 1.

33. As quoted in Morgan and Peterson, eds., *Hell Under Fire*, 185.

34. Peterson, *Hell on Trial*, 2.

35. Henry, *Matthew Henry's Commentary on the Whole Bible*, 2018.

36. *Strong's Exhaustive Concordance*, s.v. "abaddown."

37. Ibid., "shamad."

38. Alcorn, *Heaven*, 25.

39. As quoted in Peterson, *Hell on Trial*, 108–109.

40. Ibid., 107.

41. As quoted in Morgan and Peterson, eds., *Hell Under Fire*, 227.

42. John Calvin, *Commentary on Matthew, Mark, Luke*, vol. 3, viewed online at Christian Classics Ethereal Library, http://www.ccel.org/ccel/calvin/calcom33.ii.xxiii.html (accessed May 23, 2008).

43. Quoted in Peterson, *Hell on Trial*, 113.

44. Donnelly, *Heaven and Hell*, 55.

45. Jonathan Edwards, *Works of Jonathan Edwards*, vol. 2, viewed online at Christian Classics Ethereal Library, http://www.ccel.org/ccel/edwards/works2.xi.ii.html (accessed May 23, 2008).

46. Millard J. Erickson, *Christian Theology*, second edition (Grand Rapids, MI: Baker Book House, 1985), 1242.

47. Charles G. Finney, "The Loss When a Soul Is Lost," *The Oberlin Evangelist*, July 2, 1851, http://www.gospeltruth.net/1851OE/510702_loss_of_soul.htm (accessed May 23, 2008).

48. Jeffrey, *Journey Into Eternity*, 217.

49. Quoted in Peterson, *Hell on Trial*, 111.

50. Lutzer, *One Minute After You Die*, 103, 112.

51. Martin, *The Kingdom of the Cults*, 131, 128.

52. Morgan and Peterson, eds., *Hell Under Fire*, 137.

53. Peterson, *Hell on Trial*, 201.

54. A. W. Pink, *Eternal Punishment* (n.p.: n.d.), para. 10, 14.

55. Quoted in Morgan and Peterson, eds., *Hell Under Fire*, 183.

56. C. H. Spurgeon, "A Private Enquiry," sermon no. 2184, October 9, 1890, and published for reading January 18, 1891, The Spurgeon Archive, http://spurgeon.org/sermons/2184.htm (accessed May 23, 2008).

57. Quoted in Peterson, *Hell on Trial*, 99.

58. R. A. Torrey, *One Hundred Eighty Two Bible Questions Answered* (Grand Rapids, MI: Kregel Publications, 1990), 48.

59. A. W. Tozer, *The Knowledge of the Holy* (New York: HarperCollins, 1978), 38–39.

60. George Whitefield, "The Eternity of Hell—Torments," Sermon 26, Center for Reformed Theology and Apologetics, http://www.reformed.org/documents/index.html?mainframe=/documents/Whitefield/WITF_026.html (accessed May 23, 2008).

61. Quoted in Morgan and Peterson, eds., *Hell Under Fire*, 74.

62. Peterson, *Hell on Trial*, 240–241.

63. Ibid.

64. Ibid.

65. Ibid.

66. Position papers of The General Council of The Assemblies of God (USA) © Copyright 1976 by The Assemblies of God Gospel Publishing House Sringfield, Missouri, 65802-1894 GPH catalog no 34-4172, Section 15.

67. Ibid.

68. MacDonald, *Believer's Bible Commentary*, 1433, s.v. "Luke 16:19."

69. Gromacki, *New Testament Survey*, 125.

70. MacArthur, *The MacArthur Bible Commentary*, 1313.

71. Donnelly, *Heaven and Hell*, 31.

32—Are People Eventually Saved Out of Hell?—Universalism

1. Quoted in Morgan and Peterson, eds., *Hell Under Fire*, 170–171.

2. Peterson, *Hell on Trial*, 139.

3. Ibid., 140–141.

4. *Strong's Exhaustive Concordance*, s.v. "*deraown.*"

5. As quoted in Morgan and Peterson, eds., *Hell Under Fire*, 175.

6. Ibid., 186.

33—What Is "Born Again"?

1. Martin, *The Kingdom of the Cults*, 130, 585.

2. Charles Stanley, *Eternal Security* (Nashville, TN: Thomas Nelson, 2002), 24–25.

Appendix C—All Verses on Hell and Destruction

1. Quoted in Morgan and Peterson, eds., *Hell Under Fire*, 50.

BIBLIOGRAPHY

Achtemeirer, Paul J., ed. *Harper's Bible Dictionary*. New York: HarperCollins, 1985.

Alcorn, Randy. *Heaven*. Wheaton, IL: Tyndale House Publishers, Inc., 2004.

Allen, Leslie C. *The Books of Joel, Obadiah, Jonah, and Micah: New International Commentary on the Old Testament*. Grand Rapids, MI: Wm. B. Eerdmans Publishing Co., 1976.

Anton, Mike and William Lobdell. "Hold the Fire and Brimstone." *Los Angeles Times*, June 19, 2002.

Baker, David W., T. Desmond Alexander, and Bruce K. Waltke. *Obadiah, Jonah, Micah: Tyndale Old Testament Commentaries*. Downers Grove, IL: InterVarsity Press, 1988.

Barna.org. "Barna Lists the 12 Most Significant Religious Findings from 2006 Surveys." *The Barna Update*, December 20, 2006.

——— . "Beliefs: Heaven or Hell."

Bevere, John. *The Fear of the Lord*. Lake Mary, FL: Charisma House, 1997, 2006.

Bonnke, Reinhard. *Faith: The Link With God's Power*. Nashville, TN: Thomas Nelson, 1998.

Bunyan, John. *Visions of Heaven and Hell*. New Kensington, PA: Whitaker House, 1998.

Butler, Trent C. et al., eds. *Holman Illustrated Bible Dictionary*. Nashville, TN: B&H Publishing Group, 2003.

Calvin, John. *Calvin's Commentaries, Vol. 33: Matthew, Mark and Luke, Part III*. Trans. by John King. Sacred-Texts.com.

Calvin, John. *Commentary of the Harmony of the Evangelists, Matthew, Mark, and Luke*, William Pringle, trans. Edinburgh, Scotland: The Calvin Translation Society, 1846.

————— . *Commentary on Matthew, Mark, Luke, vol. 3*. Christian Classics Ethereal Library.

CBNNews.com. "Most Don't Believe in Hell." March 28, 2007.

Comfort, Ray and Kirk Cameron. *The Way of the Master*. Wheaton, IL: Tyndale House Publishers, 2004.

Comfort, Ray. *Hell's Best Kept Secret*. Springdale, PA: Whitaker House, 1989.

Donnelly, Edward. *Heaven and Hell*. Carlisle, PA: Banner of Truth, 2002.

Edwards, Jonathan. *Works of Jonathan Edwards, vol. 2*. Christian Classics Ethereal Library.

Elwell, Walter A., ed. *Baker Commentary on the Bible*. Grand Rapids, MI: Baker Academic, 2001.

Enns, Paul. *The Moody Handbook of Theology*. Chicago, IL: Moody Publishers, 2008.

Erickson, Millard J. *Christian Theology*, second edition. Grand Rapids, MI: Baker Book House, 1985.

Evans, William. *The Great Doctrines of the Bible*. Chicago, IL: Moody Publishers, 1992.

Finney, Charles G. "The Loss When a Soul Is Lost." *The Oberlin Evangelist*. July 2, 1851.

Graham, Billy. *The Classic Writings of Billy Graham*. New York: Inspirational Press, 2005.

Graham, Franklin. *The Name*. Nashville, TN: Nelson Books, 2002.

Gromacki, Robert G. *New Testament Survey*. Grand Rapids, MI: Baker Academic, 1974.

Grudem, Wayne. *Systematic Theology: An Introduction to Biblical Doctrine*. Grand Rapids, MI: Zondervan, 1995.

Hamon, Jane. *Dreams and Visions*. Ventura, CA: Regal Books, 2000.

Harrison House Publishers. *Powerful Faith-Building Quotes From Leading Charismatic Ministers of All Times*. Tulsa, OK: Harrison House, 1996.

Hayes, Norvel. *Rescuing Souls from Hell*. Tulsa, OK: Harrison House, 1983.

———— . *Understanding the Ministry of Visions*. Cleveland, TN: Norvel Hayes Ministries, n.d.

Henry, Jonathan. *The Astronomy Book*. N.p.: n.d.

Henry, Matthew. *Matthew Henry's Commentary on the Whole Bible*. Hendrickson Publishers, 2005.

Jamieson, Robert, A. R. Fausset, and David Brown. *Jamieson, Fausset, and Brown's Commentary on the Whole Bible*. Grand Rapids, MI: Zondervan, 1999.

Jeffress, Robert. *Hell? Yes!* Colorado Springs, CO: Waterbrook Press, 2004.

Jeffrey, Grant R. *Journey Into Eternity*. Minneapolis, MN: Waterbrook Press, 2000.

Josephus. "An Extract Out of Josephus's Discourse to the Greeks Concerning Hades." Wesley Center Online.

Joyner, Rick. *The Vision: A Two-in-One Volume of The Final Quest and The Call*. Wilkesboro, NC: MorningStar Publications, 2000.

Kendall, R. T. *In Pursuit of His Glory*. Lake Mary, FL: Charisma House, 2004.

———— . *Out of Your Comfort Zone*. New York: FaithWords, 2006.

———— . *Total Forgiveness*. Lake Mary, FL: Charisma House, 2002, 2007.

Koppel, Ted. "Lulling Viewers Into a State of Complicity." *Nieman Reports*, vol. 54, no. 3, Fall 2000.

Lake, John G. *His Life, His Sermons, His Boldness of Faith*. Kenneth Copeland, compiler. Fort Worth, TX: Kenneth Copeland Ministries, 1995.

Lewis, C. S. *Mere Christianity*. New York: HarperOne, 2001.

Lindsey, Hal. *Planet Earth—2000 AD*. Palos Verdes, CA: Western Front, Ltd., 1994.

Lutzer, Erwin. *One Minute After You Die*. Chicago: Moody Publishers, 1997.

———— . *Where Was God?* Wheaton, IL: Tyndale House Publishers, 2006.

MacArthur, John. "Hell—the Furnace of Fire," Tape #GC2304.

———— . *The MacArthur Bible Commentary*. Nashville, TN: Thomas Nelson, 2005.

MacArthur, John, ed. *MacArthur Study Bible*. Nashville, TN: Thomas Nelson, 2006.

Marshall, I. Howard Marshall et al., eds. *New Bible Dictionary*. Downers Grove, IL: InterVarsity Press, 1996.

Martin, Walter. *The Kingdom of the Cults*, revised and updated. Grand Rapids, MI: Bethany House, 2003.

McClure, Holly. *Death by Entertainment*. N.p.: Lions Head Press, 2001.

MacDonald, William. *Believer's Bible Commentary*. Nashville, TN: Thomas Nelson Publishers, Inc., 1989, 1990, 1992, 1995.

McDowell, Josh. *A Ready Defense*. Nashville, TN: Thomas Nelson, Inc., 1993.

——— . *Evidence That Demands a Verdict*. Nashville, TN: Nelson Reference, 1999.

Mears, Henrietta C. *What the Bible Is All About*. San Bernardino, CA: Regal Books, 1983.

Mills, M. *The Life of Christ: A Study Guide to the Gospel Record*. Dallas, TX: 3E Ministries, 1999.

Missler, Chuck and Nancy Missler. *Tomorrow May Be Too Late*. Coeur d'Alene, ID: The King's Highway Ministries, 2004.

Missler, Chuck. "Heaven and Hell," tape two.

——— . "The Nature of Our Reality," *Personal Update*, March 2008.

——— . *Prophecy 20/20*. Nashville, TN: Thomas Nelson, 2006.

Morgan, Christopher W. and Robert A. Peterson, eds. *Hell Under Fire*. Grand Rapids, MI: Zondervan, 2004.

Morris, Henry M. and Martin E. Clark. *The Bible Has the Answer*. Green Forest, AR: Master Books, Inc., 1976, 1987.

Morris, Henry. *Defending the Faith*. Green Forest, AR: Master Books, Inc., 1999.

MSNBC.com. "Belief in Hell Boosts Economic Growth, Fed Says." July 27, 2004.

Page, Franklin S. and Billy K. Smith. *Amos, Obadiah, Jonah: New American Commentary*. Nashville, TN: B&H Publishing Group, 1995.

Peterson, Robert. *Hell on Trial*. Phillipsburg, NJ: Presbyterian and Reformed Publishing Co., 1995.

Pink, A. W. *Eternal Punishment*. N.p.: n.d.

——— . *The Doctrine of Election*. N.p.: n.d.

Piper, John. "Behold the Kindness and the Severity of God," sermon delivered June 14, 1992.

Pringle, Phil. *Moving in the Spirit*. N.p.: n.d.

Rawlings, Maurice. *Beyond Death's Door*. Nashville, TN: Thomas Nelson, 1978.

Richards, Larry. *Bible Teacher's Commentary*. Colorado Springs, CO: David C. Cook, 2002.

Richards, Lawrence O. *Encyclopedia of Biblical Words*. Grand Rapids, MI: Zondervan, 1985, 1991.

Ryken, Leland et al., eds. *Dictionary of Biblical Imagery*. Downers Grove, IL: InterVarsity Press, 1998.

Smith, Chuck. *What the World Is Coming To*. Costa Mesa, CA: Word for Today, 1993.

Spurgeon, C. H. "A Private Enquiry." Sermon no. 2184. October 9, 1890. The Spurgeon Archive.

——— . "The Holy Spirit and the One Church." Sermon no. 167, delivered December 13, 1857.

——— . *The Soulwinner*. New Kensington, PA: Whitaker House, 1995.

Spurgeon, Charles, John Wesley, and Matthew Henry. *Parallel Commentary on the New Testament*. Chattanooga, TN: AMG Publishers, 2003.

Stanley, Charles. *Charles Stanley's Handbook for Christian Living*. Nashville, TN: Thomas Nelson Publishers, 1996.

——— . *Eternal Security*. Nashville, TN: Thomas Nelson, 2002.

Stoddard, Solomon. *The Fear of Hell Restrains Men From Sin*. Morgan, PA: Soli Deo Gloria Publications, 2003.

Strobel, Lee. *The Case for a Creator*. Grand Rapids, MI: Zondervan, 2005.

Strong, James. *Strong's Exhaustive Concordance*. PC Study Bible V3.2F. BibleSoft, 1998.

Sumrall, Lester. *101 Questions and Answers on Demon Powers*. South Bend, IN: Sumrall Publishing, 1983.

————. *Run With the Vision*. South Bend, IN: Sumrall Publishing, 1986.

Times Online. "Pope: Hell Is a Real Place Where Sinners Burn in Everlasting Fire." *The Times*, March 27, 2007.

Torrey, R. A. *One Hundred Eighty Two Bible Questions Answered*. Grand Rapids, MI: Kregel Publications, 1990.

Tozer, A. W. *Jesus, Our Man in Glory*. Camp Hill, PA: Christian Publications, 1988.

————. *The Knowledge of the Holy*. New York: HarperCollins, 1978.

Unger, Merrill F. *Unger's Commentary on the Old Testament* (Chattanooga, TN: AMG Publishers, 2003.

United Methodist Church, "The Sermons of John Wesley: Sermon 73, Of Hell."

Vine, W. E. *Vine's Expository Dictionary of Old and New Testament Words*. Grand Rapids, MI: Fleming H. Revell & Co., 1981.

Walvoord, John F. *Bible Knowledge Commentary: Old Testament and New Testament*. N.p.: Victor, 1985.

Whitefield, George. "The Eternity of Hell—Torments." Sermon 26. Center for Reformed Theology and Apologetics.

Wiersbe, Warren W. *Bible Exposition Commentary*. Colorado Springs, CO: David C. Cook, 2004.

————. *The Wiersbe Bible Commentary: The Complete New Testament*. Colorado Springs, CO: David C. Cook, 2007.

Youngblood, Ronald F., ed. *Nelson's New Illustrated Bible Dictionary*. Nashville, TN: Thomas Nelson Publishers, Inc., 1995.

FOR FURTHER INFORMATION:

Soul Choice Ministries
P. O. Box 26588
Santa Ana, CA 92799

Web site: www.23minutesinhell.org